# Napoleon's Infantry Handbook

# Napoleon's Infantry Handbook

## An Essential Guide to Life in the Grand Army

T.E. Crowdy

Pen & Sword
**MILITARY**

First published in Great Britain in 2015 by
Pen & Sword Military
an imprint of
Pen & Sword Books Ltd
47 Church Street
Barnsley
South Yorkshire
S70 2AS

ISBN 978 1 78346 295 7

A CIP catalogue record for this book is available from the British Library

Typeset in Ehrhardt by
Mac Style Ltd, Bridlington, East Yorkshire
Printed and bound in the UK by CPI Group (UK) Ltd,
Croydon, CRO 4YY

Pen & Sword Books Ltd incorporates the imprints of Pen & Sword
Archaeology, Atlas, Aviation, Battleground, Discovery, Family History,
History, Maritime, Military, Naval, Politics, Railways, Select, Transport,
True Crime, and Fiction, Frontline Books, Leo Cooper, Praetorian Press,
Seaforth Publishing and Wharncliffe.

For a complete list of Pen & Sword titles please contact
PEN & SWORD BOOKS LIMITED
47 Church Street, Barnsley, South Yorkshire, S70 2AS, England
E-mail: enquiries@pen-and-sword.co.uk
Website: www.pen-and-sword.co.uk

# Contents

# Tables

# Diagrams

# Foreword

Two hundred years on, the career of Napoleon Bonaparte, his *Grande Armée*, and his great adversaries continue to excite the imagination and evoke strong passions among historians and enthusiasts of military history. So much has been written about the Napoleonic wars, one would think the subject was all but exhausted; but no, the truth is we have hardly scratched the surface, particularly in the English speaking world. The Napoleonic Wars are rich in great battles, charismatic leaders, colourful uniforms, and these subjects naturally receive the greatest attention from authors and artists. However, two hundred years on, our world is so technologically and culturally removed from the one in which these men existed, how can we really understand what it was like to be a soldier for Napoleon? In a world without railways, radio, photography, or the understanding of something as basic as germs and the transmission of disease, how can we really connect with and understand their time?

There are numerous works by social historians who have studied the motivations and experiences of soldiers in the Napoleonic era, and these are important. However, having researched and written on the subject for a decade and a half, I realised there was still much to be said about the everyday habits and routines of Napoleon's soldiers, and the 'mechanics' which underpinned their experiences.

Under Napoleon alone, somewhere in the region of 2.4 million men were conscripted into the French Army. This is to say nothing of the emergency levies of the 1790s and the tens of thousands who served as National Guard Volunteers; but it gives an idea of the numbers of individual human beings who had experience of military service, who were processed, trained, uniformed and commanded by Napoleon and his marshals. In the English speaking world, much of our knowledge of this multitude originates from a handful of translated memoirs of infantrymen such as Captain Coignet, Sergeant Bourgogne and Captain Elzéar Blaze. These memoirs *are* essential reading and *are* the mainstays of any Napoleonic collection, but they are the mere blink of an eye on a colossal subject. Take the memoirs of Blaze (a personal favourite). They tell of the absurdities of military life, the throwing away of useless articles of uniform, the practice of marauding, the pursuit of the fairer sex, the drinking of drams, the smoking of pipes and so on; but are they truly reflective of the experience of 2.4 million men? Even great memoirists such as Blaze ignore the basic practices and procedures they knew too well: what time they woke, how frequently they mounted guard, what the procedure was for applying for leave, or what time they went to bed. These memoirs were written for the amusement of fellow old soldiers initiated and steeped in the same rituals of army life as the author, and such pedantic attention to detail would hardly have excited cognitive function in their greying years. In short, they are incomplete as portraits of the soldierly daily life (*vie quotidienne*); so what hope have we of better understanding this subject?

Step forward Colonel Étienne Alexandre Bardin (1774–1840). The son of a noted artist, Bardin served in one of the volunteer battalions of National Guardsmen raised after the storming of the Bastille in 1789. Intelligent and exact, Bardin quickly achieved the rank of adjutant major (a battalion-level staff officer) and bore witness to the opening battles of the war. He saw action at Hondschoote in 1793 and served in the Army of the Sambre and Meuse as a company commander in the 8th Light Infantry. He served in Italy and during the Consulate became an aide de camp to General Jean-Andoche Junot, who was, for a time, governor of Paris. For much of the imperial period, Bardin was attached to the ministry of war with the rank of major. In 1811 he held the rank of colonel with the regiment of Pupils of the Imperial Guard and then commanded the 9th Regiment of Tirailleurs of the Young Guard. After the disaster of Russia, Bardin saw active service in the Campaign of Saxony (1813) and was made a Baron of the Empire that same year. His military career concluded with an attachment to the War Depot, the forerunner of France's military archives and historical service known today as the Service Historique de la Défense. This brief biographical note is only given to establish Bardin's credentials as a soldier, and to illustrate his exposure to the different elements of the armed services, operational and administrative. He also had a parallel career as an author of military reference books, and this is what makes him such an essential figure in our understanding of the Napoleonic military machine.

This book was largely inspired by the 1813 edition of Bardin's *Manuel de l'Infanterie*. This infantry manual was first published in 1807, but the 1813 edition really captures a high mark of the development of France's infantry regiments; a process which began in the aftermath of the Seven Years War and which arguably came into real fruition during the period from the formation of the camp of Boulogne in 1804, until the British were driven out of Spain at Corunna in 1808. In this four year period, French infantry was unrivalled, besting the armies of Austria, Prussia, Russia, Spain and Britain in quick succession with only the occasional proverbial bloodied nose. Although in 1813 Napoleon's empire was about to commence upon a cataclysmic decline, the technical and theoretical knowledge of soldiering codified in this small book was the bitter fruit of two decades of near continuous warfare. There were young men reading this book in 1813 who had not been born when the conflict heard its first shots in the summer of 1792. Although in 1812 Napoleon had lost an army in Russia, in the spring of 1813, it was not beyond the French nation to raise and equip a new army. Had the so-called Marie-Louise conscripts of 1813 been afforded a summer or two of peace in which to train and perfect their military education there is no reason to suppose they could not have been as formidable in war as their predecessors from the camp of Boulogne. Alas, Napoleon's many enemies knew and feared this outcome and so refused to treat with the emperor. As a result the year 1813 was marked by the disasters of Vitoria in the south, and Leipzig in the east. Within two more summers the imperial army was dismembered and its eagles melted down for good.

Although French soldiers have a reputation for dash and flamboyancy, in fact their army was heavily regulated, bureaucratic and relied on working practices and traditions dating well back into the 18th century and beyond. As Bardin often recognised in his notes, the laws, decrees, regulations, orders and procedures which governed the French Army were often contradictory. Quite often Bardin could merely offer a Gallic shrug and diligently footnote the discrepancies and flaws in the system he sought to describe. Despite the occasional inconsistency, his infantry manual is a crucial reference for those who are interested in the mechanics of army life.

This book was supplemented in 1809 by the two-volume *Mémoiral de l'officier d'infanterie* (also revised in 1813) which was a collection of military regulations and served as a reference tool for officers. In his introduction to this book, Bardin claimed he produced the work to provide officers with a reference material pending the publishing of the *code militaire*, a work which was commissioned by Napoleon in 1805, but which never materialised. True enough, in the early part of Napoleon's reign he intended rationalising the various military regulations into a single code. Completion of the code was initially hindered by the resumption of hostilities in 1805 and the subsequent war of the Third Coalition. The project was never completed because, as some argue, Emperor Napoleon became increasingly autocratic, ruling by executive order rather than through process. In the absence of systematic reform, Bardin's 'memorial' must have proved extremely useful to diligent officers trying to master their profession.

Many of the terms used, and the items described in Bardin's manuals, have now fallen out of common use, even in French. This particularly applies to the articles of petty equipment and the products daily used for cleaning and repair. It is therefore indispensable for any student of Napoleon's army to have access to Bardin's seventeen-volume exploration of the military sciences entitled the *Dictionnaire de l'armée de terre*. This work was the fruit of thirty years work and was published posthumously in 1841. It not only sought to explain the terminology and objects which were then in use, but also to describe their practical and etymological origins. Over five thousand pages in length, this work is truly monumental.

Of course, Bardin's work does not stand alone. In 1789 Captain Lacuée of the Dauphin Infantry Regiment began work on the four volume *encyclopédie méthodique, art militaire*. This work was completed in 1797 by General Joseph Servan and is an excellent reference for the French Army in 1790s. In 1803 the first edition of Pierre Nicolas Quillet's *état actuel de la législation sur l'administration des troupes* etc. was published. Head of the bureau of pay in the war department, Quillet's work provides essential detail on the logistics and administration of the army. Captain H. Berriat's 1812, four volume *Législation militaire, ou Recueil méthodique et raisonné des lois, décrets, arrêtés, réglements et instructions actuellement en vigueur sur toutes les branches de l'état militaire* is another indispensable reference.

Also of note is Doctor Jean Jacques Martin's 1801 *Manuel de l'officier de santé*. Each of these works has been consulted in the preparation of this book, along with numerous other contemporary texts, which are referenced where relevant.

Embracing the spirit of Bardin, this book presents an eclectic selection of facts and procedures which help to explain the composition, administration and service in the infantry regiments which marched with Napoleon. The book is divided into themes, so it is often necessary to investigate different articles to fully explore a particular subject. Readers are encouraged to follow the cross references as their curiosity takes them. Wherever possible this book uses English translations of technical terms with the original French technical term given afterwards, if required. The two principal exceptions to this are *chasseur* and *voltigeur*, both of which in this book are a form of light infantry. The terms *gendarme* and *gendarmerie* are also used in their original French form. Originating from the term *gens d'armes* (men-at-arms), in the Napoleonic period the *gendarmerie* was a branch of the military responsible for policing the army. Some pieces of petty equipment defy translation, such as *astic* or *martinet*. Explanations of these terms are given in the appropriate places.

Another translated term which often causes confusion is the difference between the words 'company' and 'platoon'. In the modern armies of *le monde anglo-saxon* (as our Gallic cousins like to describe us), a platoon is a sub-unit of a company, which itself is usually a sub-unit of a battalion. In the French Napoleonic system a company (*compagnie*) was an administrative sub-unit of a battalion, while a platoon (*peleton*) was the equivalent tactical sub-unit. In other words, the terms 'company' and 'platoon' essentially refer to the same formation depending on the context. While this might at first appear confusing to those familiar with NATO definitions, it does in fact accurately reflect the military system of the era described in these pages. Another editorial decision is the use of the direct translation sub-officer (*sous-officier*), rather than the English 'non-commissioned officer' (NCO). The term could also be translated as under-officer (very much like the German *Unteroffizier*). The republican ranks *chef de brigade* and *chef de bataillon* both ought to be translated as chief of brigade, and battalion respectively. For brevity I have preferred brigade commander and battalion commander.

As a final note, I must pay my dues and acknowledge the following people: Martin Lancaster, Pierre-Yves Chauvin and Gerd Hoad have followed the progress of this book, helping me define its scope and acting as a continual sounding board for ideas. I am very grateful to Oliver Schmidt and Jakub Samek for their detailed reading of my first draft and their extensive notes and comments. I must acknowledge Bernard Coppens who first introduced me to the works of Bardin. Many others have shared in my Napoleonic journey over the years, and I thank them all for stoking my enthusiasm. I must also thank my editor Philip Sidnell for commissioning this book, and of course my wife Sarah who has patiently supported and encouraged me through this and many other projects.

T.E. Crowdy

# A Guide to Terms and Measures from Napoleonic France

Before the introduction of the metric system, France had a system of weights and measures based on Charlemagne's interpretation of the ancient Roman system. At the time of the 1789 Revolution, there were numerous regional variations and while modern readers might notice many similarities with the old French system and the Imperial System still used in the USA, they must be cautioned that the values between the French and Anglo–Saxon systems are entirely different. Where 'Imperial' measurements are given in this book, they refer to the old French versions.

The French made great use of the league (*lieue*) and the fathom (*toise*); the league being composed of 2,000 fathoms, and the fathom of six feet (*pieds*). While English speaking readers might be familiar with these terms in a nautical context, the French applied these terms terrestrially. The French did not make use of the 'yard', and there are only occasional references to the mile (*mille*) in military texts. The mile originated as a unit of measurement in Roman times (*mille passus*), and signified one thousand double paces (approximately 1.48 km). However, the French interpretation of the mile was one thousand fathoms (*toises*) – in other words, half a league.

The regularity of measurement only became a reality when the metric system was introduced by the French in 1795 and standardised in 1799. This decimal system had at its heart two essential calculations: in length, one metre was equivalent to one ten-millionth of the distance between the North Pole and the earth's equator, as measured via the Paris meridian. In weight, one gram was equivalent to the weight of one cubic centimetre (i.e. one hundredth of a metre) of water at the temperature of melting ice. From these two calculations, everything else can be computed.

The following tables give the metric equivalent of the most common old French units of weight and measurement, along with an equivalent in the Imperial System.

Alas, decimalisation was not universally popular and Napoleon's subjects hankered after their old *livres* and *toises*. Therefore in 1812 Napoleon introduced a system known as 'customary measures' (*mesures usuelles*). While official institutions were required to use the metric system, civilian traders and merchants were permitted to go back to their cherished terms of yesteryear. Of course Napoleon was sensible enough not to allow a return to the chaos of regional variations, so the new pounds and feet were assigned metric values. The 'metric pound' was conveniently deemed to weigh 500g (half a kilo), while the 'metric fathom' was measured at two metres, with one foot being 1/6th of a fathom, with an inch being 1/12th of a foot, or 1/72nd of a fathom. In terms of volume, for the purposes

**Table 1:** Units of length.

| Old unit of measurement | Composed of | Metric | Imperial |
|---|---|---|---|
| Paris league (*lieue de Paris*) | 2000 fathoms | 3.898 km | 2.422 miles |
| Mile (*mille*) | 1000 fathoms | 1.949 km | 1760 yards |
| Fathom (*toise*) | 6 feet | 1.949 m | 2.131 yards |
| King's foot (*pied du roi*) | 12 inches | 32.484 cm | 1.066 ft |
| Inch (*pouce*) | 12 lines | 27.07 mm | 1.066 in |
| Line (*ligne*) | 12 points | 2.256 mm | 88.81 thou |
| Point | – | 0.188 mm | 7.401 thou |

**Table 2:** Units of weight.

| Old unit of measurement | Composed of | Metric | Imperial |
|---|---|---|---|
| 1 hundredweight (*quintal*) | 100 pounds | 48.95 kg | 107.9 lb |
| 1 pound (*livre*) | 16 ounces | 489.5 g | 1.079 lb |
| 1 marc | 8 ounces | 244.8 g | 8.633 oz |
| 1 ounce (*once*) | 8 gross | 30.59 g | 1.079 oz |
| 1 gross (*gros*) | 72 grains | 3.824 g | 2.158 drachms |
| 1 grain | – | 53.11 mg | 0.8197 grains |

of this book, other than the metric litre (divided into one thousand millilitres) there was the archaic French pint (*pinte*), which measures at 952.1 ml. This was much larger than our Imperial one (568 ml).

The process of metrification also impacted on France's currency. At the time of the Revolution, the principal currency was the *livre*, which consisted of 20 *sous*, each of which consisted of 12 *deniers*. Other coinage included the *écu* which was valued at 6 *livres*. Until 1792 the French minted a golden Louis (*Louis d'or*) which was valued at 24 *livres*, and a double Louis (*Louis doubles*) of 48 *livres*. In 1795 the decimal *franc* was introduced, which was composed of 10 *décimes* or 100 *centimes*. The exchange rate between new and old was set at 1 *franc* to 1 *livre*, 3 *deniers*. The *écu* was replaced by a silver coin of the same name worth 5 *francs*. In 1803 the 'Napoleon' and the 'double Napoleon' were introduced as a throwback to the old *Louis*. The Napoleons were valued at 20 and 40 *francs* respectively.

The French Revolution had a profound impact on every facet of society. One of the most obvious was the rejection of the Gregorian calendar and the resetting of time itself. On 24 October 1793 the French adopted a new *calendrier républicain*. According to the new calendar, the new era had officially begun on 22 September 1791, the date on which monarchy was abolished. Each year was henceforth divided into twelve equal months, each thirty days long and given entirely new names based on the seasons and weather:

| | |
|---|---|
| Vendémiaire | (the month of grape harvests) |
| Brumaire | (the month of fog) |
| Frimaire | (the month of frost) |
| Nivôse | (the month of snow) |
| Pluviôse | (the month of rain) |
| Ventôse | (the windy month) |
| Germinal | (the month of germination) |
| Floréal | (the month of flowers) |
| Prairial | (the month of pasture) |
| Messidor | (the month giving harvest) |
| Thermidor | (the month giving heat) |
| Fructidor | (the month giving fruit) |

Each month was divided into three, ten-day weeks, called decades (*décades*). To make up the shortfall against the solar year, five extra days were added after the final month (six in a leap year). These five days were intended as a period of national holiday and were originally named *les sans-culottides* after the revolutionary party. After the demise of the *Sans Culottes* in 1795, they were referred to as the complementary days (*les jours complémentaires*).

In April 1802 the ten-day week was abandoned, and there was a return to the traditional days of the week, although the new months were retained. The Gregorian calendar was fully restored on New Year's Day 1806. In summary, the calendar represented the corresponding Gregorian dates:

| | |
|---|---|
| Year I | 22 September 1792–21 September 1793 |
| Year II | 22 September 1793–21 September 1794 |
| Year III | 22 September 1794–21 September 1795 |
| Year IV | 23 September 1795–21 September 1796 |
| Year V | 22 September 1796–21 September 1797 |
| Year VI | 22 September 1797–21 September 1798 |
| Year VII | 22 September 1798–22 September 1799 |
| Year VIII | 23 September 1799–21 September 1800 |
| Year IX | 22 September 1800–22 September 1801 |
| Year X | 23 September 1801–22 September 1802 |
| Year XI | 23 September 1802–23 September 1803 |
| Year XII | 24 September 1803–22 September 1804 |
| Year XIII | 23 September 1804–22 September 1805 |
| Year XIV | 23 September 1805–31 December 1805 |

(Note: documents written before 24 October 1793 carry the Gregorian date.)

In this book where a law or regulation was made during the period this calendar was in use, the Republican and Gregorian dates are given together. This is to make it easier for readers to look up the original document and conduct more detailed research.

It may be helpful to provide a note on the administrative structure of France. Prior to the Revolution, France was divided into various provinces. In 1790 the country was reorganised into administrative *départements* which by 1800 were divided into districts (*arrondissements*), cantons, and communes. Each department had a capital city, and each district had a capital which was called the sub-prefecture. The district which contained the departmental capital was called the prefecture. From 1793 France was also divided into a number of administrative military divisions (*divisions militaires*). Initially there were twenty military divisions, but as French territory expanded, there were twenty-five by 1800, and thirty-two by 1812, including the 30th (Rome) and the 32nd (Hamburg). These military divisions are not to be confused with 'divisions' of infantry or cavalry serving in the field armies.

It is perhaps useful to reference the various governments under which the men described in this book served. From the fall of the Bastille to the first restoration of the Bourbon monarchy there were six distinct phases of government. First was the National Constituent Assembly (*Assemblée nationale constituante* – 9 July 1789 to 30 September 1791); then the National Legislative Assembly (*Assemblée nationale législative* – 1 October 1791 to 20 September 1792); National Convention (*Convention nationale* – 20 September 1792 to 26 October 1795) during which executive power was for a time wielded by the notorious Committee of Public Safety (*comité de salut public*) and included the period known as the Terror (*la Terreur* – September 1793 – July 1794). A five member executive called the Directory (*Directoire*) then held sway from 26 October 1795 until 10 November 1799. They were replaced by the Consulate, a three man executive led by Napoleon Bonaparte as First Consul. This form of government was disbanded on 18 May 1804 when the French Empire was created. Napoleon's imperial coronation did not formally take place until 2 December 1804. The reign of Napoleon came to an end on 11 April 1814 with the Treaty of Fontainebleu and the subsequent first restoration of Louis XVIII. The period from Napoleon's return to Paris on 20 March 1815, to the second restoration of Louis XVIII (8 July 1815) is popularly known as the Hundred Days (*cent jours*).

*Part I*

# Organisation & Personnel

## Chapter 1

# The Infantry Regiments

## 1. Introduction

The word 'infantry' (*infanterie*) had its roots in Latin and came into the French language from the Spanish *infante* (an infant or little servant), a reference to the foot soldiers or recruits who accompanied a mounted *hombre des armas* (man-at-arms). The Italians had a similar expression – *fante* (boy) which came to designate a *fantaccino* (foot soldier), a word the French corrupted into *fantassin*, their generic term for infantryman. The word regiment (*régiment*) is also believed to have found its way into French from the Spanish language at the time of the Holy Roman Emperor, Charles V (1500–1558). The word had its origins in the Latin *regimentum* (administration or government) and from *regere* (control, or rule), and was synonymous with the word *régime* – in other words, it implied a body of men who were under someone's authority. Long considered the *queen of battle*, like the chess piece, infantry was a flexible force which could go anywhere. Indeed, French infantry served on land, in the colonies, and even performed the role of warship garrisons, in lieu of any specialist marine force. This first chapter summarises the basic organisation of the infantry regiments between 1789 and 1815, and also outlines the roles performed by each grade within the regiment.

## 2. Line infantry regiments

In 1789 the French Army was composed of seventy-nine infantry regiments and twenty-three foreign infantry regiments (eleven of which were Swiss, eight 'German', three Irish and one from Liege). These regiments were numbered from 1 to 104, the discrepancy in number being made up by the Royal Corps of Artillery (ranked 64th), and the Provincial Troops (ranked 97th). On 1 January 1791 all the provincial regimental titles were abolished and the regiments were henceforth identified only by number. On 21 July 1791 the National Assembly decreed the 96th Infantry Regiment (formerly titled Nassau), and all those designated as German, Irish or from Liege were henceforth to be classified, recruited, paid, and uniformed just like any other French regiment. The Swiss regiments in French pay remained in service until 20 August 1792, when they were disbanded after the massacre of the Swiss Guards at the Tuileries Palace ten days previously.

On 13 July 1789 the Constituent Assembly called for the formation of a national militia called the *Garde Bourgeoises*. This became known as the National Guard

(*Garde Nationale*) and played a very important part in the early years of the war. A law of 15 June 1791 called for a 'free conscription' of one in twenty National Guardsmen who might assemble if the state required their assistance. This was followed by a decree of 20 June 1791 which activated the National Guards in the departments bordering France's eastern frontier. Other departments were required to provide contingents of between two and three thousand men. These volunteers were organised into battalions of ten companies, each comprising of fifty men. Before long, over seventy thousand volunteers had joined the armies protecting France's eastern border. A decree of 12 August 1791 rationalised the composition of each battalion at 568 men in eight companies. On 14 October 1791 a law formally gave Louis XVI the power to incorporate the volunteers into the line. This did not occur and the volunteers retained their independence. From this point on the volunteers began to use the title National Volunteers (*Volontaires Nationaux*) to distinguish themselves from the volunteers serving in the regular army (still then recruited on a voluntary basis). They were extremely enthusiastic supporters of the new nation; their patriotism, intelligence, and generosity was often in sharp contrast to the regular army.

The law of 3 February 1792 titled the volunteers as National Guard Volunteers (*Gardes Volontaires Nationaux*). This law regulated their composition at two lieutenant colonels, one of whom commanded the battalion. All officer appointments were made by election. By 18 May 1792 somewhere in the region of 240,000 volunteers had been called up. After the country was declared to be 'in danger' on 11 July 1792 there were 257 National Guard Volunteer battalions on active service. By February 1793 there were 392 battalions of National Volunteers, plus an additional 328 volunteer corps of varying composition.

France effectively had a two-tier army: on the one hand, enthusiastic, patriotic, freedom-loving National Guard Volunteers; on the other, regular, professional soldiers whose morale was dented by the political instability around them, and irked by the better conditions enjoyed by those preferring to join the Volunteer battalions. Although the former were a symbol of everything good about the Revolution, they perhaps lacked the professionalism and sense of discipline of regular soldiers. The Volunteer battalions also lacked the supporting depots to replenish losses and to maintain the men in the field. Therefore, on 21 February 1793 the government ordered the creation of infantry half-brigades (*demi-brigades*) which united a single battalion of regulars with two battalions of volunteers. This was partly a political measure designed to obliterate the identity of the royal army, and partly a practical measure to create a single, coherent, manageable structure.

A half-brigade of the line of battle (*demi-brigade de bataille*) would be formed of a staff commanded by a brigade commander or *chef de brigade* (the rank of colonel was suppressed), three field battalions (each containing eight companies of fusiliers and one of grenadiers), an artillery company with six 4-pounder guns, and, in wartime, an auxiliary company which formed a depot. As it happened, the formation of the half-brigades was adjourned on 31 March 1793 due to the approaching campaign season. Their composition was further clarified in a decree of 12 August 1793, particularly in terms of the composition of the staff, and how the amalgamation would actually be accomplished. The law of *2 Frimaire II* (22 November 1793) further clarified the composition of the companies (see Table 1). On *19 Nivôse II* (8 January 1796) a decree was issued finally enacting the reform proposed eleven months before.

Two years later, on *18 Nivôse IV* (8 January 1796) a further rationalisation took place, reducing the number of infantry corps to one hundred line half-brigades, and renumbering them by lottery. A second order ten days later raised the number to one hundred and ten. The basic structure of the half-brigade was barely changed by this second formation, consisting of three battalions and an artillery company (albeit reduced in size to three 4-pounders). Two notable changes were the addition of a second quartermaster treasurer who would remain with the depot and also the addition of a fourth battalion commander who was charged with overseeing the accounting, instruction and discipline of the corps. The auxiliary company comprised of three supernumerary officers, the craftsmen of the corps and the surplus of the men left over from the amalgamation process.

There was in fact a third amalgamation of sorts which occurred in 1799. On *10 Messidor VII* (28 July 1799), the government ordered the formation of an auxiliary battalion (*bataillon auxiliaire*) in each department of France. Each auxiliary battalion contained ten companies (eight of fusiliers, one of chasseurs and one of grenadiers). These battalions were formed from the newly raised conscripts and were equipped locally and trained by veterans. Towards the end of the year, these auxiliary battalions were incorporated into the line, with the chasseur companies being sent to reinforce the light infantry half-brigades.

When he was First Consul, on *1 Vendémiaire XII* (24 September 1803), Napoleon restored the title 'regiment' to the French infantry and also the title of colonel. Napoleon also reintroduced the rank of major, a senior grade which had been omitted since 1 January 1791. On 19 September 1805 each battalion of line infantry was instructed to convert its second company to one of voltigeurs, a form of light infantry skirmisher recruited from men of short stature who could never qualify for service in the grenadier companies. In many cases the implementation of this decree was interrupted somewhat by the Ulm and Austerlitz campaigns. The main change of the imperial period came on 18 February 1808 when each regiment was brought to a strength of five battalions. The first four battalions contained only six companies – four of fusiliers and one each of voltigeurs and grenadiers. The size of each company was increased, being more than twice the size of the peacetime companies formed in 1791. The fifth company formed the regimental depot and consisted of four fusilier battalions only. By adopting this measure Napoleon significantly increased the number of field battalions available to him, without having to employ significantly more sub-officers and officers. On 12 April 1811 twenty-five regiments were assigned a sixth battalion.

One of the features of Napoleon's army was the creation of a number of ad hoc regiments. The depot companies were often collected to form provisional regiments. These might be classed as a half-brigade (*demi-brigade*), a provisional regiment (*régiment provisoire*), or a battalion of march (*bataillon de marche*). Often they would be returned to their parent regiment at the end of a campaign or particular mission, or incorporated into the battalions already in the field. Napoleon's army also saw the creation of so-called grenadier divisions made from collections of elite companies removed from their parent battalions. Elite soldiers serving in the same brigade or division might also be collected to form 'special battalions'.

After Napoleon's first abdication in 1814 the line regiments were reorganised on 12 May 1814. The Royal Army was reduced to ninety line infantry regiments, each organised into 3 battalions of six companies, with a cadre of officers and sub-officers for a fourth battalion. This meant some regiments were renumbered or even merged. Even with prisoners of war returning to France, only six regiments actually had enough soldiers to form the third battalion. When Napoleon returned from exile in Elba in 1815, he undid the reforms of the Bourbons, restoring the renumbered regiments back to their original identities in the decree of 25 April 1815. Previous to this on 13 April 1815, he announced a provisional organisation of the infantry regiments, ordering them to form five battalions each (one depot, four field battalions). However, by the time of the Hundred Days campaign, few regiments could field more than two battalions, and these were much weaker than the 1808 equivalents (see Table 3). After Waterloo the imperial army was utterly

**Table 3**: Line infantry organisation 1791–1815.

| A. The Staff | 1 Jan 1791 | 8 Jan 1794* | 8 Feb 1808 | 12 May 1814 | 13 Apr 1815 |
|---|---|---|---|---|---|
| Colonel | 1 | – | 1 | 1 | 1 |
| Brigade commander | – | 1 | – | – | – |
| Major | – | – | 1 | 1 | 1 |
| Lieutenant colonel | 2 | – | – | – | – |
| Battalion commanders | – | 3** | 4 | 3 | 4 |
| Adjutant majors | 2 | 3 | 5 | 3 | 5 |
| Quartermaster treasurer | 1 | 1*** | 1 | 1 | 1 |
| Paymaster officer | – | – | 1 | – | 1 |
| Clothing officer**** | – | – | – | – | 1 |
| Chaplain | 1 | – | – | – | – |
| Eagle / standard bearer | – | – | 1 | 1 | 1 |
| Surgeon major | 1 | 3 | 1 | 1 | 1 |
| Surgeon aides | – | – | 4 | 1 | 4 |
| Sub-aide surgeons | – | – | 5 | 1 | 5 |

* This composition was set on 12 August 1793
** A fourth battalion commander was added between 1796 and 1799.
*** A second QMT was added in 1796.
**** Prior to 1815 this rank was an appointment only.

| B. Petty staff | 1 Jan 1791 | 8 Jan 1794* | 18 Feb 1808 | 12 May 1814 | 13 Apr 1815 |
|---|---|---|---|---|---|
| Adjutant sub-officers | 2 | 3 | 10 | 3 | 10 |
| 2nd and 3rd eagle bearers | – | – | 2 | – | 2 |
| Drum major | 1 | 1 | 1 | 1 | 1 |
| Drum corporal | 1 | 1 | 1 | 1 | 1 |
| Musicians | 8 | 8 | 8 | 8 | 12 |
| Master tailor | 1 | 1 | 1 | 1 | 1 |
| Master armourer | 1 | 3 | 1 | 1 | 1 |
| Master cobbler | 1 | 1 | 1 | 1 | 1 |
| Master gaiter-maker | – | – | 1 | – | – |
| Baggage master | – | – | 1 | – | – |

* This composition was set on 12 August 1793.

| C. The companies | 1 Jan 1791 | | 8 Jan 1794* | | 18 Feb 1808 | 12 May 1814 | 13 Apr 1815 |
|---|---|---|---|---|---|---|---|
| | F. | G. | F. | G. | | | |
| Captain | 1 | 1 | 1 | 1 | 1 | 1 | 1 |
| Lieutenant | 1 | 1 | 1 | 1 | 1 | 1 | 1 |
| Sub-lieutenant | 1 | 1 | 1 | 1 | 1 | 1 | 1 |
| Sergeant major | 1 | 1 | 1 | 1 | 1 | 1 | 1 |
| Sergeant | 2 | 2 | 4 | 2 | 4 | 4 | 4 |
| Quartermaster corporal | 1 | 1 | 1 | 1 | 1 | 1 | 1 |
| Corporal | 4 | 4 | 8 | 4 | 8 | 8 | 8 |
| Chosen men | 4 | 4 | – | – | – | – | – |
| Men | 53 | 40 | 104 | 64 | 121 | 56 | 80 |
| Drummers / cornetists | 2 | 2 | 2 | 2 | 2 | 2 | 2 |

* This composition was set on 22 November 1793.

broken up by the Bourbon government, creating new formations with no links to the army of the republic or empire.

Table 3 sets out the key changes in the effective strength of the line infantry corps over the period from 1791 to 1815. Throughout the period each regiment contained a number of staff officers who were classed as the *état-major*. There were also a number of soldiers and specialists who held the rank of sub-officer and were classed as the petty staff (*petit état-major*). Finally there were the officers and men who formed the individual companies. In addition to the positions shown in the table, each regiment would have a number of supernumerary officers (*officiers à la suite*), sutlers, laundresses and children. These groups and other specialist roles will be discussed later in the appropriate chapters.

A line infantry grenadier typical of the
1790s and early part of the First Empire.

## 3. Light infantry regiments

The wars of the 18th century saw the development of infantrymen who fought
outside of the line of battle and formed part of an army's advanced guard. France
initially relied on irregulars to fulfil this function, often recruiting foreigners for
the role. They also experimented with mixed 'legions' of light horse and infantry,
or adding light infantry companies to the regiments of the line. It took until
1788 for independent battalions of foot chasseurs (huntsmen) to be formed in the
manner of Frederick the Great's *jaeger* corps. The purpose of these light battalions
was to provide an advanced guard service to the army, scouting, protecting camps
and covering retreats. Light infantry also came to play an increasingly important
role on the battlefield. When originally conceived, light troops tended to be posted
on the periphery during battles, guarding the flanks of the army and the camp.
However, the field service regulations of 1792 assigned light infantry with four
specific roles on the battlefield, namely:

1. Screen the deployment of the line infantry and artillery batteries.
2. Discover enemy dispositions.
3. Target enemy batteries and kill the gunners.
4. Pursue retreating enemy troops.

Unlike troops of the line, light infantry were to fight outside of regular troop formations and to exploit cover as it could be found.

At the outbreak of war there were fourteen battalions of light infantry; by the time of Napoleon's first abdication in 1814 thirty-five regiments existed (numbered 1st to 37th; numbers 20 and 30 not having been used). In 1791 the composition of a light infantry battalion included a staff of two lieutenant colonels (one of whom commanded), one adjutant major, one quartermaster treasurer, an adjutant, one surgeon major, one drum major, four musicians, a master tailor, one master armourer and one master cordwainer. The eight companies each included a peacetime complement of one captain, a lieutenant, a sub-lieutenant, one sergeant major, two sergeants, one quartermaster corporal, four corporals, four chosen men, one drummer, six riflemen (*carabiniers*) and forty chasseurs.

Light infantry immediately proved their worth in the opening stages of the war, serving in the outposts in advance of the armies and skirmishing in battle. In order to meet the demand for light infantry, on 28 July 1792 the government decreed the formation of National Volunteer Chasseurs (*Chasseurs Volontaires Nationaux*) to serve with the light troops in the forward posts. This led to the formation of numerous free companies of light infantry irregulars and battalions of chasseurs. As with the line infantry, this led to the formation of light infantry half-brigades (*demi-brigade d'infanterie légère*) in 1794, with a further amalgamation in 1796 to rationalise the light infantry arm into thirty half-brigades, each with three battalions organised in the same manner as the infantry, but without an artillery company. The fact France went from fourteen to ninety light infantry battalions in five years clearly demonstrates their utility.

In the Napoleonic period the light infantry regiments underwent significant changes. In 1804 each light infantry battalion converted its second company into voltigeurs (a move copied by the line the following year). Following the changes of 18 February 1808 (see Table 3), the special nature of light infantry regiments appears to have diminished. During the later imperial period in particular, voltigeurs were widely recognised as the true light infantry of the French Army, with a different recruitment process, armament and tactics. Whether they came from line or light battalions, the voltigeurs were often combined at divisional or brigade level into special battalions which performed the traditional advanced guard role and took on an increasing burden when it came to battlefield skirmishing.

In the reforms of 12 May 1814 the Bourbons consolidated the surviving light infantry into fifteen regiments, each consisting of three battalions, with a cadre for a fourth battalion in reserve. On Napoleon's return in May 1815, most regiments could only provide two combat battalions and the shortness of the campaign did not allow the depots sufficient time to provide the remaining two battalions. The organisation of light infantry regiments during the Hundred Days followed that of the line (see Table 3).

## 4. Regimental artillery

Before the Revolution, the ordinance of 28 April 1778 had attached two artillery pieces to each line infantry battalion. The decree of 21 February 1793 attached six 4-pounders and an artillery company to each half-brigade of the line, with two guns allocated to each battalion. The artillery company was composed of two captains, three lieutenants, one sergeant major, five sergeants, one quartermaster corporal, five corporals, one drummer, thirty-five first gunners (*premiers canonniers*), four artificers and thirty-two second gunners (*seconds cannoniers*). In the second formation of the half-brigades of 1796, the artillery company was reduced to three 4-pounders with a complement of three officers, one sergeant major, three sergeants, one quartermaster corporal, six corporals, one drummer and thirty-five gunners. A law of *5 Pluviôse VI* (24 January 1798) reversed this decision and disbanded the regimental artillery companies.

Regimental artillery was revived by Napoleon during the imperial period. The decree of 9 June 1809 awarded regiments earmarked for service against Austria with two pieces of captured Austrian artillery (3 or 4-pounder) plus a substantial train of three ammunition caissons, a campaign forge, an ambulance caisson, one caisson for the regimental papers, two caissons per field battalion for infantry cartridges and the transport of bread. These vehicles would be served and conducted by a company of regimental gunners included one lieutenant, one sub-lieutenant, three sergeants, three corporals, twenty gunners, forty soldiers of the train, and two craftsmen. A decree of 11 April 1810 ordered the regiments returning from Germany to surrender all such vehicles, equipment and horses on their arrival in France or Italy. Those regiments remaining in theatre retained their guns and in 1811 increased their number to four. On 17 April 1811 the regiments in France were ordered to reconstitute their artillery detachments. Those regiments which took part in the ill-fated invasion of Russia in 1812 lost their artillery during the winter retreat. Napoleon drew a line under the experiment in 1813.

In terms of its tactical employment, the regulation of 1 August 1791 mentioned using regimental artillery to protect the intervals between battalions when fending off cavalry attacks. The principal use was to bolster the firepower of the line and give close support against fixed positions. Gunners were instructed to concentrate on enemy troop formations rather than engaging in counter battery fire. The problem with regimental artillery was the difficulty of transporting it across the battlefield on drag ropes. On balance this difficulty outweighed its usefulness. If fire support was required at a particular point, a general was probably better served by horse artillery which was able to move at speed and arrive at an important point relatively quickly.

[**See also:** 2. Line infantry regiments; 85. Wagons and horses; 165. Infantry squares.]

*Chapter 2*

# Officers of the Staff

## 5. Colonel (*colonel*)

The colonel was the commanding officer of an infantry regiment. The title originated from the Italian *colonnella* – the commander of a column of soldiers. Traditionally appointed by the sovereign, during the early republican era the title colonel was suppressed and replaced with the title *chef de brigade* (21 February 1793) with this post falling to the most senior battalion commander in the half-brigade. The title of colonel was readopted in 1803. Regardless of the title, the colonel took a leading role in every aspect of the regiment's administration, instruction and training, police and discipline and led it in the field in wartime. He was the chairman of the regiment's council of administration; he set the objectives for training for officers and men alike. Colonels chose the regimental musicians and the regimental children. Colonels made the nominations for promotion and made recommendations for entry into the Legion of Honour.

[**See also:** 20. Chief musician; 24. Captain; 34. Grenadier; 37. Drummer; 43. Recruitment captain; 45. Ensign bearer; 47. Master-at-arms; 48. Orderly; 51. Worker; 52. Fifer; 53. Uniform – general description (introduction); 64. Epaulettes; 68. Shako; 71. Plumes; 84. Tents; 85. Wagons and horses; 94. Flags and eagles; 95. Ensigns; 107. Council of administration; 109. The regimental chest; 110. Pay; 114. Auditing and reviews; 115. Leave; 118. Promotion to the officer corps; 119. Awards and national recognition; 132. General disciplinary measures; 135. Councils of War; 139. Honouring dignitaries; 141. Funerary honours; 149. Tactical placement of senior officers and staff; 183. The daily routine; 205. Cleaning & maintenance (introduction); 213. Basic training; 214. Instruction of officers; 219. General education; 234. After the battle.]

## 6. Major (*major*)

The rank of major was introduced by Bonaparte on *15 Floréal XI* (5 May 1803). It is important to note this rank had existed before 1 January 1791, but previously the major was placed below the lieutenant colonel in seniority. Napoleon placed the majors second only to the colonel in rank. While the colonel was in charge of personnel, the major was placed in charge of material and administration. The major was not a field officer, but remained in command of the regimental depot. They were specially charged with administrative inspections, the uniform of the regiment, its discipline, police, and the accounting of the regiment and its companies. In many respects there was a degree of crossover with the duties of the quartermaster treasurer and the adjutant major. In the council of administration, the major took on the role of 'reporter' and had a consultative voice in the debates, although he was not a formal member. However with colonels increasingly away in the field for extended periods, majors took on the role of chairman of the permanent council of administration. Majors were responsible for reporting acts of heroism to the minister of war; they would also report births, deaths and marriages which occurred in foreign lands. From 1811 there was also the title of major in second (*major en second*). With regiments having anything up to five field battalions, it was common for a single regiment to be providing battalions to different theatres. The major in second would therefore command those battalions not under the colonel's direct control.

[**See also:** 48. Orderly; 64. Epaulettes; 71. Plumes; 85. Wagons and horses; 107. Council of administration; 118. Promotion to the officer corps; 141. Funerary honours.]

## 7. Lieutenant colonel (*lieutenant colonel*)

In the regulation of 1 August 1791, infantry battalions were commanded by a lieutenant colonel. In the original light infantry battalions and National Guard Volunteers there were two lieutenant colonels, one of whom was the commanding officer. When the battalion was in line formation, the battalion commander was mounted on a horse and located thirty paces behind the file closers rank at the centre of the battalion, directly behind the flag. During battalion fire he would decide if firing should be oblique or direct. If formed as part of a brigade he would repeat commands of the brigadier general. In a square he would be at the centre and able to look over his men's heads to direct their fire. The rank of lieutenant colonel ceased to be recognised after 1793.

[**See also:** 2. Line infantry regiments; 8. Battalion commander.]

## 8. Battalion commander (*chef de bataillon*)

After the creation of the half-brigades on 21 February 1793, the rank of lieutenant colonel was suppressed in favour of the term chief of battalion, or battalion commander. Generally speaking, prospective battalion commanders first had to serve as captains. On *15 Floréal XIII* (5 May 1805) Napoleon stipulated battalion commanders must have eight years' experience as an officer, including four years as a captain. The most junior battalion commander in the regiment would command the first battalion because it was supposed the colonel would always be with his first battalion. If a battalion was broken up into detachments, the battalion commander would remain with the largest portion of it. When the battalion commander was absent he was deputised by the most senior captain who took on the title commanding captain (*capitaine commandant*). On *23 Fructidor VII*

(9 September 1799) an additional battalion commander was appointed to look after administration of the corps. This practice appears not to have been universally recognised and ceased after the creation of the post of major in 1803.

[**See also:** 7. Lieutenant colonel; 24. Captain; 48. Orderly; 51. Worker; 64. Epaulettes; 68. Shako; 71. Plumes; 85. Wagons and horses; 107. Council of administration; 117. Promotion; 118. Promotion to the officer corps; 127. Wills; 131. The hierarchy of command; 135. Councils of War; 141. Funerary honours; 149. Tactical placement of senior officers and staff; 169. Volley firing; 171. Firing by rank; 173. Firing from the cross-bayonets position; 183. The daily routine; 184. Police; 226. Arrival at camp; 227. Duties in camp; 229. Outpost duty; 231. Battle tactics.]

## 9. Adjutant major (*adjudant major*)

The adjutant major was the officer charged with all details relating to the instruction, movement, discipline and police of a regiment, with particular concern for their own battalion. Reporting directly to the senior officers, the adjutant major was known simply as 'the major' in order to distinguish him from the adjutant sub-officer.

The position of adjutant major was typically awarded to a lieutenant by the regiment's council of administration. After eighteen months in the role, the adjutant major would be automatically raised to the rank of captain and would retain this grade until promoted to the rank of battalion commander. Although this was a means of fast tracking the careers of promising junior officers, critics of the system pointed out the potential pitfalls of having battalion commanders with no first-hand experience of the command and administration of their own company.

The adjutant major's tactical position was behind the right half of the battalion. When the battalion was formed with other battalions, if the brigade commander's voice was drowned out by the noise of battle, or lost in strong winds, the adjutant major was permitted to repeat the words of command. In terms of administration the adjutant major was specially responsible for maintaining the book of orders (*livre d'ordres*). They were also able to deputise for the quartermaster treasurer.

[**See also:** 16. Adjutant; 25. Lieutenant; 37. Drummer; 42. Clothing officer; 48. Orderly; 64. Epaulettes; 85. Wagons and horses; 131. The hierarchy of command; 132. General disciplinary measures; 149. Placement of senior officers and staff; 183. The daily routine; 185. The police guard; 191. Rations & supplies (introduction); 215. Instruction of sub-officers; 227. Duties in camp.]

## 10. Quartermaster treasurer (*quartier maître trésorier*)

The regimental quartermaster treasurer (QMT) was an officer responsible for the management of funds and accounting. Traditionally they were 'officers of fortune', which is to say they were selected on merit and competence rather than a noble pedigree. In many cases they were given the rank of sub-lieutenant and were considered non–combatants. By 1788 they were allowed to progress to the rank of lieutenant and after the decree of 3 August 1792 they were allowed to hold the rank of captain. The law of *18 Nivôse IV* (8 January 1796) recognised a second QMT; one remaining with the corps in the field, while the first remained at the depot. After the reforms of 18 February 1808 only a single QMT was recognised. He would remain in the depot while a paymaster officer accompanied the regiment.

The principal duties of the QMT were to ride ahead on the march and prepare the regiment's lodgings and to oversee distributions. This officer held the accounting books and other records such as annual registers of troops and movement records. He was secretary of the regimental council of administration and sat opposite the chairman, although he was not granted a vote. The QMT was one of three key holders for the regimental chest. Under the civil code introduced by Napoleon (*code Napoléon*) the QMT performed the role of civil officer when the corps was on campaign. This made the QMT responsible for the register of births, deaths and marriages within the regiment.

[See also: 107. Council of administration; 109. The regimental chest; 110. Pay; 112. Deductions and funds.]

## 11. Paymaster officer (*officier payeur*)

This role was created on 18 February 1808 and was, in essence, a lieutenant who performed the role of treasurer to the field battalions while the regiment's quartermaster treasurer remained at the depot. The paymaster officer would maintain a register detailing all receipts and expenditure and submit this to the quartermaster treasurer on their eventual return to the depot. In the absence of the quartermaster treasurer the paymaster officer would also assist at distributions.

[See also: 10. Quartermaster treasurer; 110. Pay.]

## 12. Chaplain (*aumônier*)

The decree of 1 January 1791 recognised one chaplain per infantry regiment attached to the staff. Chaplains were not provided for the battalions of foot chasseurs, nor for the battalions of National Guard Volunteers; although this is not to say some may have had chaplains on an unofficial basis. As the Catholic Church increasingly became a rallying point for counter-revolutionaries, public worship was forbidden in October 1793. Therefore by 1794 the post of regimental chaplain ceased to exist. Although Catholic worship was officially restored in France in 1801, the post of regimental chaplain was not officially re-established until after the Napoleonic Wars, on 24 July 1816.

[See also: 140. Honours to religious parades and services.]

Grenadiers of the 84th Line proclaiming their tattered eagle standard.

## 13. Eagle bearer (*porte-aigle*)

In the order of *11 Messidor XII* (30 June 1804), there was one eagle standard per battalion, carried by a sergeant major. The decree of 8 February 1808 only recognised one eagle per regiment, carried by an eagle-bearer chosen from the lieutenants or sub-lieutenants, and attached to the regimental staff. The eagle standards were carried in a holster attached to a belt worn on the left shoulder. Salutes were made when the emperor or the princes of empire, grand dignitaries, ministers and marshals were present. Traditionally the flag would be tilted forwards and lowered so the tip of the lance was six inches from the ground. However, when the eagles were introduced in 1804, the weight of the eagle made this type of salute extremely difficult, so at the Camp of Boulogne an order was issued by Marshal Berthier that the pole only had to be inclined forward by 45 degrees.

[See also: 17. Second and third eagle bearers; 94. Flags and eagles; 146. Placement of the colour guard.]

## 14. Surgeon major (*chirurgien-major*)

Although surgery was basic by modern standards, the role of regimental surgeons became increasingly important during the Napoleonic wars. A medical service had been created in 1708 under Louis XIV, but through much of the century surgery was typically performed at regimental level by the company barbers. It was generally considered the skills and tools required for shaving and cutting a man's hair were a good basis for performing surgery. By the time of the Napoleonic wars matters had advanced somewhat, with a qualified doctor serving as the chief medical officer in a regiment. Appointed by the minister of war the surgeon major made up part of the regimental staff and was on a similar pay scale to a captain. During the wars of the Revolution, there was typically one surgeon major per battalion, although between 1794 and 1803 the position was termed medical officer (*officier de santé*). By 1808 only one surgeon major was recognised, although he was supported by four surgeon aides and five sub-aides.

During formal reviews of the regiment, the surgeon major would be positioned in front of the battalion commander, twenty paces behind the battalion. However, in battle, the surgeon major would generally set himself up somewhere in the rear, in a place sheltered from enemy fire, or in a building where he might give aid to the wounded. Each army would have a surgeon, doctor and pharmacist in chief. In theory the chief surgeon could pool the regimental medical officers together, but in practice the surgeons remained with their regiments and organised immediate first aid, stabilising casualties before arranging their evacuation to the army's field hospitals.

In garrison the surgeon major would manage the infirmary and issue bills exempting men from service. He would also report those who had feigned sickness or injury as a ruse. He would make periodic inspections of the barracks to ensure sanitation was being maintained. Recruits and conscripts would be examined to ensure they had arrived in a state fit for service. He would also examine soldiers returning from leave; sub-officers who were found to have contracted venereal disease or scabies might well be demoted. The surgeon major could make recommendations for sending officers and men to civilian hospitals to be treated, or to take the waters at a thermal spa.

[**See also:** 15. Surgeon aide; 85. Wagons and horses; 126. Registering deaths; 183. The daily routine; 236. The medical officer's manual; 253. Medical treatment in garrison; 254. Military hospitals.]


## 15. Surgeon aide (*chirurgien aide*)

Assistants to the surgeon major, these medical officers were paid in line with lieutenants and made up the part of the regimental staff. According to the decree of 18 February 1808 there were four aides, who were in turn assisted by five sub-aides. Like the surgeon major, the first category would have been qualified doctors with a fair knowledge of their craft. However the sub-aides tended to be trainees let loose on the army after just a few months study in a medical school.

[**See also:** 14. Surgeon major.]

# Chapter 3

# Men of the Petty Staff

## 16. Adjutant (*adjudant sous-officier*)

The adjutant was the senior sub-officer of a battalion and made up part of the regimental petty staff. Their duties were onerous and great pains were made in selecting the best possible candidate for this role. The qualities sought were outlined in the ordinance of 1 July 1788: adjutants had to be well trained and possess a good spirit. The commanders of regiments and senior officers were advised to observe potential candidates for at least one month before selecting one.

The adjutant was responsible for the training of the sub-officers and examining candidates for the role of sergeant and corporal. He was also responsible for overseeing the various instructional classes established in the regiment, such as the schools of drumming, music, fencing and dance. He would make checks on the battalion's camping equipment, gunpowder and munitions, and direct the workshops for making cartridges. He was responsible for policing the battalion and was the soul and embodiment of discipline. He kept watch over the guardhouse and the cells and made ad hoc roll calls of men confined to quarters. He kept hold of the police guard's register and signed it off every day. Morning and night, he would receive and collate the company roll calls and make a general roll call which he presented at night for the signature of the captain of police. Working closely with the adjutant major, he would help communicate orders within the regiment. Adjutants were given a supplement of 1 *franc* 50 *centimes* per month for paper, ink and quills.

On active service the adjutant was responsible for assembling the battalion under arms and equalising the strength of the platoons. His tactical position was behind the centre of the left half of the battalion. The adjutant also commanded guards of honour. He set the routine guards in garrison, on the march and in camp. On the march he assembled the police guard and nominated a sub–officer to look after the walking wounded. He nominated the time for distributions, decided how many men were required by each company to receive them and maintained order. In 1808 a second adjutant was added to each battalion, and was placed behind the right hand file of the battalion.

The adjutant's uniform was similar to that worn by the officers. He wore boots when under arms rather than shoes and gaiters, and carried an épée which was worn on a bandolier over the right shoulder. However, unlike officers he carried a cane, only drawing his épée for personal defence in action. The cane served no useful purpose and was an affectation which survived from earlier times. The cane consisted of a staff with some form of pommel and base, but there was no regulation length for them. In 1807 Bardin suggested they should be one metre in length so they could serve as a tool for measurement. This practical suggestion does not appear to have been universally adopted until after the Napoleonic wars.

[**See also:** 9. Adjutant major; 28. Sergeant; 37. Drummer; 40. Cantineer; 47. Master-at-arms; 63. Footwear; 64. Epaulettes; 68. Shako; 107. Council of administration; 112. Deductions and funds; 113. Credit and debt; 117. Promotion; 136. Military executions; 138. Salutes; 145. Assembling the battalion; 149. Tactical placement of senior officers and staff; 183. The daily routine; 184. Police; 185. The police guard; 186. Making the rounds; 187. The sergeant of police; 188. Duties of the corporal of the guard; 191. Rations & supplies (introduction); 215. Instruction of sub-officers; 227. Duties in camp.]

## 17. Second and third eagle bearers (*deuxième et troisième porte aigles*)

The decree of 8 February 1808 instituted the posts of second and third eagle-bearers in the infantry regiments. These posts were awarded to 'old, illiterate soldiers'. They were armed with a spontoon (*esponton*) and pistols in an 'oriental' holster attached to a belt worn across the chest. In the decree of 25 December 1811 the escorts were described as wearing a metal helmet and 'protective' epaulettes. They were armed with a spear decorated by a small swallow-tailed pennon (*flamme*) or a decorative parade spontoon with a brace of pistols for defence.

[**See also:** 13. Eagle bearer; 65. Distinctive markings; 88. Pistol; 146. Placement of the colour guard.]

## 18. Drum major (*tambour major*)

Chosen by the regiment's council of administration the drum major was chief among the corps of drummers and cornetists. The role of drum major was one of the most prestigious in the regiment. He had the rank of sergeant major and was almost always chosen from one of the tallest men in the regiment. The drum major conducted the drum corps using a cane with a heavy, ornate pommel mounted on a veneered wooden staff which tapered towards the base. The staff was often decorated by a metal chain which was wrapped round its length and fixed to the pommel and base cap by studs. The dimensions of the staff varied from corps to corps, but were eventually regulated in 1818 at 1.3 metres in length, pommel and base cap included.

The regulation of 1 August 1791 described the signals used by the drum major as follows:

- *La générale* – extend the right arm, holding the cane in the middle and raising the pommel level with the collar.

- *L'assemblée* – extend the arm, raising the cane about one foot off the ground, the thumb resting on the pommel.
- *Le rappel* – place the cane on the right shoulder, the base inverted.
- *Aux drapeaux* – raise the arm, turn the wrist inwards, so the cane crosses horizontally in front at the height of the cravat.
- *Aux champs* – raise the cane perpendicularly, the base at the top, the arm held level with the right shoulder.
- *Le pas accéléré* – carry the cane directly in front, the base forward, the arm extended.
- *La retraite* – pass the cane across behind the back.
- *La messe* – carry the pommel of the cane on the right shoulder.
- *La breloque* – take the cane by the cordon and hold it level with the shoulder.
- *Aux armes* – carry the cane across the left shoulder, the base behind.

The cane would also be used for signalling the direction of march for the drummers:

- To march to the right flank, the cane was held in the middle and the arm extended to the right.
- To march to the left flank, the same, but held in the left arm.
- To dismiss the platoon, allow the base of the cane to fall in the left hand level with the eyes.
- To form the platoon, allow the pommel of the cane to fall in the left hand level with the eyes.

A drum major leads his half-brigade in a march through the streets of Paris.

- To change direction, the drum major would make a half turn and indicate by a movement of the cane which side the drummers should turn towards.
- To march obliquely to the right, the right arm level was held level with the shoulder, holding the cane at an angle, while the left hand grasped the base of the cane level with the hip.
- To march obliquely to the left, the reverse was done, the pommel of the cane indicating always the side towards which one should oblique.

[See also: 19. Drum corporal; 20. Chief musician; 37. Drummer; 64. Epaulettes; 107. Council of administration; 147. Placement of drummers and musicians; 182. Lodgings and the arrangements of the bedchamber; 183. The daily routine; 227. Duties in camp; 233. Duties of sub-officers in battle.]

## 19. Drum corporal (*caporal tambour*)

Traditionally known as the master drummer (*tambour maître*), the title of drum corporal was created by the law of 29 October 1790, which allowed the colonel to nominate a drum corporal from among his corps of drummers. Although the drum corporal was equipped with a drum and was required to beat signals he could lead the drum corps in the absence of the drum major. In a two battalion regiment, the drum corporal would always lead the drum corps of the second battalion so would therefore require a drum major's cane, although this might be less ornate than the one used by the drum major, for example only having silk or woollen cords rather than chains. The drum corporal was responsible for forming a school of drumming, which included lessons on enemy drum beats. The drum corporal would also teach how to disassemble the shell of the drum and to prepare new skins. The decree of 3 July 1811 allowed regiments to nominate a second drum corporal who would remain in the regimental depot and train the student drummers.

[See also: 18. Drum major; 37. Drummer; 147. Placement of drummers and musicians.]

## 20. Chief musician (*chef de musique*)

Military music had two principal functions. The first was as accompaniment to the drum signals used to communicate orders, or to aid soldiers marching on parades. The second function was ceremonial, playing martial music to add a sense of occasion and pomp to parades and reviews. Music was also sometimes played in battle to encourage soldiers and, presumably, take their minds off the chaos and tumult around them. The law of *26 Messidor III* (14 July 1795 – the sixth anniversary of the Bastille) encouraged military bands to play patriotic and civil airs in battle. True enough, French soldiers had sung in battle since before William of Normandy's men chanted *chansons* at the battle of Hastings in 1066 (allegedly the famous *chanson de Roland*). The repertoire of regimental bands was extremely varied. Firstly, there were the great patriotic airs written in the Revolutionary period. After a séance of the National Convention on *26 Messidor* III (14 July 1795) the 1792 *la Marseillaise* was adopted as the 'civic song'. After Napoleon's coronation in 1804, *la Marseillaise* was supplanted by the 1791 *Veillons au Salut de l'Empire* (Let us watch over the Safety of the Empire), and the 1794 *chant du départ* (Song of the Departure). Overtly revolutionary songs such as *Ah! ça ira* did not survive after the establishment of the Consulate, despite being extremely catchy. Band leaders might also interpret various historical and contemporary classical pieces, popular operas, not to mention popular folk songs, drinking songs like *fanchon*, or silly songs like *chanson de l'oignon* (the onion song) allegedly sung by the grenadiers of the Guard at Marengo in 1800. Another popular song played to the beat of the charge was *On va leur percer le flanc* (we're going to break through their flank). In some respects these battlefield songs were akin to naval capstan shanties, helping the men act in unison; to march in step and to excite their courage.

Regimental bands were led by a chief musician. An honorary sub-officer, the chief musician was ordinarily a hireling (*gagiste*) appointed by the colonel. The role was created in 1788 and confirmed by the law of *23 Fructidor VII* (9 September 1799) which recognised one chief musician per half-brigade, numbering as one of the eight musicians allowed. The chief musician wore the same uniform as the other musicians with the distinction of gold or silver braiding around the coat collar and the stripes of the sergeant major. When the band was assembled, the chief musician would stand in the ranks and generally play one of the instruments of harmony such as a clarinet. Chief musicians were responsible for the instruction of the band, and also for teaching music for cornets and bugles, the fife and percussion. Tactically, the chief musician and the band came under the orders of the drum major; administratively the chief musician was under the orders of an 'officer of music'.

[**See also:** 5. Colonel; 18. Drum major; 21. Musicians; 38. Cornetist.]

## 21. Musicians (*musiciens*)

In the 18th century the first military bands were attached to the regimental drum corps and were normally composed of no more than a fifer or two, and a clarinettist. As regimental bands became more popular after the Seven Years War, horn players and bassoonists were added, sometimes taking the place of drummers on the regimental rolls, all down to the whim of the colonel. The ordinance of 17 March 1788 allowed each infantry regiment to employ eight musicians plus a bandmaster (*maître de musique* – the forerunner of *chef de musique*). Light infantry battalions were allowed to hire four musicians who played the cornet or other similar brass instruments. In 1791 and throughout the remainder of the 1790s, the size of the band was reduced to eight men, including the chief. The composition of a regimental band would likely include a minimum of two clarinettists, two hornists, two bassoonists, a bass drummer and a cymbalist. However, during the Consulate and First Empire regimental bands began to grow in size.

Although there were officially only eight musicians allowed on the books (twelve in 1815), many colonels wished to enhance the prestige of their regiment by imitating the grandeur of Napoleon's Guard and fielding a large band. The additional numbers might be enhanced by fifers provided by the regimental corps of children, but it was equally common for the colonel to employ a number of supernumerary musicians, who were hirelings (*gagistes*). These might be professional musicians who would be offered a written contract for a year or two, or they might be serving soldiers who were capable of playing an instrument and who would be issued an unofficial high pay for their services. To meet these unauthorised expenses, the colonel would institute a private fund known as the *masse de musique* into which each officer would contribute for the upkeep of the band from deductions to his wages. This typically amounted to a day, or day-and-a-half's pay per month. A captain or lieutenant would be designated as officer of music (*officier de musique*), who, in addition to his usual duties, would manage the band and supervise the collection of funds.

A circular of 2 November 1807 criticised the practice of employing hirelings on limited contracts and having them draw pay and subsistence as if they were serving soldiers. The state would only pay for eight musicians, so if the colonel wished to have more, the musicians should be signed up as proper soldiers, or hired on a contract and clothed and provided for entirely at the officers' expense, with a cap of no more than one day's pay per month, per officer.

Musicians officially wore the same uniform as drummers throughout the period. After *17 Frimaire XI* (8 December 1802) they were allowed a single braid ten lines wide on the cuff. After *11 Fructidor XII* (29 August 1804) infantry musicians were armed with a short musketoon and bayonet.

[See also: 20. Chief musician; 39. Regimental children; 52. Fifer; 107. Council of administration; 147. Placement of drummers and musicians; 182. Lodgings and the arrangements of the bedchamber.]

## 22. Master craftsmen (*maître ouvriers*)

Each infantry regiment contained a number of non-combatant craftsmen who were appointed by its council of administration. They came under the supervision of the clothing officer (*capitaine d'habillement*) and were responsible for the manufacture of uniforms and petty equipment, as well as the upkeep of weapons. The master craftsmen wore the same uniforms as sub-officers and were armed with an infantry sabre. Their workshops were normally located in the regimental depot and after the law of *7 Thermidor VIII* (26 July 1800) each craftsman would take at least two of the regiment's children as apprentices and would employ soldiers with appropriate trades. The master craftsmen included:

**Master tailor** (*maître tailleur*) – Ranking as a sergeant, the master tailor was the senior craftsman in the regiment, responsible for manufacturing uniforms and making repairs. The master tailor would measure each man and produce a uniform in the approved model. When complete the new uniforms would be tried on by the men in the presence of their officers and anything which was not in order had to be made good on the spot at the master tailor's own expense. Once the new uniforms were manufactured and issued, the master tailor would concentrate on making repairs. He was seconded by a number of tailors. Although not officially recognised as such, there are indications every company would have at least one tailor. The 1810 *cours d'administration militaire* states the company funds were used to pay the salary of the *tailleur de compagnie*. This tailor was most likely one of the authorised workers (*travailleurs*) excused normal duties to pursue their trade.

**Master armourer** (*maître armurier*) – Armourers were chosen by the Council of Administration and ranked as corporals, wearing the same coat and stripes. When weapons were taken to the armourer for repair, they were paid for in two ways. Firstly, if there were pieces missing, broken due to poor quality or an event which occurred in service, the general fund would pay for the repair. If the damage was due to the negligence of the soldier, he would pay for it himself.

**Master cordwainer** (*maître cordonnier*) – The master cordwainer held the rank of corporal and was responsible for making and repairing shoes and cartridge pouches. The word *cordonnier* derives from the popularity of using cordouan leather (i.e. from Cordoba in Spain) for the manufacture of shoes. (Note: a cobbler is technically someone who only repairs shoes, not a manufacturer of them).

**Master gaiter-maker** (*maître guêtrier*) – This self-explanatory role originally came under the remit of the master tailor, but was officially recognised as an independent role on *23 Fructidor VII* (9 September 1799).

[**See also:** 39. Regimental children; 42. Clothing officer; 51. Worker; 53. Uniform – general description (introduction); 54. Materials; 57. Coat; 59. Greatcoat; 70. Forage cap; 99. Voluntary enlistment; 107. Council of administration; 112. Deductions and funds; 182. Lodgings and the arrangements of the bedchamber; 205. Cleaning & maintenance (introduction); 210. Maintaining the musket.]

## 23. Baggage master (*vaguemestre*)

A member of the regimental petty staff, the origin of the word *vaguemestre* is believed to be German (*Wagen Meister* – wagon master). This function was given to a trusted sergeant or a quartermaster corporal. He was commonly known as the first sub-officer of the corps (other than the adjutant). However he only received particular pay on campaign, otherwise the role was carried out as part of the ordinary duties of a sub-officer (the role of *vaguemestre* was only officially established from 1808 to 1814).

On campaign the baggage master came under the orders of a baggage master general and was inscribed on a list of authorised persons. When ordered to march, the baggage master would inspect the regiment's wagons and carts and on the eve of departure, gather the regiment's baggage and have it loaded. He was responsible for the safety and security of the wagons on the road and for having them unloaded at the destination. The baggage master would also have the officer's orderlies under his command.

In his quality as regimental postman (*facteur*) he was authorised to draw letters from the army's post office addressed to officers, sub-officers and soldiers of the corps. He would maintain a register of all post coming in and out of the regiment, as well as return unclaimed letters, citing the reason for the recipient's absence, or if the person was unknown to the regiment. He also looked after the postal service, had the right to collect one *sou* per letter and one *sou* per *livre* of coin sent by post.

[**See also:** 85. Wagons and horses; 107. Council of administration; 116. Military postal service; 224. Duties of the baggage master; 225. Arrival at a *gîte*; 227. Duties in camp.]

# Chapter 4

# Company Personnel

## 24. Captain (*capitaine*)

Captains were the senior company officer. Prior to the Revolution they enjoyed a feudal privilege of having the company named after them. Like the regimental provisional titles, this feudal practice ceased after 1 January 1791. Captains were responsible to the superior officers, and above all, to the colonel, for all aspects of the discipline, training, administration and uniform of their companies. Captains were required to visit their companies daily. They would receive a daily report from the duty officer and consider all requests for leave, late arrival, and any form of exemption before submitting this to the battalion commander for approval.

The law of *23 Floréal V* (12 May 1797) created three classes of captain. The captain first class had the right to command the battalion in the absence of the battalion commander. This was important because in war, everyone needed a deputy. There was therefore one first class captain per battalion. This raised a question: what if the captain of grenadiers was the senior captain, should he command the battalion? In many cases the question was academic, because the grenadiers were often detached from their parent battalion, but it lead to examples where there was no first class captain present. Napoleon resolved the issue (or further muddied the waters, depending on your viewpoint) by declaring in 1808 that all captains of grenadiers would be held as first class regardless of their rank. In effect, each battalion would therefore have two first class captains. The creation of the third class of captains was seen as less beneficial and became a constant source of complaint by those labelled thus.

The captain of grenadiers was typically chosen by the colonel. In 1788 the colonel was required to select an officer from the six most junior captains; however this practice changed during the Revolution. In 1808 it was confirmed the captain was selected at the choice of the colonel. Moreover, this captain would always be in the first class of captains, as explained above. The captain of grenadiers enjoyed some prerogatives, such as being exempt from police and guard duties. This recognised that the grenadier captain above all would be most likely to come in harm's way leading assaults or commanding desperate rearguard actions. Voltigeur captains did not enjoy the same treatment, even though they were recognised as commanding an elite company. Again this double standard was a common source of complaint and resentment for officers.

Light infantry captain. This uniform
and hair style is typical for the period
between 1794 and 1800.

[**See also:** 8. Battalion commander; 9. Adjutant major; 25. Lieutenant; 27. Sergeant major; 34. Grenadier; 42. Clothing officer; 43. Recruitment captain; 48. Orderly; 50. Barber; 51. Worker; 64. Epaulettes; 68. Shako; 85. Wagons and horses; 106. Administration & pay (introduction); 107. Council of administration; 112. Deductions and funds; 115. Leave; 117. Promotion; 118. Promotion to the officer corps; 131. The hierarchy of command; 132. General disciplinary measures; 135. Councils of war; 143. Tactical composition of a battalion; 144. Assembling the platoon; 151. Composition of detachments; 183. The daily routine; 185. The police guard; 213. Basic training; 253. Medical treatment in garrison.]

## 25. Lieutenant (*lieutenant*)

Deriving in French from *lieu* (place) and *tenant* (holder), the word lieutenant meant someone who held the place of another. In its most general sense it refers to the second officer in command after the captain. Lieutenants were graded as first or second class, there being an equal number of each class within the regiment. They were not assigned to companies by order of seniority. They might be promoted to the rank of captain, or be appointed as adjutant major, from where they could gain a captain's rank and be fast-tracked to battalion commander. Lieutenants might also serve as quartermaster treasurers, or from 1808, as eagle bearers or paymaster officers. They were administratively in charge of half of the company and were required to share the role of duty officer with the sub-lieutenant, with whom they shared their quarters. Tactically the lieutenant was located in the rank of file closers, behind the second section of the platoon. In a column of sections the lieutenant would quit the file closers rank and stand at the head of the second section as section commander.

[**See also:** 9. Adjutant major; 10. Quartermaster treasurer; 11. Paymaster officer; 13. Eagle bearer; 26. Sub-lieutenant; 64. Epaulettes; 84. Tents; 106. Administration & pay (introduction); 118. Promotion to the officer corps; 144. Assembling the platoon; 183. The daily routine; 184. Police; 226. Arrival at camp.]

## 26. Sub-lieutenant (*sous-lieutenant*)

The rank of sub-lieutenant was the most junior officer grade. Their functions were essentially the same as the lieutenant, taking administrative oversight of half the company and sharing the role of weekly duty officer. Their tactical position was behind the centre of the first section. If the sections of a company were split, the sub-lieutenant would remain with the captain's section. If the captain and lieutenant were both absent, the sub-lieutenant was considered too junior to take command of a company. In this situation a lieutenant from another company would be seconded over.

[**See also:** 25. Lieutenant; 64. Epaulettes; 112. Deductions and funds; 118. Promotion to the officer corps; 144. Assembling the platoon; 184. Police.]

## 27. Sergeant major (*sergent-major*)

Below the battalion's adjutant, the stalwarts of each company were the sergeant majors. Selected by the captain, the sergeant major was effectively responsible for running the company's administration, police, training and maintaining discipline. He was responsible for forming the platoon and ensuring everyone was correctly placed within it and appropriately attired. The sergeant major held eight registers and books which governed the administration, police, discipline and training of the company. A digest of these registers demonstrates the breadth of detail the sergeant major was concerned with:

1. *Livre de signalement* – this was a summary of the regimental roll which contained the date of incorporation into the company, promotion and the date of leaving the corps.
2. *Contrôle annuel* – the annual company roll listed the names of the men actually serving and the post they held.
3. *Livre d'ordre* – this was a record of orders issued daily to the company. When the book was full, it was deposited with the captain.
4. *Inscription du service* – the purpose of this register was to ensure men each took turns at mounting guard duty.
5. *Cahier d'appel* – this register listed the men by length of service and contained the names of the officers, sub-officers, drummers, sappers, fifers and children included in the company. Separate sections listed the men by height order, recorded which men were bedmates (they slept two to a bed in this period), and noted which weapons had been issued to them (weapons were numbered).

6. *Livret des travailleurs* – this was a record of the men granted the right of taking work, with details of their work and pay. It also recorded the name of the soldier charged with looking after the workers' weapons and equipment. This register would also record the men granted leave, and the date on which they were due to return.
7. *Livre de punitions* – colloquially known as the 'red book' (*livre rouge*) this was a record of misdemeanours and the punishments inflicted for them.
8. *Livre d'instruction* – this record held details of the training men had received, the names of instructors and the passage from one lesson to the next.

Every five days the sergeant major would make a record of the wages due to the men. Once prepared it would be signed by the company commander and the duty officer, who would go and collect the money from the quartermaster treasurer at the hour fixed by the daily orders. He would make a weekly check on the furnishings of the bed chambers and check the company's camping equipment and tools. The sergeant major would also look after the arms and effects of the men in hospital. He lodged with the quartermaster corporal and enjoyed the right to sleep alone in a single bed. The tactical position of the sergeant major was to the rear of the platoon in line with the officers, behind the right of the second section. One sergeant major per battalion would hold the battalion's colour or ensign.

[**See also:** 2. Line infantry regiments; 3. Light infantry regiments; 13. Eagle bearer; 29. Quartermaster corporal; 45. Ensign bearer; 56. Weight of arms and equipment; 65. Distinctive markings; 94. Flags and eagles; 95. Ensigns; 96. Pennants; 106. Administration & pay (introduction); 108. The Ordinary; 110. Pay; 112. Deductions and funds; 114. Auditing and reviews; 116. Military postal service; 117. Promotion; 131. The hierarchy of command; 144. Assembling the platoon; 145. Assembling the battalion; 182. Lodgings and the arrangements of the bedchamber; 183. The daily routine; 184. Police; 221. On the march; 226. Arrival at camp; 227. Duties in camp; 229. Outpost duty; 234. After the battle; 253. Medical treatment in garrison.]

## 28. Sergeant (*sergent*)

Originally deriving from the Latin *servientem* (someone who was the servant of a lord) the rank of sergeant was one of the most long established ranks in the French Army. In the Napoleonic era sergeants had to be sufficiently instructed to command a platoon, and to have a good standard of literacy. In the administration of a company, sergeants were responsible for a subdivision comprising two squads. In the field, a sergeant might command a post numbering between twelve and eighteen men; or twenty-four men if two corporals were present (any unit numbering over thirty men had to be commanded by an officer).

The duties of a sergeant were manifold. His primary duty was one of supervision. He would undertake the evening roll call, hold the list of the petty equipment issued to the men and assist with writing in the men's account books. In garrison he would take turns as sergeant of the week (*sergent de semaine*), in other words, the company's duty sergeant. He might also be given the assignment of *sergent de planton*. The word *planton* derived from the verb *planter* – to plant; in this context it referred to a soldier who was assigned a fixed post for a period of up to twenty-four hours. This might include overseeing the details in the hospital, infirmary, bakery, workshop or magazine. He might also be assigned to the quarters of a general or superior officer, the town gates, etc. The adjutant would issue the *plantons* with their instructions and watch over them; sergeants assigned to *plantons* only carried their sabre. A sergeant might also be assigned to the regiment's police guard, or be the sergeant of the round (*sergent de ronde*) responsible for checking on the sentries, posts and touring round the ramparts.

A sergeant might also be assigned the role of instructor to those men granted permission to practice a civilian trade. The training sergeant would provide the workers lessons twice a week between 1 May and 1 August and three times per week at other times to ensure they maintained their martial competencies.

Sergeants also had an important tactical role. The position of replacement sub-officer (*sous-officier de remplacement*) was assigned to the first sergeant of each company. This was behind the platoon commander in the third rank. During firing, the replacement sergeant would fall back onto the line of the file closer's rank. Another important role was the *sergent de encadrement*. Although in the modern sense *encadrement* refers to the body of managerial or supervisory staff, in this sense it is closer to its other meaning, which is a frame. The second sergeant of the leftmost platoon would act as the left hand guide to the battalion, thus marking the extent, or framing the end of the line.

After 1811 when each battalion was issued with an ensign, two sergeants per battalion would flank the sergeant major bearing it. The main role of these sergeant guard-ensigns was to help regulate the pace of the battalion. The ensign itself was assigned no specific honours.

In garrison the sergeants lodged together and formed an 'ordinary' (i.e. they messed together). They paid 5 *centimes* more than the men, which meant they could afford to hire a civilian or sutleress to perform the cooking for them. They slept singly in garrison and two by two on route.

Although sergeants wore the standard infantry uniform there were several variations worth noting. Since the time of Louis XV sergeants wore moustaches. They carried a smaller version of cartridge pouch because they did not take part with the various species of platoon firing and therefore only needed to fire in extreme cases. In some regiments the sergeants carried *épées* rather than infantry sabres. When the use of shakos became universal, sergeants were allowed to wear a bicorn as part of their petty dress. Another important duty assigned to sergeants was to carry the vinegar canteens and, between them, a supplementary cooking pot (*marmite*) for the company.

[See also: 40. Cantineer; 65. Distinctive markings; 73. Beards and moustaches; 80. Petty equipment; 108. The Ordinary; 117. Promotion; 131. The hierarchy of command; 136. Military executions; 141. Funerary honours; 144. Assembling the platoon; 146. Placement of the colour

## 29. Quartermaster corporal (*caporal fourrier*)

The French word *fourrier* has no direct equivalent in English, being derived from the French term for a merchant of forage; however the term quartermaster corporal is perhaps the best translation of the role. In the Napoleonic era, the quartermaster corporal was responsible for holding the company registers, performing book keeping duties on behalf of the sergeant major and for being present at all distributions. The quartermaster corporal also arranged lodgings for soldiers on the march. He worked under the direct supervision of the sergeant major and lodged and ate with him. They had no specific tactical post in the platoon, but when the battalion was united for manoeuvres, the regulation of 1 August 1791 assigned them to the colour guard. This decision was often called into question. Firstly the battalion colours tended to become a fulcrum of the action in battle. It was not entirely sensible to place young men there who were used to a fairly sedentary life, and whose talents were better served organising the administration and lodgings for their comrades.

[**See also:** 23. Baggage master; 27. Sergeant major; 42. Clothing officer; 50. Barber; 65. Distinctive markings; 99. Voluntary enlistment; 106. Administration & pay (introduction); 112. Deductions and funds; 114. Auditing and reviews; 117. Promotion; 131. The hierarchy of command; 146. Placement of the colour guard; 183. The daily routine; 191. Rations & supplies (introduction); 192. Bread and biscuit; 198. Fuel for heating and cooking; 199. Food preparation (introduction); 221. On the march; 225. Arrival at a *gîte*; 226. Arrival at camp.]

## 30. Corporal (*caporal*)

The role of the corporal (archaically *cap d'esquad* – head of a squad) was to supervise a squad (*escouade*) of soldiers. Corporals would ensure their men remained at their post; they would take roll calls and ensure the men were dressed correctly; that housekeeping duties were performed and the uniform, arms and equipment were kept clean and in good repair. Corporals were cautioned against allowing their men to shave or comb their hair in the bedchambers, and they were not to permit their men to smoke, unless the weather was extremely cold. They would keep order among the men, resolving quarrels and ensuring the barracks remained free of 'strangers' such as brokers and 'suspect women'. They would also ensure the men did not gamble, nor sing obscene songs, or brag about licentious scenes, or past desertions. The corporal would put a stop to quarrels by conciliation or punishment.

As a qualification, corporals were required to be literate, and while they were required to share quarters with their men, they were cautioned against becoming too familiar with them. At the same time they were forbidden from injuring or maltreating their charges. When new recruits joined the squad, corporals took charge of their instruction and it was common for corporals to share a bunk with the newcomer to ensure he was not bullied.

Tactically, corporals fought within the ranks of the platoon, taking position in the front and third ranks on the flanks of each section. This tactical placing caused some debate about corporals being classed as sub-officers as they were technically 'men of the ranks'. However, the regulations of 1 August 1791 classed them as 'sub-officers', and this distinction remained throughout the period described in this work.

[See also: 65. Distinctive markings; 77. Gun tools; 79. Haversack; 106. Administration & pay (introduction); 117. Promotion; 131. The hierarchy of command; 144. Assembling the platoon; 146. Placement of the colour guard; 183. The daily routine; 184. Police; 186. Making the rounds; 188. Duties of the corporal of the guard; 205. Cleaning & maintenance (introduction); 216. Target practice; 218. Gymnastic and fitness exercises; 226. Arrival at camp; 229. Outpost duty; 233. Duties of sub-officers in battle.]

## 31. Chosen man (*appointé*)

This rank was awarded to the senior man in a squad after the corporal, or the senior drummer after the drum corporal. In the Royal Army the chosen man was a long-serving soldier of good conduct, perhaps blocked from promotion by illiteracy, but who was trustworthy and deserving of high pay. The chosen man could deputise for the corporal, but he was not exempt from fatigues or guard duty; nor did he fulfil any tactical function. In 1788 chosen men were stripped of their high pay. The grade was eliminated by the decree of *2 Frimaire II* (22 November 1793), but was later used by Swiss regiments in French service.

[See also: 30. Corporal; 151. Composition of detachments.]

## 32. Fusilier (*fusilier*)

Derived from the name of the weapon they carried (*fusil* was the French word for a flintlock musket), fusilier was the generic term for soldiers in the line infantry regiments who did not hold rank or belong to one of the elite companies. The companies of fusiliers were known more commonly as the 'centre companies', a description which derived from elite companies being assigned so-called places of honour on the wings of the battalion.

[See also: 2. Line infantry regiments; 56. Weight of arms and equipment; 64. Epaulettes; 71. Plumes; 86. Musket; 110. Pay; 136. Military executions; 143. Tactical composition of a battalion; 144. Assembling the platoon; 145. Assembling the battalion; 216. Target practice.]

## 33. Chasseur (*chasseur*)

Derived from the French word 'hunt' (*chasse*), the word chasseur was analogous with the German *jaeger* (hunter); indeed the inspiration for the first chasseur battalions came from Frederick the Great of Prussia who recruited the sons of gamekeepers skilled in marksmanship. Mounted or on foot, the first chasseurs were found in the mixed legions of Louis XV. Chasseurs were soldiers noted as being dependable, hardy, good shots, being skilful at fighting outside the ranks, and trusted not to desert. During the Seven Years War some colonels created their own chasseur units by selecting three marksmen per company who could act as scouts, protect the flanks and search woods. Initially these men remained attached to their parent companies, but by 1784 every infantry regiment had its own dedicated company of chasseurs – a precursor of the Napoleonic voltigeur companies. By 1788 there were twelve independent foot battalions of chasseurs and these formed the nucleus of the light infantry half-brigades which saw action in the wars of the Revolution.

In a proposed instruction for light infantry written in 1804, Colonel Guyard described the perfect chasseur as being young, between five foot (French) and five foot four (between 1.62 and 1.73 metres), with a good constitution and of robust health. Based on the experiences of the wars of the Revolution, smaller men were preferred for light infantry service because, Guyard claimed, they were more compact in their strength than tall men, better at resisting the fatigues of war, and were more *nerveux*, a word we might translate as on-edge, or aggressive. They also enjoyed the practical advantages of presenting a smaller target and found it easier to pass through copses and other difficult terrain than someone who might be five foot seven or eight.

[**See also:** 3. Light infantry regiments; 35. Carabineer; 57. Coat; 58. Coatee; 62. Gaiters; 64. Epaulettes; 68. Shako; 71. Plumes; 176. Skirmishing (introduction); 231. Battle tactics.]

## 34. Grenadier (*grenadier*)

During the reign of Louis XIV there was a type of light infantry known as the 'lost children' (*enfants perdues*) who during siege operations would volunteer for the perilous task of running forwards to throw hand grenades into enemy defences. Initially they were not armed with muskets, only a satchel of grenades, each the equivalent in size to a four pound cannon ball. This practice of throwing grenades gave rise to the term 'grenadier', and although the practice of using grenades stopped as musketry became more effective, the word remained in use and came to symbolise elite troops. (Grenades remained in use by engineer sappers and the navy.)

Grenadiers enjoyed a higher rate of pay, colloquially known as the '*sou* of the grenade'. Until 1812 they wore bearskin caps. In general, they never performed fatigues, except for themselves, such as making soup, and they were the first in the queue at distributions. Grenadiers never took part in routine guard duty, police guard, pickets or fatigues and could only be commanded by their own officers and sub-officers, who in turn were exempt from making rounds.

As a mark of distinction, they were issued with sabres, a throwback to the time when they needed a weapon for close protection after throwing their grenades. They were the first soldiers in the French Army to be awarded straps for their muskets, again, a throwback to the time when they needed their hands free for throwing grenades or scaling siege ladders. In the *ancien régime* grenadiers also enjoyed the dubious distinction of being punished by flogging from a leather musket strap, rather than being beaten by metal ramrods like common soldiers. Another archaic prerogative awarded to grenadiers was the right to torture men condemned to death, and blood their weapons at executions. Such grisly privileges did not survive beyond the Revolution.

By the 1790s a selection process was in place for nominating grenadiers. On the first of September each year, every captain would choose three fusiliers from his company who he thought deserved promotion into the grenadiers. The candidates were to be men who had displayed examples of valour, good conduct and subordination; always chosen from among soldiers of proven merit, with more than two years' service in the regiment and standing over 5ft 4 inches tall (approximately 1.73 m). The candidates would be forwarded to the quartermaster treasurer who would draw up a list presented to a delegation of grenadiers made

Grenadier and voltigeur of line infantry circa 1809.

up of the officers, sub-officers and the two longest serving grenadiers in the company. If there were vacancies in the company, the delegation would examine the list together, debate the merits of the candidates proposed and select two candidates for each post available. The colonel of the regiment would then review the selections and, based on the accounts of valour and good service, would choose his preferred candidates. This system continued until 1808 when the imperial decree of 18 February stipulated grenadiers had to be drawn from the tallest men in the regiment and to have served for four years or taken part in two of the four campaigns of Ulm, Austerlitz, Jena or Friedland.

[**See also:** 2. Line infantry regiments; 24. Captain; 35. Carabineer; 46. Sapper; 56. Weight of arms and equipment; 57. Coat; 64. Epaulettes; 69. Bearskin cap; 71. Plumes; 73. Beards and moustaches; 76. Cartridge pouch; 91. Infantry sabre; 111. High Pay; 139. Honouring dignitaries; 140. Honours to religious parades and services; 143. Tactical composition of a battalion; 146. Placement of the colour guard; 164. Battalion formations and manoeuvres; 165. Infantry squares; 176. Introduction (skirmishing); 216. Target practice; 220. Opening the campaign (introduction); 227. Duties in camp; 231. Battle tactics.]

## 35. Carabineer (*carabinier*)

When originally constituted on 17 March 1788 the battalions of foot chasseurs had no elite companies. In lieu of a grenadier company, each chasseur company selected twelve *chasseur-carabiniers*, the first six of whom would qualify for a high pay of

Light infantry voltigeur and carabineer. Note the bearskin does not have a brass plaque.

an additional daily *sou*; the six others would only receive an additional sixpence. Unlike grenadiers in the line regiments, these soldiers were chosen 'without a single regard for their height, from among the best soldiers in the battalion, giving equal preference to the most skilful shooters and never admitting recruits.' As their name suggests, it is believed these marksmen were armed with rifled carbines rather than smoothbore muskets.

When the number of chasseur companies was doubled from four to eight per battalion in 1791, each company was assigned six carabineers. By the time of the formation of the half-brigades in 1794, carabineers came to form an independent company in their own right. Through the remainder of the wars of the Revolution, they moved away from their traditional marksman role and adopted the same function as grenadiers in the line infantry. In the reforms of 8 February 1808 the function of carabineers was identical with that of grenadiers and the same selection criteria applied. The bearskin caps worn by carabineers did not have a brass plaque at the front.

[**See also:** 3. Light infantry regiments; 34. Grenadier; 64. Epaulettes; 68. Shako; 69. Bearskin cap; 71. Plumes; 87. Carbine; 91. Infantry sabre.]

## 36. Voltigeur

A type of light infantryman. The word voltigeur has no direct equivalent in English, and was commonly (and erroneously) translated as 'rifleman' in many English texts. The word also refers to a circus performer, specifically an acrobat or tumbler. However its principle origin was from the French equestrian term *voltige* – the performance of gymnastics on horseback, or 'vaulting' in modern English. This unusual term is better understood when one learns that the original purpose of voltigeurs was to be transported into action by cavalry, riding pillion-style on the backs of horses (a feat witnessed by de Fezensac in fighting at the Berezina River in November 1812), or jogging alongside trotting horses.

In 1776 French infantry regiments were given a light company of chasseurs, which took the place of the second battalion's grenadiers. In 1791 the regimental chasseur companies were suppressed, but during the 1790s, some half-brigades formed unofficial units of scouts (*éclaireurs*) to replace them. These perhaps formed a precedent for Napoleon introducing a company of voltigeurs to each battalion of light infantry on *22 Ventôse XII* (13 March 1804), suppressing the second company to accommodate them. Voltigeurs had elite status and received 'high pay'. Napoleon stipulated voltigeurs had to be less than 1,598 mm tall (officers could be up to 1,625 mm or 5 French feet). There were two reasons for this selection process. Firstly, short soldiers (of which there plenty) could never qualify for service in the grenadiers, but they could aspire for service in the voltigeurs. Secondly, Bardin estimated this measure increased the pool of those eligible for conscription by about 40,000 men.

Line infantry fusiliers wade through a river to fire on an enemy held bridge.

Each company would comprise of three officers, one sergeant major, four sergeants, one quartermaster corporal, 104 voltigeurs and, in place of drummers, two military instrumentalists who played a small hunting horn called the *cornet*. The imperial decree of 8 February 1808 retained the voltigeur companies, setting their composition at three officers, one sergeant major, four sergeants, a quartermaster corporal, 121 voltigeurs and two cornetists.

This innovation was extended to line infantry regiments in the imperial decree of *2nd Complementary Day XIII* (24 September 1804). This decree clarified the recruits must be of a sound constitution, vigorous and nimble, but short in stature. Voltigeurs were initially issued with the infantry sabre (withdrawn after 1807) and the shorter dragoon model musket; officers and sub-officers were issued with rifled carbines. Their uniform was the same as the rest of the corps except a buff (*chamois*) coloured collar and yellow or green epaulettes and plume.

[**See also:** 2. Line infantry regiments; 3. Light infantry regiments; 24. Captain; 38. Cornetist; 56. Weight of arms and equipment; 57. Coat; 64. Epaulettes; 71. Plumes; 73. Beards and moustaches; 76. Cartridge pouch; 86. Musket; 87. Carbine; 111. High Pay; 143. Tactical composition of a battalion; 167. Musketry (introduction); 174. Independent fire; 176. Skirmishing (introduction); 177. Skirmishing – the Davout instructions of 1811; 179. Skirmishers: movement and communication; 218. Gymnastic and fitness exercises; 221. On the march.]

## 37. Drummer (*tambour*)

The drum was adopted as a military instrument in France during the 14th century. Drummers were chosen from among suitable fusiliers by the colonel (officially they were never children). There were two drummers per company, but when the battalion formed, the drummers would unite, standing in two ranks fifteen places behind the fifth platoon. They only marched in front of the battalion during parades – in combat they were too important to be exposed to the worst of enemy fire. Their principal role was to communicate orders through a variety of rolls and beats, the most important of which were known as the ordinance calls, and included:

- *La générale* – this signal announced the gathering of all the troops in a garrison or a camp; it was also used as a call to arms in an alert. When drummers were practising the various signals, they would play this drum call last so there would be no mistake of its intention.
- *L'assemblée* – this was the call for troops to assemble by company and hold themselves ready. It would be played in several circumstances. For example, if the regiment was to march out or conduct exercises, there would be a warning of the *la générale* or *aux champs*, followed half an hour later by *l'assemblée* at which the companies would assemble, roll calls be given and an inspection of arms and equipment performed. In garrison this call would also be used at nine o'clock in the morning to instruct the guard to take post.
- *Le rappel* – this call was used for rendering honours to senators, grand officers of the Legion of Honour, generals of divisions and inspector generals. It was sometimes used in place of *la générale* when only a portion of a garrison or camp was being called to arms. It also used as a signal for troops to reform if their order had been broken up in combat. On night marches it was used as a signal to halt the head of the column because part of the troops had become separated. It was also played when a city raised the white flag and surrendered.
- *Au drapeau* – after assembly and inspection, this was the call for the colours to be made ready and to take position in the line. It could also be used in battle when the regiment had become dispersed to rally around the flag.
- *Aux champs* – this was generally the call for a body of troops to proceed at the ordinary pace of 76 paces per minute. It was used in parades where honours were rendered; to announce the closure of a town's gates and on night marches to signal the column was ready to resume its march. It was also used when a condemned man was brought to the place of execution.
- *Le pas accéléré* – this was the signal to increase the speed of the march, nominally up to 100 steps per minute. It was used for conducting guards to their posts and was preferred for parades by Napoleon rather than the traditional *aux champs*.
- *La retraite* – in garrison and in camp the retreat was the signal to return to quarters at night. It could also be used in the event of a fire, or brawls, to order the men to return quickly to their barracks. It was also used as a signal for a regiment in line formation to retire.

- *La messe* – this drum call fell out favour after the Revolution. Its traditional purpose was to call the men together without arms on Sundays and fête days for Mass.
- *La breloque* – The breloque was a curious drum call. Soldiers likened it to the staggering motion of someone in the process of falling over. It was not the sort of beat you could easily march in step to, and it gave rise to the expression 'beating the breloque' (*battre la breloque*), meaning to talk nonsense. Contemporary Anglo-French dictionaries describe a *breloque* as a 'toy', 'geegaw' or 'whim wham', in other words, something showy and ornamental. In practical terms it was used to summon working parties, or to announce general fatigues, and the distribution of weapons. It was also used as a sign the soldiers were free to break ranks.
- *Aux armes* – This drum signal alerted the guards, posts and piquets.

Other common drum calls included *la Diane*, which was played at daybreak when the gates to a town were opened, or to greet a new officer at his reception by the company; *la charge*, which was the signal to march at the charge pace (often beaten in battle to drive the men forwards); *le rigodon*, a celebratory call signifying a direct hit during target practice, or played during the procession of men sentenced to be chained to a ball; *le ban* was played when an important announcement was to be made, for example orders on entering a town, or the reading of a sentence following a trial.

There was also a basic, short drum roll (*roulement*) which instructed troops to render themselves immobile and to observe silence. This was also used as a signal to cease fire. Daily life in garrison was also regulated by these *roulements*, with a duty drummer assigned to the police guard. The standard daily drum calls included:

- 06.00 (07.00 in winter) One drum roll for reveille
- 09.30 Two rolls for the duty sergeant's inspection
- 10.00 One roll for morning soup.
- 10.30 Three rolls for the duty officer's inspection.
- 17.00 (16.00 in winter) one drum roll for evening soup

Later in the evening there would be three drum rolls for roll call half an hour after the beating of the retreat, and a single drum roll half an hour after this for 'lights out'.

There were various calls which could be ordered by superior officers, the captain of police, the adjutant major, the adjutant, and the commander of the police guard:

- To call the men confined to barracks – one roll, one *breloque*, one *rappel*
- The sergeant majors – one roll followed by four individual beats
- The sergeants – one roll and three beats
- The quartermaster corporals – one roll and two beats

- The corporals – one roll and a single beat of the drum
- The duty sergeants and corporals – one roll plus the *rappel*

In order to distinguish their drum calls from those of other units, some regiments would add a flourish to the end of each signal. Regiments also had their own 'night march' calls, used for assembling the soldiers to their corps during darkness or in fog.

Until October 1792 drummers in the regular army wore a blue coat decorated in braid sporting the king's livery. Through the remainder of the 1790s and into the early part of the First Empire, they wore the same coats as the rank and file; although some wore lapels, cuffs and collars in a different colour (usually red, but other colours were occasionally observed). Napoleon introduced an imperial livery with the decree of 30 December 1811 which formed part of the uniform regulations of 19 January 1812. It was a coat in 'dragoon green' with a green braid bordered with red, and with yellow squares which were embroidered alternatively with an eagle design, or the letter 'N'. On the march, drummers would carry their instruments over their backpacks. The Napoleonic drum weighed at least 6 kg, with another kilo added for the protective leather apron and harness every drummer wore. The body of the drum was blue, with brass rims.

[**See also:** 16. Adjutant; 18. Drum major; 19. Drum corporal; 31. Chosen man; 39. Regimental children; 56. Weight of arms and equipment ; 82. Packing the haversack; 119. Awards and national recognition; 139. Honouring dignitaries; 140. Honours to religious parades and services; 145. Assembling the battalion; 147. Placement of drummers and musicians; 164. Battalion formations and manoeuvres; 178. Deploying skirmishers; 179. Skirmishers: movement and communication; 182. Lodgings and the arrangements of the bedchamber; 183. The daily routine; 185. The police guard; 187. The sergeant of police; 191. Rations & supplies (introduction); 223. Night marches; 227. Duties in camp; 233. Duties of sub-officers in battle.]

## 38. Cornetist (*cornet*)

This was a type of musician who played a small horn (*cornet*), rather like a post horn. There were experiments with using cornetists as signallers in the light infantry battalions in 1792 but this innovation failed to spread. The decrees of *22 Ventôse XII* (13 March 1804) and *2nd Complementary Day XIII* (19 September 1805) revived the experiment of 1792 by introducing cornetists into the new voltigeur companies attached to light and line infantry regiments respectively. There were two cornetists per company in place of the usual drummers. The calls were primarily for reassembly and manoeuvre. Education was slower and more difficult than with using a drum, and lessons were generally provided by the chief musician. Whereas any intelligent soldier could pick up a drum and beat it in the thick of battle, they could not do the same with a cornet. Therefore if the cornetists were killed or injured, the commander had to rely on voice commands alone, something which often proved problematic over distance or in the din of battle. Whistles do not appear to have been widely used by the French, although they had been used in 1792 by Batavian (Dutch) troops in French service to good effect.

[**See also:** 18. Drum major; 21. Musicians; 56. Weight of arms and equipment; 82. Packing the haversack; 178. Deploying skirmishers; 179. Skirmishers: movement and communication.]

A cantineer takes up arms to defend herself and a wounded soldier. On campaign, cantineers shared the fate of the soldiers they served, for better or worse.

*Chapter 5*

# Non-Combatant Personnel

## 39. Regimental children (*enfants de troupe*)

Around the fringes of the regimental depot were the children of serving soldiers and officers, regimental orphans, and even the children of retired veterans. Traditionally a number of the boys would be admitted into the corps and given a military upbringing after which they would be given the chance to sign up. Although the practice lost its official sanction during the 1790s, it was restored after a law of *7 Thermidor VIII* (26 July 1800).

In each company there would be two children on military pay, each at least two years old and the issue of a legitimate marriage between a 'defender of the fatherland' and a woman attached to the corps as a laundress or sutleress. There were two classes of child: the second class children would be on half pay, with the first class children on two thirds pay. To gain promotion to the first class, the children would have to demonstrate progress in reading, writing, arithmetic, swimming, running, military exercises, gymnastics, and in a trade useful to the army. Both classes would receive clothing, lodging, bread and a heating fuel allowance. Their garments were cut in a military fashion by the regimental tailors using the off-cuts of uniform manufacture.

When a vacancy for a child arose, there was a strict selection process to determine those most in need:

1. If a simple soldier's son was not available, a sub-officer's son might be considered; if a sub-officer's son was not available, an officer's son might be considered.
2. In each case, preference would go first to orphans who had lost their mother and father; then to those who had lost one parent. If there were two children with the same qualification, those with the most brothers or sisters would be selected first.

The children would be under the care of an officer of the corps, two sergeants and four corporals. These supervisors would be from among the most instructed, distinguished men available. They were specially charged with teaching the children to read, write, calculate, swim, run, etc. They were in charge of their military instruction and provided moral guidance. Additionally, each of the regimental master craftsmen was obliged to always have at least two children as apprentices. Other children would be taught to play musical instruments by members of the regimental band.

When the regiment went to war, the regimental children would remain with the depot. The minimum age for children to accompany the regiment as musicians was set at 14 years. At this age children who had made good progress in music were able to join the regimental band and serve on full pay; but they were not allowed to serve as drummers. When the boys reached the age of 16 they were allowed to sign up (two years earlier than usually permitted) and serve as soldiers on full pay.

[**See also:** 5. Colonel; 22. Master craftsmen; 52. Fifer; 99. Voluntary enlistment; 224. Duties of the baggage master.]

## 40. Cantineer (*cantinière*)

Sutlers (*vivandiers* – from *vivres* – foodstuffs) in the French Army were originally male merchants known as *brandeviniers*, or soldiers who would sell everyday necessities, such as tobacco, ink, writing paper, vinegar, and alcohol at reasonable prices. Their wives tended to work as laundresses and also would carry out minor uniform repairs for fixed fees. When the sutler was a serving soldier he was required to serve on campaign. His wife would therefore take over the business. Such female sutlers were termed *vivandières*. Through the wars of the Revolution, the title *vivandière* fell out of use at regimental level and came to refer to the merchants attached to the army at headquarters level. The regimental sutlers became known as cantineers instead.

The origin of the word cantineer dates to the latter half of the 18th century. When it became more common for soldiers to be quartered in barracks rather than among the general population, certain garrison towns allowed regiments to establish their own canteens. These were places where soldiers might drink and smoke at a fair price without being exposed to the debauched antics of the neighbouring *cabarets* and taverns. The wives of the sutlers began to take on the role of canteen-keepers and thus the role of the cantineer was born. These regimental canteens could also be taken on campaign, with the brandy barrels and supplies stacked in a wagon or carried on horseback, and sold from a tent or other makeshift shelter. The utility of each battalion having its own portable drinking establishment hardly requires explanation. The cantineer's tent quickly became the social hub of a regiment on campaign.

The 1792 field service regulation allowed one cantineer with a four-horse cart for the staff of each regiment and two sutlers for each battalion, each with a bat horse. These would be provided with an oval plaque with the name of the army they belonged to. The centre of the plaque would give their role, and their patent number would be recorded at the bottom. These patents would only be issued after the receipt of a certificate from the council of administration attesting the subject was of good life and habits and irreproachable in their conduct. In this regulation, soldiers were not allowed to practice the trade of being a sutler and those with wives who were sutlers were not to be exempted from any service in order to help out.

Unlike the cantineers of later periods, those of Napoleonic vintage wore ordinary civilian clothing, not a quasi-military uniform. Granted, the cantineers of the 1790s may have embellished their costume with tricolour devices, but so did all good citizens. They may also have acquired articles of military uniform during a campaign in harsh weather, but such practices were exceptional rather than the norm. If they had anything resembling a uniform at all, it was usually a small barrel (*tonnelet*) carried on a strap over the shoulder from which they could dispense tots of brandy.

In the First Empire, cantineers were typically the wives of serving soldiers, most commonly married to a sub-officer. In addition to the various regulations and orders governing their behaviour, it was believed a husband would also exercise a level of control over his wife. When the husband was killed in action, it appears the status of 'regimental widow' was also recognised and cantineers continued to trade. Out of practical necessity the cantineer would usually remarry, but a marriage ceremony could not legally be performed until ten months after the husband's demise. On the reverse, the link between the cantineer and sub-officer created scope for various abuses. A sub-officer might bully his subordinates to drink at his wife's establishment; the sub-officer might neglect his soldierly duties; he would likely end up drinking with his sub-ordinates; and, worst of all, he might overlook

Cantineer with child and infantryman with distribution sack. Note the cantineer's large gold earrings and feathered bonnet. (Beyer)

222222222

certain breaches of discipline on the part of his subordinates, lest they take their money elsewhere.

Canteens came under the surveillance of the adjutant and the sergeant of police. Cantineers caught selling drinks after the beating of the retreat would be fined 12 *francs* on the first offence, and then be expelled from the army at the second offence. Those caught robbing the dead and wounded on battlefields would be expelled from the army with their merchandise and money seized and sold off, the profit going to hospitals. If applied there were laws for imprisoning sutlers for looting, with a maximum penalty of 20 years in irons.

[**See also:** 39. Regimental children; 85. Wagons and horses; 113. Credit and debt; 134. Military justice; 183. The daily routine; 186. Making the rounds; 220. Opening the campaign (introduction); 224. Duties of the baggage master; 226. Arrival at camp; 227. Duties in camp.]

## 41. Laundress (*blanchisseuse*)

A non-combatant role performed by the wife of a serving soldier or sub-officer. The order of *7 Thermidor VIII* (26 July 1800) and the regulation of 11 October 1809 allowed two laundresses per battalion. In garrison the laundresses would collect the dirty linen on a Monday and return it on the Saturday. Laundresses wore typical civilian clothing and would have had equipment such as buckets, washboards, brushes and soap for performing their tasks. They would receive a patent in the form of an oval plaque which would carry the name of the army and their role (i.e. laundress) in the centre. Below this would be a registered number. In garrison they were issued with two bedchambers, furniture, but received no rations or pay. On campaign the laundresses were permitted a bat horse to carry their equipment and were issued with rations.

[**See also:** 39. Regimental children; 40. Cantineer; 84. Tents; 85. Wagons and horses; 108. The Ordinary; 206. Cleaning the uniform; 226. Arrival at camp.]

# Chapter 6

# Special Roles & Appointments

## 42. Clothing officer (*capitaine d'habillement*)

The clothing officer was a captain appointed for a one year term by the regimental council of administration. Candidates could be a company captain, or the commander of an auxiliary company or the depot. After the reforms of 18 February 1808, the captain would also command one of the four depot companies of the 5th Battalion. A decree of 14 October 1811 passed the role of clothing officer to a captain with the rank of adjutant major (*capitaine-adjudant-major d'habillement*), who was specially charged with the uniform of the corps and who was independent of commanding a company. This position was assumed by the existing clothing officer, who relinquished his company command. In the draft organisation of 13 April 1815, a *capitaine d'habillement* was also included among the officers of the staff as a formal position.

The term 'clothing officer' was somewhat inexact, because he also supervised the other master craftsmen of the corps, including the armourer. He received a quarterly report from the quartermaster corporals on the state of each company's uniforms and had under his guard the stores of cloth for manufacturing uniforms. He was also responsible for the purchase of cloth and the book keeping related to the manufacture of uniforms and the purchase of cloth and equipment. The clothing officer was also responsible for ensuring the master tailor manufactured uniforms according to the regulations. To this end, each regiment was required to develop one complete set of uniform and equipment and to present this to an inspector at a review for authorisation. The clothing officer would ensure the master tailor followed the agreed pattern. The clothing officer was allowed to choose two other officers to assist him. One of these assistants would concentrate on the details of manufacture and distribution of uniform; the other on equipment and arms.

[**See also:** 22. Master craftsmen; 54. Materials; 107. Council of administration.]

## 43. Recruitment captain (*capitaine de recrutement*)

During the Napoleonic period, conscripts were raised locally by department. In order to ensure the conscripts were suitable for service and, more importantly, they arrived at the regimental depot safely and promptly, the post of recruitment captain was created. The law of *28 Floréal X* (18 May 1802) stipulated each corps would send a captain and a sufficient number of lieutenants and sub-officers to conduct conscripts 'to the colours'. The recruitment captain would be selected by the ministry of war and would reside in the departmental capital from where the regiment's conscripts were drawn. The captain would assist in the recruitment councils where conscripts could plead to be exempted, but he did not get to vote on the final decision.

There would be at least one officer or sub-officer per *arrondissement*, depending on the size of the department. According to the law of *18 Thermidor X* (6 August 1802), the composition of the party would be chosen by the colonel, and sub-officers would be replaced every year. The imperial decree of 31 July 1806 further refined the process, stating recruitment captains must have held their rank for at least two years and only a maximum of two lieutenants could join the recruitment party, the remainder being composed of sub-lieutenants only. This decree also stipulated a single infantry regiment would provide the recruitment party for each department.

[See also: 101. Recruitment council.]

## 44. Supernumerary officer (*officier à la suite*)

It was extremely common for officers to be attached to a regiment without having an effective role. In wartime a good example of this was when officers were returned from enemy captivity, or if an officer had returned from a long convalescence. While waiting for a suitable position to become vacant, it was common for supernumerary officers to carry out various administrative duties and to take turns in the various services, such as being the duty officer.

[See also: 118. Promotion to the officer corps.]

## 45. Ensign bearer (*porte-ensigne*)

Traditionally each field battalion would have its own flag, but after the reforms of 8 February 1808, each regiment was limited to a single eagle standard. In the regulation of 1 August 1791 the battalion colour guard had a tactical roll, acting as a guide for the battalion, showing the direction of march and also acting as a rallying point in danger. Therefore Napoleon allowed battalions to carry an ensign as a marker flag. The flag was intended to be a simple marker and not bestowed with any special importance. The roll of ensign was exactly the same as the old post of standard bearer (*porte drapeau*) which had existed prior to the 1808 reform. The ensign/standard was entrusted into the hands of a sub-officer selected by the colonel, normally the best instructed sergeant major. The ensign was typically carried in the right hand with the base of the pole resting against the right hip. When the battalion was in line formation, the ensign was carried over the right shoulder with the right arm straight along the pole, the heel of the pole resting in the right hand.

[**See also:** 94. Flags and eagles; 95. Ensigns; 96. Pennants; 146. Placement of the colour guard.]

## 46. Sapper (*sapeur d'infanterie*)

In the French Army the word 'sapper' traditionally described those soldiers equipped with axes, spades, picks and other tools for the purpose of creating a 'sap' – a ditch or excavation made for the purpose of demolishing a building or other edifice. However, by the Napoleonic era such tasks would have been undertaken by engineering troops (*la genie*). The Napoleonic infantry sapper therefore had his origins in the latter half of the 18th century, when there was a practice of issuing ten 'hammer axes' to each grenadier company for the purposes of smashing a path through palisades, town gates and other obstacles. The roll was therefore less of an engineering role, but more of performing assault demolitions.

The practice of selecting robust and brawny men for this task was maintained in the *Gardes Françaises* regiment and eventually copied by infantry regiments of the line. At the outbreak of the American Revolution (1776) sappers were only appointed during wartime; but from 1780 until the outbreak of the French Revolution they existed in peacetime also. By the outbreak of war in 1792 there is no official mention of sappers, and Bardin indicates they did not reappear until the Consulate period, albeit in an unofficial capacity. The formal establishment of regimental infantry sappers was not confirmed until the decree of 18 February 1808, when each grenadier company was ordered to select four men who would be under the command of a corporal. In addition to their combat role, sappers were often given an important role in ceremonies, leading the regiment on parade, marching in two ranks in front of the drum major.

The ordinance of 19 April 1766 gave sappers a leather apron which was an unfinished chamois-coloured hide (a type of yellowy beige, similar to buff). The uniform was more firmly established by the ordinance of 25 April 1767, which described infantry sappers as being equipped with an axe, a sawtooth sabre, a black hide apron and a bearskin cap without a plaque and three inches shorter than those issued to grenadiers. The regulation of 1 October 1786 described the apron as being of whitened sheepskin. Sappers were also issued with heavy gauntlets known as *gants à la Crispin* (St Crispin is the patron saint of leather workers). These were very thick and were generally considered useless when it came to handling weapons or tools. On *11 Fructidor XII* (29 August 1804) sappers were issued with a musketoon, bayonet and, until 1812, they wore the Corsican style cartridge pouch which was worn over the midriff on a waist belt.

[**See also:** 56. Weight of arms and equipment; 69. Bearskin cap; 65. Distinctive markings; 73. Beards and moustaches; 148. Placement of sappers.]

## 47. Master-at-arms (*maître d'armes*)

This was an unofficial role performed by a soldier or sub-officer who was particularly skilled in the use of bladed weapons (*armes blanches*). Sometimes known as the fencing master (*maître d'escrime*) the master-at-arms was seconded by one or more deputies known as provosts-at-arms (*prévots d'armes*). The master-at-arms would serve as an instructor at the regimental fencing school and might also represent the regiment in tournaments against other units. Like many aspects of the Napoleonic army, this role was not governed by a regulation, but was something which had grown organically through need and tradition. Fencing schools had been established by Louis XIV and fencing masters became commonplace in most regiments. The 1792 police regulations allowed colonels to set up a regimental fencing school in an arms hall (*salle d'armes*). Under the supervision of an adjutant, the regimental master-at-arms would teach swordsmanship and provide private lessons to soldiers and officers alike for a fee, or at least a dram in return. Perhaps the only formal instruction given to the master and his provosts was to withdraw lessons if the men became stormy and querulous rather than reserved and polite.

[**See also:** 16. Adjutant; 212. Training (introduction); 218. Gymnastic and fitness exercises.]

## 48. Orderly (*domestique*)

As was common practice in other armies, each officer would have a bat-man or orderly to carry out menial domestic tasks such as cleaning the uniform and equipment, or grooming the officer's horse. This practice was age old and typically unregulated. During the *ancien régime*, officers had employed valets to accompany them on campaign in the capacity of servants. These were non-combatants and were sometimes required to dress in a uniform different to the corps. After the Revolution the feudal connotations of master and servant were incompatible with political dogma, but the requirement for orderlies continued out of practical necessity. The provisional field service regulation of 5 April 1792 envisaged domestics being civilian non-combatants authorised, like sutlers, to follow the army. However, such an arrangement would require the officers to pay their orderlies from their own purse, something most could not afford. In practice therefore, orderlies were selected from among the serving soldiers. This practice was not ideal as it theoretically robbed the line of a significant number of combatants. However it was widely accepted some soldiers were more useful to the regiment if spared from the rigours of combat.

One gets an idea of how many men might be assigned orderly duties by studying the regulation of 12 October 1791 on the lodging and barracking of troops. This regulation set out how many beds were required in the officers' quarters for their orderlies. The colonel would have three orderlies; the quartermaster treasurer, captains, adjutant majors, surgeon majors and chaplain would each have one, while the lieutenant and sub lieutenant appeared to share one between them. A second document dated 20 November 1807 describing military beds indicates that during the empire colonels and majors had two orderlies, while battalion commanders, captains, etc. had one.

According to Blaze, during the empire French officers colloquially referred to their orderlies as *Tartars*. This was presumably a derogatory reference inferring the common soldiers were nothing but barbarians – a far cry from the days when everyone was addressed as *citizen*.

[**See also:** 23. Baggage master; 84. Tents; 85. Wagons and horses; 226. Arrival at camp.]

## 49. Secretary (*secrétaire*)

On *28 Nivôse VI* (17 January 1798) the quartermaster treasurer was assigned two soldiers as secretaries who were appointed by the regiment's council of administration. These secretaries were sometimes described as office clerks (*commis de bureau*). They were exempt from service and ordinarily classed as non-combatants. The volume of paperwork in a regiment should not be underestimated. For a regiment of four battalions the sum of 2,160 *francs* per annum was granted for office supplies including registers, papers, writing implements and lighting. The colonel would also typically appoint a secretary to manage his papers and correspondence.

[**See also:** 10. Quartermaster treasurer; 84. Tents.]

## 50. Barber (*frater*)

This was an unofficial role performed by a soldier at company level. In the last half of the 18th century each company would have a barber who would dress the men's hair and keep them relatively clean shaven. This same man would also be skilled in the use of scalpels and would perform minor surgery (the name *frater* derives from the Latin word for 'brother' and perhaps originated from monks who gave medical care). In 1764 each company was assigned a surgeon barber, while the ordinances of 1776 and 1779 also recognised a barber. Although this role was no longer mentioned in the statues after 1782, the practice of having company barbers continued out of necessity through the Revolution and First Empire.

Each captain would nominate a barber and exempt him from fatigues while he performed his duties, which were shaving the men every other day (or at least twice a week) and, in regiments which maintained the queue, dressing the men's hair. Soldiers would pay a deduction which went towards supplies of soap and razors. The rate was set on a regimental basis (in the 1790s it had been 1 *sou* per month) and this money would be paid to the barber by the quartermaster corporal.

During the Napoleonic Wars it became increasingly common for men to shave themselves. The 1792 campaign service regulations stated men should each possess a razor. In the 1813 Infantry Manual, it was also recommended each sub-officer and soldier should possess a razor and they ought to shave themselves every day. As the fashion of wearing short hair was adopted by individual regiments the post of barber died out, so did the practice of being shaved. However, an 1810 text book for the cadets at St Cyr (*cours d'administration militaire*) taught how barbers at the time were paid from company funds.

[**See also:** 72. Hairstyles; 73. Beards and moustaches; 110. Pay; 112. Deductions and funds.]

## 51. Worker (*travailleur*)

The ordinance of 1 March 1768 allowed up to six 'workers' per company. If a man had a skill or trade which he wished to practice, the battalion commander would ask the colonel's permission, outlining the potential benefits to the man. Permission was only given to men of good conduct and the colonel's word was final. To qualify for work, these men had to have completed the training schools up to battalion level. They would also receive intensive refresher training from a sergeant instructor through the week. Each regiment maintained a statute detailing who was working, their whereabouts and what they were being paid.

Workers were deducted 30 *centimes* per day for their food (if they did not take part in preparing soup), 10 *centimes* for linen and shoe allowance, and a further 5 *centimes* to the man who looked after his arms and equipment while away working.

Workers in town were required to present themselves at evening roll call, unless their captain had given permission, and this was approved by the colonel. Even if given permission to sleep away from their quarters, workers had to be present at evening roll call the night before fête days and on Sundays, when there would be a general inspection of the corps.

Workers going into town would leave their uniform coats in the bedchamber and would wear a jacket or smock frock with cuffs in the regiment's facing colour. In some regiments the workers had the letter 'T' (for *travailleur*) sewn on the left sleeve of their jacket.

[**See also:** 22. Master craftsmen; 27. Sergeant major; 28. Sergeant; 70. Forage cap; 182. Lodgings and the arrangements of the bedchamber.]

## 52. Fifer (*fifre*)

Fifers were a throwback to the days before regimental bands, when each drum corps would have several clarinettists and fifers to accompany the drummers. These instrumentalists eventually became the musicians and the role of fifer fell from the regulations. Following the example of the Consular Guard, some colonels decided to unofficially add a number of fifers to accompany their regimental band and drum corps. Fifers tended to be drawn from the regimental children, with those aged over fourteen years being allowed to accompany the regiment on campaign. The fife was a small cylindrical instrument pierced with six holes. It had a range of two octaves. The fife was carried in a cylindrical tube with leather bands at top and bottom. It was carried in a brass plaque with the regimental number.

[**See also:** 20. Chief musician; 21. Musicians.]

A military family: the soldier, his wife the cantineer, and their two sons, both children of the corps being trained for a life of soldiering.

*Part II*

# Uniform, Arms & Equipment

# Chapter 7

# Uniform – General Description

## 53. Introduction

Uniform has long been an essential part of what makes a soldier, providing him with a military identity and the legitimacy to bear arms and kill in the name of the state. In the French Army of the Revolutionary era, the uniform also became something of a political statement; a manifestation of the national colours. The uniform was also an essential part of the discipline of a corps. Therefore in addition to regulations which described the dimensions and manufacture of the uniform, the police regulations of 24 June 1792 described *how* and *when* the various articles should be worn.

Standardised uniforms began appearing in the French Army during the 1660s and by the mid-18th century the French infantry had adopted a white uniform. At the beginning of the Napoleonic period the uniform worn by French infantrymen differed very little in cut from the one described in the regulation of 1 October 1786. This consisted of a felt cocked hat, a long-tailed coat (*habit*), and a light jacket known as a *veste* (often described as a sleeved waistcoat). Infantrymen wore breeches which extended just below the knee and long gaiters which extended above the knee, and were held in place by buttons and garter straps.

Except for the chaotic years in the mid-1790s, regiments generally manufactured their own uniforms and purchased the necessary cloth directly. Although the master tailor was required to follow a model agreed by an inspector general, variations arose between the regiments depending on the state of the unit's finances, the local availability and quality of cloth, and of course the personal preferences of the colonel. There were also significant differences between the uniforms worn by line and light infantry. It was only with the release of the ordinance of 19 January 1812 that a standardised uniform was adopted by the French Army, and even then certain distinctions remained.

An infantry officer's uniform was essentially the same as that worn by the men, albeit better tailored and made from finer materials. At the beginning of the period, officers wore a felt cocked hat, but this was gradually replaced by the shako as its use became prevalent, or the imperial style bicorn. Around their neck officers wore a white collar, which could be substituted by one of black silk on the march or on campaign. They wore a coat, jacket and breeches. In summer the officers could wear a jacket made from dimity (*basin uni*) or linen (*toile*). When on duty, officers were required to wear a gilded gorget *(hausse col)* and boots. Superior officers were allowed to wear their belt over the top of the jacket with the buckle decorated by a gilded plaque. They wore an épée suspended from this belt with a golden wrist-strap (*dragonne*). When off duty, the belt was to be worn beneath the jacket with a wrist-strap of white thread.

The exact garments worn varied for the different duties and tasks the soldiers were required to perform. In French the word used to describe the various dress codes was *tenue*, a word which does not directly translate into English. Deriving from the French verb 'to hold' (*tenir*) it does not simply refer to the garments one wore, but also the general bearing of the person. In the military sense, it described an assemblage of garments, the correct manner of arranging them and keeping them maintained.

When in full dress (*grande tenue*) the men would be dressed in their coats, jackets, breeches and gaiters with their crossbelts, equipment and arms. As described in the 1792 police regulations, the hat would be raised slightly over the right eye, with the 'cocked' part directly above the left eye. Bearskin hats were to be placed squarely on the head (as were shakos when later introduced), with the brass plaque squarely over the face. The soldiers' collars were to be black, or white on grand parades only. The collar of the shirt was always covered by the neck collar and was not allowed to protrude above it. Equally the cuffs of the shirt were not to protrude beyond the cuffs of the coat.

The soldier's petty dress (*petite tenue*) consisted of a fatigue cap (*bonnet de police*), black collar, jacket, breeches and gaiters. The marching dress (*tenue de route*) was similar to full dress except the men wore grey gaiters and linen trousers. When the issuing of greatcoats became more commonplace, some regiments may have removed their coats on the march, folding them up and carrying them in their packs to preserve them. Soldiers who were punished with confinement to barracks were ordered to remove one gaiter, thus making their status obvious to the sentries at the gate. Those locked in a cell had to wear their fatigue caps, which is where the French term *bonnet de police* originated.

It is fair to say successive changes in uniform were not always mirrored by the administrative regulations which provided for them. Therefore articles might be budgeted for which were no longer required. Regulations such as the service regulation of 1 March 1768, which had not been repealed as late as 1813, required men to wear white gaiters on parades and black ones when on guard duty. However, from 1 January 1792 onwards, the administrative regulations did not provide infantry regiments with funds for white gaiters, and so only the Consular and Imperial Guard were actually provided with them by the state.

## 54. Materials

Articles of uniform were made from a variety of types of woollen cloth and linen, with the shoes and equipment manufactured from leather. Some of the most commonly used fabrics included:

- *Basin.* A light strong cotton fabric woven with a striped or squared pattern known as 'dimity' in English.
- *Cadis.* A type of coarse woollen fabric or *serge* typically used for the lining and 'skirt' of a coat. Known in English as caddis or caddice, it was a superior quality to *drap.*
- *Drap.* A heavy woollen-cloth typically used in the manufacture of uniform coats and greatcoats.
- *Serge.* A twill-woven woollen fabric, which was softer and finer than *drap.*
- *Toile.* This was a linen cloth typically used as a lining material, or in its heavier canvas form for making gaiters and protective coverings.
- *Tricot.* A light woollen fabric traditionally produced in the regions of Picardy and Champagne and used for jackets, gilets, breeches and trousers. *Tricot* is typically a knitted woollen fabric used in the manufacture of stockings and gloves. The variety of *tricot* used in uniform manufacture was actually a type of *serge* originally produced in the town of Tricot, Picardy.

According to the second volume of Quillet's *l'administration des troupes*, the width of the bolts of cloth used in uniform manufacture were as follows:

- 119 cm for woollen cloth to be used in the manufacture of coats, greatcoats, redingotes, etc.
- 89 cm for *tricot* and cotton material for manufacturing breeches, the backs and sleeves of jackets and black gaiters.
- 79 cm for linen for shirts.
- 104 cm for the cloth used in lining material and for sacks.

A table in Damesme and Varinot's 1810 *cours d'administration militaire* (a textbook for St Cyr cadets) detailed the lengths of material required for the manufacture of line and light infantry uniforms:

*Line infantry uniform (circa 1810)*
1.34 m of blue woollen-cloth for jacket.
0.12 m of white woollen-cloth for coat lapels.
0.15m of madder red woollen-cloth for cuffs, collars, and piping.
2.60 m of white caddis for the coat lining.
1.83 m of white *tricot* for the jacket.
1.44 m of white *tricot* for the breeches.
2.40 m of beige woollen-cloth for the greatcoat.
1.30 m of linen for the coat lining.
1.15 m of linen for lining the breeches.
1.15 m of linen for lining the greatcoat.

*Light infantry uniform (circa 1810)*
1.29 m of blue woollen–cloth for the coat.
1.29 m of blue woollen–cloth for the sleeved gilet.
0.06 m of white woollen–cloth for the coat piping.
0.04 m of scarlet woollen–cloth for cuff flaps and short collar (*petit collet*).
1.63 m of blue caddis for the coat lining, not including the sleeves.
2.50 m of beige woollen–cloth for the *redingote*.
1.93 m of blue tricot for the trousers.

Tailors were advised to cut the cloth amply to ensure freedom of movement and have the greatest possible lifespan. However, tastes in fashion and expediency sometimes led to tighter cuts. The best quality materials were used for officers' uniforms, and sergeants generally enjoyed better quality cloth than the men. In the latter case the ordinance of 25 March 1776 stated sub-officers would receive better quality uniforms. During the chaotic years following the Revolution, this was not observed; but as order resumed under Napoleon, Bardin states the practice was re-adopted.

[**See also:** 22. Master craftsmen; 42. Clothing officer; 53. Uniform – general description (introduction); 112. Deductions and funds; 206. Cleaning the uniform.]

## 55. Lifespan of uniforms

When manufactured, all clothing was stamped with the year of its manufacture. The various garments and items of equipment were each assigned a life expectancy, which helped regiments budget for expenditure on uniforms.

**Table 4:** Lifespan of uniforms

| | | | |
|---|---|---|---|
| Bearskin cap | 6 years | Greatcoat | 3 years |
| Breeches | 1 year | Jacket | 2 years |
| Belts | 20 years | Linen draws | 1 year |
| Cartridge pouch | 20 years | Musket and sabre | 50 years |
| Coatee (1812 pattern) | 2 years | Sapper's apron | 20 years |
| Coat (traditional) | 3 years | Sapper's axe | 10 years |
| Drum and belt | 20 years | Shako | 4 years |
| Fatigue cap | 2 years | | |

[**See also:** 53. Uniform – general description (introduction); 54. Materials.]

## 56. Weight of arms and equipment

In his infantry manual Bardin calculated the weight of equipment carried by infantrymen of varying classes. These weights are exclusive of camping equipment such as pots and mess pans and additional ammunition or personal property, but nevertheless serve as a useful guide.

**Table 5**: Loads carried by individual soldiers.

| Rank/class | Metric | Imperial (American) |
|---|---|---|
| Voltigeur cornetist | 19.929 kg | 43lb 14oz |
| Voltigeur sub-officer | 23.940 kg | 52lb 12oz |
| Voltigeur | 23.960 kg | 52lb 13oz |
| Fusilier | 24.172 kg | 53lb 4oz |
| Fusilier corporal | 25.730 kg | 56lb 11oz |
| Fusilier drummer | 26.231 kg | 57lb 13oz |
| Fusilier quartermaster corporal | 26.403 kg | 58lb 3oz |
| Fusilier sergeant major | 26.403 kg | 58lb 3oz |
| Grenadier | 27.354 kg | 60lb 4oz |
| Fusilier sergeant | 27.628 kg | 60lb 14oz |
| Grenadier drummer | 27.707 kg | 61lb 1oz |
| Grenadier sergeant major | 28.087 kg | 61lb 14oz |
| Grenadier sergeant | 29.312 kg | 64lb 9oz |
| Sapper | 32.975 kg | 72lb 11oz |

The following individual weights (in grams) were also provided for various items:

**Table 6**: Weight of individual articles (grams).

| | | | |
|---|---|---|---|
| Account book | 15 | Carbine charge measurer | 245 |
| Axe holder | 1,468 | Carbine mallet | 245 |
| *Astic* | 42 | Cartridge pouch | 526 |
| Awl | 22 | Cartridge pouch cover | 48 |
| Ball extractor | 7 | Clothes whip | 87 |
| Bearskin cap | 947 | Coat | 1,210 |
| Belt & bayonet scabbard | 372 | Collar | 45 |
| Bottle of oil | 28 | Comb | 8 |
| Bread for 4 days | 2,937 | Dismounting spring | 60 |
| Breeches | 78 | Draws, linen | 397 |
| Breeches | 780 | Drum | 5,384 |
| Brush for coat | 76 | Drummer's apron and | 1,733 |
| Brush for leather | 30 | sticks | |
| Buckles | 42 | Fatigue cap | 167 |
| Button-pull | 28 | Gaiters, 1 pair, black | 353 |
| Button-stick | 22 | Greatcoat | 1,549 |
| Canteen, filled with water | 675 | Grey gaiters | 333 |

| | | | |
|---|---:|---|---:|
| Handkerchief | 72 | Sergeant's vinegar bottle | 1,958 |
| Haversack, hide | 1,072 | Shako | 672 |
| Hoop | 26 | Shako cover | 79 |
| Jacket | 658 | Shirt | 534 |
| Linen sack | 718 | Shoe brush | 72 |
| Meat for 2 days | 489 | Shoes, 1 pair | 611 |
| Musket and bayonet | 4,725 | Socks, 1 pair, woollen | 152 |
| Musket sling | 89 | Spare flint and lead | 37 |
| Musket, voltigeur | 4,493 | Spoon | 489 |
| Night cap | 52 | Stockings, cotton | 122 |
| Oily rag | 5 | Turn-screw | 38 |
| Pair of shoes | 611 | Twill bearskin bag | 152 |
| Pennant | 733 | Two packets of cartridges | 1,323 |
| Plume | 259 | Vent pick | 8 |
| Polisher | 98 | Whitening brush | 41 |
| Carbine powder horn | 244 | Voltigeur cornet and cord | 815 |
| Repair kit | 137 | Waxed bearskin cover | 118 |
| Sapper's axe | 4,489 | Wooden practice flint | 5 |
| Scraper | 19 | Woollen epaulettes | 208 |

[**See also:** 79. Haversack; 247. Marching.]

## Chapter 8

# Articles of Uniform

### 57. Coat (*habit*)

The origins of the Napoleonic infantry coat (*habit*) dated back to the time when medieval soldiers wore a long coat with heraldic colours or devices over the top of their armour. The first true infantry coat (*habit*) came into being during the 1660s when the royal bodyguard (*Garde du Corps*) and the French Guards (*Gardes Françaises*) standardised the coats they wore. This practice was gradually adopted by other elements of the army.

   During the reign of Louis XIV the coat had a long skirt or *basque* which reached almost to the knee. As fashions changed, the skirt was pinned back forming into tails, a practical concession towards horse riding. As the 'tailcoat' fashion became more pronounced, the coat was cut so it was open over the stomach (thus revealing the waistcoat or jacket) and fastened only at the chest and collar. In 1767 the tails became slightly shorter. They were measured from the floor when the soldier was at the kneeling position. Previously they had been one inch from the ground, but in 1767 they were shortened to three and a half inches from the ground. The regulation of 21 February 1779 refined the coat further, stating it had a life span of three years. False pockets were indicated with piping on the exterior face of the tails, covering the real pockets which were inside the tail and made of linen. Line and light infantry were initially dressed in the same style of coat. Line infantry adopted white coats in 1762 and the chasseur battalions were later dressed in green. At the outbreak of war, the line and light infantry arms both employed a system of distinguishing colours worn on the collar, cuff, and lapels, and had an identifying number on their buttons.

   The French Army of the Revolutionary and Napoleonic wars is most famously depicted in the national colours of blue, white and red. The origin of the blue coats is one of history's little ironies and worth recounting. On 14 July 1789 the French Guards garrisoned in Paris mutinied and joined the protestors supporting the fledgling National Constituent Assembly. The French Guards went on to form the nucleus of the new Paris National Guard. Unlike the white-coated regiments of the line, the French Guards wore a coat in the King's livery blue (*bleu de roi*), with scarlet cuffs and collar (the civic colours of Paris are blue and red). Given the prominent role of the guards on 14 July, this colour scheme was adopted by other local National Guard units. On 13 July 1791 the National Assembly decreed all National Guard units would formally adopt a uniform with a coat in the King's blue, a scarlet collar and cuffs, with white lapels and piping. This colour scheme was universally applied to all line infantry during the creation of the half-brigades after 1793. Of course, by then it was politically unacceptable for the army of the French Republic to be dressed in the blue livery colour of the decapitated king. Rather than change the colour of the uniform, the colour itself was conveniently renamed. King's blue became 'national blue' and in turn 'imperial blue'.

Although the 1786 regulation described the uniform coat, there was a great deal of variation in the way master tailors interpreted these instructions. For example the cuffs (*parements*) generally were a band of cloth with a cuff flap (*patte de parement*) which contained three buttons, two of which were below the line of the cuff and the third on the sleeve. The cuff could be piped with a straight or pointed band; the cuff flap might also be piped squarely or have a pointed design. The cuff flap might be the same colour as the cuff, or the facing colour; an extra button might also be added. The coat's collar might be cut straight so it buttoned squarely at the neck, or it might be open at an angle to reveal the neck stock or cravat. The lapels (*revers*) of the coat might finish in a point, following the natural flow of the tail, or they might be cut squarely at the waistline. The piping of the false pockets on the tails might be horizontal or vertical, and the tails might be cut squarely or pinned to form a triangular finish. Finally, on the turnbacks there were a variety of badges. Grenadiers would have a flaming grenade device; voltigeurs and chasseurs hunting horn symbols; in the empire there were the ubiquitous N's (with an imperial crown above), but hearts, diamonds, stars, Phrygian caps were also used at various times.

To muddy the waters further, in 1806 Napoleon experimented with dressing his infantrymen in the traditional white coat of the Royal Army. The regiments affected by this were numbered 3, 4, 8, 12, 14, 15, 17, 18, 19, 21, 22, 24, 25, 27, 28, 33, 34 and 86. Along with the white coats came the return of distinctive colours worn on cuffs, collars and lapels in various combinations. This decision was reversed on 2 October 1807 and the regiments affected resumed issuing blue coats.

Light infantry battalions had begun the war in a dragoon green coloured coat which was cut to the same pattern worn by the infantry. A blue coat was adopted from 1794 when the amalgamations of regular and volunteer battalions was enacted. The majority of light infantry half-brigades adopted a short-tailed version of the coat, which had first been worn by Belgian light troops in French service who were influenced by the more functional garments worn by Austrian and British light troops.

It was only with the introduction of the coatee (*habit veste*) on 19 January 1812, that a real attempt was made to standardise the infantry coat. However, with a three year lifespan of the old style coats and the disruptions caused by the collapse of the empire, it is unlikely the 1812 coatee was fully introduced until the period of peace between Napoleon's abdication and the Hundred Days campaign of 1815.

The coats worn by officers were essentially the same as those worn by the men. Officers' coats began to lose their luxurious embroidery in the 1720s, and by the 1780s the only real difference was the quality of the tailoring and material. Officers

Debonair infantryman
(possibly a drummer)
enjoys a moment of repose.

had a second coat called a *surtout* or *frac*, which was worn on campaign and also as a form of 'undress'. This was very similar to the English Regency dress coat which did not have lapels and was fastened at the front by a single row of buttons.

[**See also:** 20. Chief musician; 22. Master craftsmen; 37. Drummer; 51. Worker; 53. Uniform – general description (introduction); 54. Materials; 55. Lifespan of uniforms; 56. Weight of arms and equipment; 58. Coatee; 64. Epaulettes; 65. Distinctive markings; 80. Petty equipment; 82. Packing the haversack; 110. Pay; 132. General disciplinary measures; 133. Regimental prisons; 134. Military justice; 182. Lodgings and the arrangements of the bedchamber; 189. Duties of sentries at the gates; 206. Cleaning the uniform.]

## 58. Coatee (*habit-veste*)

On 19 January 1812 France adopted a new type of infantry coat. Known as the *habit-veste*, the proper English term for this garment is a coatee – a coat which fastens from the neck to the waistline and has an upstanding collar. The coatee had been proposed as early as 1776 and had been temporarily adopted by French troops on Napoleon's Egyptian expedition (1798–1801). In essence it was a copy of the utilitarian uniform which had been worn by Austrian troops throughout the Napoleonic wars and which had been adopted by the British at the turn of the 19th century.

One should note how prior to the 1812 uniform the short-tailed coat worn by light infantry was often referred to as a *habit-veste* to distinguish it from the more amply cut line infantry coat. This description is not entirely accurate, because the light infantry coat was essentially the same pattern as worn by line infantry, but with shorter tails. It did not fasten at the waist as a proper coatee should.

[**See also:** 33. Chasseur; 53. Uniform – general description (introduction); 55. Lifespan of uniforms; 57. Coat.]

## 59. Greatcoat (*capote*)

The French word for greatcoat (*capote*) was a derivative of the word *cape*. By the latter part of the 18th century greatcoats were generally only issued to soldiers on sentry duty in poor weather or at night. They therefore formed part of the guardhouse equipment rather than being general issue, and tended to be made of thick cloth in natural colours. On campaign they tended only to be worn in colder regions during winter, and were often fabricated locally rather than by the regimental tailors.

After 1806 the issue of greatcoats to soldiers on campaign became increasingly common. When not being worn the greatcoat was usually attached to the top of the haversack. To prepare it, the greatcoat was laid flat and the edges folded inwards so it did not exceed the width of the haversack. It was rolled very tightly, starting with the collar, and then attached to the haversack by means of two buff belts which were buckled tight. Some soldiers wore their greatcoats rolled up like a bandolier over the shoulder, right to left. As well as a comfortable means of carrying the coat, the tightly rolled coat was known to afford soldiers some level of protection in combat.

Although the garment was in use since the regulation of 25 April 1767, their form was not officially described until the regulation of 19 January 1812. The 1812 pattern greatcoat was beige in colour with a double row of five buttons up the front. The greatcoats worn by elite companies had buttons on the shoulders to allow epaulettes to be worn. Until then the cut of an officer's riding coat was somewhat arbitrary and typically tailored in the regimental colour (i.e. national blue), rather than the beige worn by men of the ranks.

Greatcoats were sometimes described as a *redingote* – the French mispronunciation of the English riding coat, a garment which came into use in the early 1700s. Properly speaking, the greatcoat of an officer was a *redingote*; while the *capote* was a common soldier's *redingote*.

[**See also:** 53. Uniform – general description (introduction); 55. Lifespan of uniforms; 56. Weight of arms and equipment; 65. Distinctive markings; 76. Cartridge pouch; 79. Haversack; 82. Packing the haversack; 187. The sergeant of police; 238. The effect of clothing; 254. Military hospitals; 199. Food preparation (introduction).]

## 60. Jacket (*veste* or *gilet*)

The infantryman's jacket (*veste*) was a tight-fitting, sleeved garment with a *basque* or 'skirt' (i.e. it was tailored to extend below the waistline over the hips). Although worn under the coat, the jacket could be worn in its own right as fatigue jacket. The jacket had a collar and cuffs and was fastened at the front by small uniform buttons. Additional buttons were provided for epaulettes and for fastening the cartridge pouch over the small of the back. There were two small pockets at the front of the jacket, either side of the opening.

Light infantry tended to wear a jacket which was cut less amply. The *gilet* was a jacket without the *basque* (i.e. it was tailored to sit on the hips). It was originally designed as a sleeveless garment worn underneath the jacket to provide an additional layer of clothing in cold weather, but by the Napoleonic era it was an alternative to the jacket. The Napoleonic *gilet* was usually sleeved, with a collar, cuffs, pockets, etc. This style of jacket was universally adopted in the uniform regulation of 19 January 1812.

[**See also:** 51. Worker; 53. Uniform – general description (introduction); 54. Materials; 55. Lifespan of uniforms; 56. Weight of arms and equipment; 65. Distinctive markings; 182. Lodgings and the arrangements of the bedchamber; 191. Rations & supplies (introduction); 206. Cleaning the uniform.]

## 61. Breeches and pantaloons (*culottes/pantalons*)

Breeches were widely worn in the 18th century. The 1779 uniform regulations described breeches as being made from *tricot* and lined in linen. The leg extended past the knee and finished at the top of the calf muscle where buttons or buckles held the garment tight to the leg. The lower leg was protected by stockings and gaiters. The waist band sat on the haunches. The garment was tightened by buttons at the front and by an adjustable vent at the back which could be tightened by buckles or a lace. For convenience, the front of the breeches could be quickly opened by means of a square buttoned flap called a drawbridge (*pont-levis*). Although supposed to be amply cut, breeches were often extremely rigid when newly issued; so much so a man would require the help of two fellows to help put them on. This problem appears to have continued into the Napoleonic period when fashion dictated breeches should be tailored to fit as tightly as possible. The wearing of underwear was not then prevalent in society and many regiments did not issue separate linen long drawers (*caleçon*) because the breeches were already lined with linen and it was felt an undergarment might further impede movement, or gather up and form visible creases in the breeches. Some regiments did issue draws, because it was generally recognised that separate underwear was easier to keep clean, and was therefore more salubrious than lined breeches. Soldiers issued with drawers also benefitted from being able to use them as part of their fatigue dress, particularly when cleaning weapons.

From 1792 officers were permitted to adopt a summer dress with breeches made of dimity, or whitened linen. Soldiers were also authorised to wear white linen. Each soldier was issued with a new pair of breeches every year. The old pair was generally retained for another year as a second pair. Prior to the Revolution, sergeants allowed their men to blacken the old pair for use as a winter petty dress. It is unclear if this practice continued into the Napoleonic era or not.

As fashions began to change at the turn of the century, trousers or pantaloons (*pantalons*) became more common. These garments covered the whole leg and initially had an association with the *sans-culottes* political movement – breeches being associated as a garment worn by the aristocracy, pantaloons the common man. In the army, pantaloons were particularly popular with Belgian light infantry volunteers in 1792 and 1793. By Years III and IV many light infantry half-brigades had also adopted them as a form of over-trousers (*surculotte*) which were worn with short gaiters. These over-trousers were secured on the outer leg by a line of buttons down the seam in the style of light cavalry stable dress.

Although long draws (*caleçon*) had been used for fatigue dress, linen trousers became increasingly common as part of the infantry's fatigue or marching dress. This practice was acknowledged on *17 Frimaire XI* (8 December 1802) by an instruction authorising the wearing of linen pantaloons if the corps' funds could afford it. Further to this, a circular of *4 Vendémiaire XII* (27 September 1803) stated all troops destined for the expedition to Britain should have linen trousers paid for by the state.

As the Napoleonic period progressed the use of pantaloons became much more prevalent, so much so, the 1812 pattern uniform formally abandoned the use of breeches. This had a knock on effect removing the need for long stockings and long gaiters. The 1812 pattern pantaloons were not lined. Instead the men were issued with a pair of linen draws (*caleçon*) which were the same length as the pantaloons, and were cut amply to allow kneeling. The draws were fastened over the fly by two buttons, and secured around the waist by a drawstring. The adoption of pantaloons also saw the formal issuing of braces to hold them up. Men had previously worn waist belts to best secure their breeches.

[See also: 51. Worker; 53. Uniform – general description (introduction); 54. Materials; 55. Lifespan of uniforms; 56. Weight of arms and equipment; 82. Packing the haversack; 238. The effect of clothing; 254. Military hospitals.]

## 62. Gaiters (*guêtres*)

Gaiters were adopted by the French Army during the War of Spanish Succession (1701–1714), in imitation of Basque costume. They became a symbol of service, or *guet* (watch, surveillance, or the process of making the rounds), one not putting on gaiters unless one was taking up arms. By 1786 gaiters were an integral part of the uniform, with white gaiters for parades, blackened canvas gaiters on general service and marches in the summer, and black woollen gaiters for winter. They rose above the knee and were fastened with twenty to twenty-four small buttons, depending on the length of the leg. At the top they were attached by two buttons to the breeches, and were further secured by a buckled garter strap. This restricted leg movement considerably and French soldiers stopped using garters well before long gaiters were abolished in 1812. When kneeling was first introduced, some regiments added a leather pad inside the gaiter to protect the knee, however this practice was outlawed in the ordinance of 25 April 1767 and does not appear to have resumed. The gaiter was held to the shoe by a *sous-pied*, a strap which passed under the shoe in front of the heel (one of the reasons shoes could not have flat soles and required a heel).

The tradition of wearing white gaiters at parades also fell from favour after 1792, and the requirement for this was officially removed in the circular of *29 Frimaire XIV* (20 December 1805). Of course, this is not to say some troops were not issued with white gaiters at the discretion of the colonel, and the tradition was maintained by the Imperial Guard. On 19 January 1812 a half gaiter was universally adopted. Light infantry ought to have worn long gaiters until 1812, a decision confirmed by an instruction of *11 Thermidor VII* (29 July 1799). However, well before this, the majority of light infantry half-brigades had adopted a style of half-gaiter popularised by independent light companies in the early part of the 1790s. This official edict appears to have been ignored and light infantry of the Napoleonic period are most commonly depicted with short gaiters which were cut to resemble hussar boots, complete with piping and tassels.

[**See also:** 53. Uniform – general description (introduction); 54. Materials; 55. Lifespan of uniforms; 56. Weight of arms and equipment; 61. Breeches and pantaloons; 63. Footwear; 80. Petty equipment; 82. Packing the haversack; 112. Deductions and funds; 187. The sergeant of police; 238. The effect of clothing.]

## 63. Footwear (*chaussures*)

The regulation of 21 February 1779 stated officers and men alike were to be issued with shoes and gaiters. Shoes (*souliers*) came in three standard sizes, had a square front and, initially at least, could be worn on either foot. The sole was reinforced by metal hobnails (*clous de souliers*). The nails (*clous à vis*) had a screw thread on the shaft to give more purchase into the leather. Bardin gave the diameter of the head of each nail as 7–8 mm, with a length of 6 mm. Each sole would have seventy, sixty, or fifty nails, depending on the size of the shoe.

The ordinance of 1 October 1786 confirmed the buckles on these shoes ought to be brass for soldiers and silver for officers. During the 1790s the use of buckles waned in favour of fastening shoes with a leather lace. The Consular Guard issued its soldiers with silver buckles as a form of 'society dress' (*tenue de société*) because, as Bardin ruefully recorded in his dictionary, 'laws are not made for privileged corps'. Although forbidden by the 1779 regulations, low fronted shoes called *escarpins* were worn by infantry officers as part of their undress uniform. These shoes could be buckled or worn as a slipper, in which case they were very similar in appearance to the modern female court shoe.

The instruction of *16 Ventôse III* (6 March 1795) confirmed each soldier would have two pairs of shoes, one of which was carried in the haversack. However there were numerous local orders which required soldiers to have two spare pairs of shoes in their packs. Despite the best intentions, this was rarely achieved. The expected lifespan of a shoe was fixed at three months by a circular of *29 Frimaire V* (19 December 1796). However, there was widespread abuse in the manufacture of shoes and enormous sums of money were made by contractors and suppliers who passed off shoddy goods to the army. An investigation in 1793 found the soles of one batch of shoes were made of cardboard. It was little wonder the soldiers at the front were often barefoot and forced to make local requisitions, or to resort to clogs or sandals. The abuses continued and this led to the circular of *4 Brumaire VI* (25 October 1797) stating corps should manufacture their own footwear in future.

The regulation of 24 June 1792 required infantry officers and adjutants to wear turndown boots known variously as *bottes à retroussis* and *bottes à l'anglaise*. The turndown section of these boots was a yellowish leather, the idea of which was to stop the boot black rubbing off on the white breeches. However, this turnback section was easily scuffed and stained, and so, as breeches began to fall out of favour, shorter, all black boots (*bottes courtes*) became fashionable and were adopted as standard in 1812. On an unofficial basis, mounted infantry officers tended to wear riding boots (*bottes à l'écuyère*), which were designed to give protection to the knee. However as the fashion changed from breeches to trousers, these were also replaced by short boots, albeit with spurs attached. Light infantry officers may have also worn so-called Hungarian boots (*bottes à la hongroise*) in the fashion of hussar officers.

[**See also:** 16. Adjutant; 22. Master craftsmen; 54. Materials; 55. Lifespan of uniforms; 56. Weight of arms and equipment; 62. Gaiters; 79. Haversack; 80. Petty equipment; 82. Packing the haversack; 110. Pay; 112. Deductions and funds; 182. Lodgings and the arrangements of the bedchamber.]

## 64. Epaulettes

Epaulettes were an ornamental shoulder strap worn by officers, sub-officers, elite troops and light infantry. Generally speaking they took the shape of a rectangular strap, finished with a crescent section which sat over the top of the arm and was decorated by a twisted cord edging and a fringe. Fringes could be made of twisted bullion (these were reserved for senior officers), a bullion thread, silk thread or wool. They were fixed to the coat by passing them through a shoulder strap which was located parallel with the shoulder seam, and a button which was located near the collar. Like many decorative garments, epaulettes had their origins in practicality. They were initially nothing more than a detachable shoulder strap which held the cartridge pouch bandolier on the shoulder. In the 18th century, when company level officers were armed with muskets, they also required a shoulder strap to hold their cartridge pouches in place. During the Seven Years War they became associated with being a symbol of rank, apparently at the instigation of Marshal de Belle-Isle in 1759.

The distinctive marks carried on epaulettes during the Napoleonic era were based on those of the uniform regulation of 21 February 1779. Colonels wore a pair of epaulettes made of bullion, either gold or silver to match the colour of the uniform button. The fringes of the epaulette were made from twisted bullion thread in a style known in French as *cordes à puits*. The epaulettes were edged with a twisted thread *torsade*. The rank of colonel in second wore the same epaulettes, but with a bar of red silk running down the centre of both.

Majors wore bullion epaulettes on both shoulders, but with the body and fringe in two different metals – the fringe matching the button colour. A major in second was distinguished by a red silk bar down the centre. Battalion commanders wore a colonel's epaulette on the left shoulder only, with a fringeless counter-epaulette on the right shoulder.

Captains wore a single epaulette on the left shoulder made from braid in the same colour as the uniform buttons. The epaulette was decorated with a fringe of bullion thread (*grains d'épinard*) only. Captains wore a fringeless counter-epaulette on the right. Lieutenants wore the same style, but with a single bar of red silk across the centre of the epaulette; sub-lieutenants a double bar of red silk. Adjutant majors wore the epaulettes of a captain or lieutenant (depending on their rank) but reversed (i.e. the epaulette was on the right shoulder). Adjutants wore a red silk epaulette with two braids in the same metal as the uniform button. The fringe was red mixed with metal in the button colour.

According to the 1786 uniform regulation, grenadiers did not have epaulettes, but were issued instead with red woollen shoulder straps piped in white, identical in shape to those worn by fusiliers. However, after 1789, red, fringed epaulettes became very popular with the National Guard and these were adopted by the regular army after the instruction of 1 April 1791. In general, fusiliers continued to wear simple shoulder straps throughout the period. Voltigeurs were supposed to wear epaulettes coloured yellow or 'sunrise' (*aurore*), a shade described in the 1814 edition of Boyer's *Royal Dictionary* as 'golden yellow', and elsewhere as 'yellow with light red tones' (i.e. a pale orange). The exact description of this shade is somewhat academic, as many colonels decided to issue their voltigeurs with green epaulettes instead. This was partly because yellow hues faded quickly in sunlight, but mostly because the light infantry of the Imperial Guard wore green epaulettes and colonels wanted to imitate them. On 27 December 1807 the Ministry of War decided it would reject all expenditure claims for green epaulettes for voltigeurs. The decree of 19 January 1812 clarified the colours of shoulder straps and epaulettes for infantry as given in Table 7.

The usefulness of epaulettes is a matter of debate. From even short distances the distinguishing marks on company officers' epaulettes were indistinguishable. They were ruined by a combination of wet weather and hard usage. On active service officers would often sleep fully clothed and the epaulettes suffered from

**Table 7:** Distinguishing colours 19 January 1812.

|       | *Company* | *Base colour* | *Piping* |
|-------|-----------|---------------|----------|
|       | Grenadier | Red           | Madder red |
| Line  | Fusilier  | Blue          | Scarlet  |
|       | Voltigeur | Chamois       | Blue     |
|       | Carabineer | Scarlet      | Red      |
| Light | Chasseur  | Blue          | White    |
|       | Voltigeur | Chamois       | Blue     |

this. They were also difficult to replace on campaign, and spare sets and their storage boxes took up too much valuable space in a portmantle (*portmanteau*). Some might say their status was somewhat diminished when the commanders of the Consular Guard infantry (who recognised no regulations other than their daily orders) decided to award their drum major with a pair of colonel's epaulettes. The Guard was always held as an example of excellence, so colonels of the line felt justified in dressing their own drum majors as lavishly as they pleased. The matter appears to have been exacerbated by foreign ambassadors dressing their lackeys in epaulettes modelled on the colonel's style for hunting expeditions attended by senior French generals. This increased the clamour for bigger, bulkier epaulettes all round – a fashion realised later in the 19th century. As a further aside, Bardin indicates regiments bought in epaulettes rather than manufacture them in-house. The craft of *passementerie* was an extremely specialist skill in itself, requiring an apprenticeship of seven years.

[**See also:** 17. Second and third eagle bearers; 36. Voltigeur; 56. Weight of arms and equipment; 65. Distinctive markings; 112. Deductions and funds.]

## 65. Distinctive markings

In addition to epaulettes, rank and other distinguishing marks could be worn as stripes (*galons*) or chevrons. For example, a sergeant major wore two braids in gold or silver (depending on the button colour) positioned obliquely on each forearm. These metallic braids were often mounted on a red or yellow fabric braid. Sergeants had a single metal braid positioned obliquely on the forearm. Corporals had two stripes on each forearm made from woollen braid, either red or yellow in colour. The quartermaster corporal wore the same distinctive markings as a corporal, with the addition of a sergeant stripe worn on the upper part of each arm.

Long service chevrons (*chevrons d'ancienneté*) were first introduced in 1771. Up to three chevrons could be awarded, each representing eight years of service. After twenty-four years soldiers were awarded an oval medallion worn on the left breast as a mark of veteran status. These distinctions were prohibited on 6 August

1791. Napoleon reintroduced distinctive marks for veterans on *3 Thermidor X* (22 July 1802) although this law only included men and corporals. Sergeants were not included until *2 Fructidor XI* (20 August 1803). Under the new system, one chevron represented 10 years' service; two chevrons 15 years; three chevrons 20 years. After 25 years' service, veterans had the right to be admitted into the Legion of Honour. The chevrons were made from a braid of scarlet wool ten lines thick (approximately 22 mm) in an inverted 'V' shape. Some sub-officers used gold braid instead of scarlet wool. They were worn on the upper sleeve (between the shoulder and elbow) of the left arm on the coat and greatcoat, with five millimetres spacing between them. This distinctive mark was also worn on the jacket, although the braid was half the normal size.

Created in the decree of 18 February 1808, the second and third eagle bearers wore a combination of chevrons and stripes. In the original decree, they were instructed to wear four chevrons on each arm. However, in his 1813 infantry manual, Bardin cited a circular of 18 March 1811, and confirmed only two chevrons should be worn on each arm. They were to be made from red woollen braid, 30 cm long. They also wore a stripe in gold or silver (line and light respectively), presumably on both arms, in the same position as a sergeant. Sappers wore a badge formed of two crossed axes on the mid-section of the upper sleeve.

[**See also:** 20. Chief musician; 21. Musicians; 22. Master craftsmen; 37. Drummer; 57. Coat; 64. Epaulettes.]

Veteran with long service stripes flatters a conscript who has bought him a drink: 'You have honour, you have principles; you will be a hero!' (after Raffet).

*Chapter 9*

# Headgear & Hairstyles

### 66. Infantry helmet (*casque*)

At the beginning of the war in 1792 French infantry wore a helmet (*casque*) similar to the British Tarleton. The French *casque* was made of boiled leather which was blackened, varnished, and surmounted by a crest which ran from front to back. This crest was shaped like a caterpillar and made of bearskin for the officers and black horsehair for the men. Around the base of the helmet was a band, or turban, approximately 6 cm high which was made of fake 'big cat' skin (leopard, or panther). The head was protected from sabre cuts by a brass band which passed from one side of the helmet to the other, perpendicular to the crest. A leather visor gave some protection to the eyes. Around the time of the amalgamation of the regular and volunteer battalions in 1794, the infantry began to adopt the felt cocked hat (*chapeau*) worn by the National Guard volunteers.

[**See also:** 17. Second and third eagle bearers; 67. Cocked hat; 71. Plumes.]

Infantryman in leather *casque* helmet with cantineer, early 1790s.

## 67. Cocked hat (*chapeau*)

The *chapeau* was a broad-brimmed, black, felt hat which had been the traditional headgear of French soldiers since the latter part of the reign of Louis XIV. Initially the tricorne style had been popular. The rear half of the brim was turned up and pinned to the cap forming a semi-circular 'fan'. The right and left front halves were then turned upwards so the brim formed a triangular shape. As the century progressed, the triangular shape became less pronounced, with the 'cock' of the hat moving so it was over the left eye. The hat was normally adorned on the left side with a cockade in the national colours (white before the Revolution and tricolour after 1789), sometimes surmounted by a pompom, a flat lentil shaped ornament, or even a tumbling horsehair plume. While regular infantry adopted the leather helmet at the beginning of the 1790s, the National Guard continued to wear the felt cocked hat.

As a military garment, Bardin believed the *chapeau* was utterly useless. The hat had to be worn so the right corner was a little lower and advanced than the left in order to accommodate the musket at the shoulder arms position. When loading and firing, the hats of the men in the front and second ranks might obstruct the musket of the man behind them. As a result of this hats would be knocked off the soldiers' heads. The weight of the pompom worn over the left eye would cause the hat to sag in that direction. The hat did not have a visor to protect the eyes from sunlight and rain, and it offered no protection to the neck either. Nor did the hat afford any protection against blows to the head. However, the hat was very popular and being ever practical, during the wars of the Revolution, French troops spontaneously turned their hats about by ninety degrees from the *en bataille* position (i.e. parallel to the line of battle) so the right or left corner faced to the front (a style known as *en colonne*). Worn in this manner the hat did not get in the way of shouldering the weapon, or loading, and it provided shade to the eyes and neck. By the mid-1790s this hat was worn almost universally by French infantrymen.

After shakos were universally adopted during the early part of the empire, the *chapeau* was transformed into a bicorn hat worn by officers, or sub-officers as their petty dress. The cocked section over the left eye disappeared, and the brim was expanded in size forming a tall crescent shape.

[See also: 28. Sergeant; 53. Uniform – general description (introduction); 71. Plumes; 239. Hairstyles and headgear.]

## 68. Shako (*schako*)

The Napoleonic infantry shako originated from a tall, felt, semi-conical hat worn by hussars known as a *mirliton*. The earlier patterns had a decorative 'flame' wound round them; in other words, a triangular piece of black felt lined with *serge* in a variety of different colours. The flame could be wrapped either to the left or right of the shako to appear black or in the facing colour. Eager to adopt the flamboyant and fashionable costume of the hussars, during the early 1790s the *mirliton* was adopted by horse artillery and mounted chasseurs. In 1794 the hat was also adopted by some light infantry carabineers who wore a model 11 inches high and which tapered inwards at the top.

The *mirliton* fell out of favour during the Consulate in favour of a simpler pattern. By then light infantry had adopted a cylindrical leather shako which had a detachable leather visor, a cockade in the national colours, a plume on the left side, and a brass plaque (normally in the shape of a lozenge) at the front. Although this design was widely adopted in Year VI, the shako was only officially recognised as the headgear of light infantry by the decree of *4 Brumaire X* (26 October 1801).

The shako was adopted by line infantry regiments on 25 February 1806. A circular of 27 March 1806 described the shako being made of felt, 18 cm high, and 23 cm wide at its largest diameter. Where the light infantry shako had been cylindrical, the line infantry pattern was semi-conical, with the top of the hat being wider than the brim. This shape gave marginally more protection to the face from rain, snow and sabre cuts. The plume moved to the front of the hat, positioned over a 7 cm tricolour cockade. Ornate cords and tassels (*raquettes*) were suspended from the sides of the shako, but these decorations proved extremely inconvenient when chin scales were later added to the design.

A circular of 9 November 1810 redefined the dimensions and decorations of the shako. The shako would be 19 cm high and made of felt, with a hard leather top piece which had a diameter of 24.4 cm, and formed a band around the circumference of the shako 4 cm deep. At the bottom of the felt body was a second band 2.7 mm wide. At the rear of this band was a gusset and buckle so the shako could be adjusted to fit. At the front of the shako was a leather visor and a plaque in the shape of a lozenge bearing the regimental number, and surmounted by a 7 cm tricolour cockade. Chin scales were attached to each side of the shako, brass for line infantry, and white metal for light. All decorative cords were forbidden. They were replaced by decorative bands (*galons*) in gold or silver around the top circumference of the hat as follows: colonels, a 34 mm band with a 14 mm band located 20 mm below; majors, a single 34 mm band; battalion commanders, a single 27 mm band; captains, a single 20 mm band; lieutenants, 18 mm; sub–lieutenants, 14 mm. Adjutants would have the same distinctive band as sub-officers, but with a red silk lozenge pattern woven in to it. There are examples of red or yellow braid being added to these bands for the elite companies.

[See also: 53. Uniform – general description (introduction); 55. Lifespan of uniforms; 56. Weight of arms and equipment; 71. Plumes; 72. Hairstyles; 80. Petty equipment; 138. Salutes; 239. Hairstyles and headgear.]


## 69. Bearskin cap (*bonnet à poil*)

The bearskin caps worn by certain elite troops originated in the days when grenadiers would sling their muskets over their backs while scaling ladders and throwing grenades. The wide-brimmed felt hats of the period would be knocked by the musket while in the process of doing this, so certain grenadiers began wearing a triangular bonnet which resembled a flame. Over time, this triangular shaped hat began to take on the form of a mitre, and then over more time still, the cap came to be manufactured from bearskin.

In 1791 grenadiers were issued with a bearskin and a cocked hat. The bearskin caps worn by line infantry grenadiers had a brass plaque over the brow with a grenade device. The bearskin worn by light infantry carabineers did not have a plaque. The top of the bearskin was finished with a fabric 'skullcap' (*calotte*), usually red fabric with a white cross.

On the march, bearskin caps were often placed in a twill bag which was worn above the haversack and greatcoat. In order not to disturb the appearance of the cap, the twill bag opened at both ends, allowing the cap to be introduced and removed without the hair being brushed back. The ends of the bag were sealed by cords, which were pulled tight and then tied to greatcoat straps.

The decree of 19 January 1812 withdrew the bearskin for line and light infantry. At the time France was making sixty thousand bearskins per year at a cost of four million *francs*. They were generally considered ridiculous, incommodious, heavy, without rigidity, and offered no defence to the wearer. In winter they would be covered in frost, and snow would settle on them. In compensation for losing their bearskins the shako worn by grenadiers was 15 mm taller than the model worn by fusiliers.

One should also mention a version of the bearskin called the *colback*. Deriving from the Turkish Kalpack, this bonnet was more squat, and broader than the regular *bonnet à poil*, with a fabric *flame* on top, rather than the skullcap. The hat was first adopted by the Horse Chasseurs of the Consular Guard after the Egyptian campaign, but it is sometimes seen in prints worn by infantry sappers, particularly those of light infantry regiments. Bardin claims it was not widely adopted by drum majors until after the Bourbon restoration.

[**See also:** 34. Grenadier; 35. Carabineer; 46. Sapper; 55. Lifespan of uniforms; 56. Weight of arms and equipment; 71. Plumes.]


## 70. Forage cap (*bonnet de police*)

In 1767 the French Army adopted a pie-shaped Polish cap called a *pokalem* as part of their petty dress. This cap was variously described as a traveller's, or courier's bonnet. It had a cloth plaque at the front on which the regimental number was displayed, and side flaps which could be lowered to protect the ears and sides of the face in bad weather. On 1 April 1791 the *pokalem* was replaced by the *bonnet à la dragonne* which was a triangular bonnet popularised by the cavalry. The *queue* of the new bonnet had a tassel and was worn to the left or right side of the head. This bonnet lacked the *pokalem's* practical attributes, but was considered more elegant. The *pokalem* was reintroduced in 1812.

Conscripts on campaign circa
1813/14. Note the soldier carrying
potatoes in his shako is wearing a
pokalem fatigue cap, with the side flaps
lowered. The figure on the right is
wearing his shako back to front. (Beyer)

Known collectively as a *bonnet de police*, these caps were worn as morning dress; the men cooked wearing them, performed fatigues and ate soup wearing them too. Workers wore them in the workshops; sentries wore them at night after retreat. They were traditionally made by the master tailor from the material taken from old coats. However, as the period went on, they were made from new cloth and replaced every two years. The pattern for officers was the same, but the caps were made of finer material. When on the road, officers were allowed to wear their bonnets in the evening after dinner.

[**See also:** 53. Uniform – general description (introduction); 132. General disciplinary measures; 191. Rations & supplies (introduction).]

## 71. Plumes (*plumet*)

During the wars of the Revolution, even at the hardest times, when soldiers were ill-fed, barefoot and reduced to rags, one thing which appears not to have suffered was the French penchant for wearing decorative plumes. With the exception of the Normans of Guillaume le Bâtard's time (who were perhaps not Frenchmen in the true sense), French soldiers had worn adornments in their hats since the time of the Gauls. One of France's best loved kings, Henri IV was famous for wearing a white *panache* into battle, crying out to his soldiers 'follow my white plume' (perhaps the origin of the French white infantry flag?). In

1767 the Ministry of War tried to prohibit the practice, but was thwarted by the hussars, who pointed out theirs was a foreign costume and therefore not subject to the ban. In the infantry the practice was continued unofficially by officers going on leave, by the recruiting agents (*raccoleurs*) and drum majors. Finally, when the National Guard came into being, all manner of plumes were adopted, often in patriotic colours. The instruction of 1 April 1791 allowed infantrymen to wear plumes in their *casques* on parade days only. In effect, this instruction opened the floodgates and plumes were worn on *casques* and cocked hats all the same. Apparently the Egyptian campaign of 1798 was a particular high point in the fashion of plume wearing, with Bardin claiming (perhaps with a hint of exaggeration) officers purchased plumes so elaborate they were sold for as much as a good Arab horse.

The most elaborate plumes were worn on shakos in the early period of the empire. They consisted of a long stem (no official length was set) onto which a number of feathers were added. They could be dyed a multitude of colours, but the most common were red (for grenadiers) and green for light infantry. Chasseurs sometimes had their green plumes decorated with a dark red tip; voltigeurs a yellow tip. When not being worn, they were often bound in a protective ribbon and tied to their sabre scabbards using the shako's decorative cords.

More common were the so-called pompoms which variously took the form of balls, ovals, lentils and carrots. The word pompom is believed to have been a frivolous word in Southern French dialect to describe a lady's *panache*. It entered army jargon during the war of the Revolution, and was used freely with the officially recognised terms, *houpe* and *houpette*. The *houpe* was issued to all soldiers after 1 April 1791. They were made of wool which was formed over a sort of egg-shape mandarin with a wire protruding from the bottom which allowed it to be inserted into a small leather tube sewn inside the brim, behind the cockade. By the time of the empire, a round pompom was perhaps most common, sometimes with an *aigrette* inserted on top (an *aigrette* was a type of feathered tuft or crest – in effect, a shortened plume). Fusiliers tended to wear blue pompoms, grenadiers/carabineers had red, chasseurs green, and voltigeurs yellow.

It is only in 1810 that specific instructions appear to have been issued on the matter. On 9 November of that year a decision stated colonels ought to wear a white plume; majors, half white, half red, with red at the top; battalion commanders, all red. All other grades would receive a woollen *houpette* which would be white for the staff, red for grenadiers, yellow for voltigeurs, and various colours for the different centre companies. These colours were confirmed in a circular of 21 February 1811 as dark green (*vert foncé*) for the 1st company; sky blue (*bleu céleste*) for the 2nd; 'sunrise' (*aurora*) for the 3rd; and violet for the 4th. Although not stipulated in the circular, grenadiers and voltigeurs added an *aigrette* on top of their *houpettes* to remind everyone of their elite status.

A circular of 21 February 1811 added some important details, confirming the dimensions of plumes and *houpettes*. The plumes of senior officers would be 56 cm high, while the *houpettes* would be 5.5 cm in diameter and 1 cm thick. All other officers would have a conical *houpette* (colourfully described as 'pyramidal') in the relevant colour, 8 cm high.

[**See also:** 67. Cocked hat; 68. Shako; 80. Petty equipment; 112. Deductions and funds.]

## 72. Hairstyles

The official hairstyle of the French Army was described in the 1792 police regulations. Officers were required to wear their hair in a queue, covered with a silk ribbon held in place with a simple pin and not a rosette or bow. The sides of the hair were styled into a single curl which descended to the middle of the ear. The queue was to be no longer than eight inches in length and the tail of the queue was to protrude no more than one inch from the end of the ribbon.

Soldiers also wore their hair in a queue held in place with a black woollen ribbon in a similar manner to the officers, but did not have the sides of their hair curled, but had them layered (*étagées*), not protruding beyond the mid-point of the ear. This style was known as *à l'avant-garde*. The hair around the crown of the head and the fringe was cut short *en vergette*. In the latter half of the 1790s a style known as 'dog ears' (*oreilles du chien*) was fashionable, where the hair was allowed to grow long at the sides, covering the ears and framing the face. However, perhaps the biggest change to hairstyles occurred in the consular period when the short, cropped *à la Titus* style came into vogue and was supported by the First Consul and many officers.

At the beginning of the imperial period, the majority of regiments maintained their queues cutting the hair around the head in a style called *en brosse* (like a brush). This style continued until the shako was universally adopted by line infantry in 1806 after which short hair became more popular. Even then, there was no official ruling on hair and the decision to cut off the queues was made by individual regiments on the whim of the colonel. For example the 2nd Line Infantry retained their queues as late as 1812 when the regiment was serving in Spain. Even in the Imperial Guard there was not a single policy: the foot grenadiers doggedly hung onto their queues, while the foot chasseurs were more disposed to fashion and cut their hair short. In fact, short hair was not officially sanctioned until the ordinance of 25 September 1815, by which time the Imperial army was in the final throes of disbandment.

The Hungarian style braids known as *cadenettes* were principally worn by hussars and had the practical aspect of partially protecting the side of the face from sabre cuts (Hussars might also insert wooden mandarins into their queue to protect the neck). The practice of wearing *cadenettes* was also common among grenadiers in the latter part of the *ancien régime*.

Since the time of the American Revolution, white hair powder was reserved for grand parades, Sundays and fête days. This practice continued at least until the Consulate, and until 1814 in the foot grenadiers of the Imperial Guard.

[**See also:** 50. Barber; 73. Beards and moustaches; 110. Pay; 112. Deductions and funds; 134. Military justice; 239. Hairstyles and headgear.]

## 73. Beards and moustaches

In the main, French soldiers of the period were required to be clean shaven. Men were shaved at least twice a week by the company barber (*frater*) with the act of shaving taking place outside the bedchambers. Even the men in hospital and in detention were shaved at least once a week by the company barber. The moustache was allowed for elite and senior troops. Grenadiers and voltigeurs wore moustaches, as did sergeants and, increasingly so towards the end of the period, officers also. Men authorised to wear moustaches were forbidden from 'polishing' them or applying any lotion or grease to style them. This practice was considered improper and unhealthy.

It was generally unusual for men to wear beards at this epoch, except perhaps those of the Jewish faith or certain monastic orders; but in the latter half of the 18th century the fashion of sappers wearing beards became established, giving them a certain primitive and masculine appearance. There was no regulation for this, but permission to grow a beard was granted at the colonel's whim.

During the Revolution and Empire, the practice of growing sideburns (*rouflaquettes*) became popular. From contemporary prints, the sideburns could extend in a straight line as far as the jawbone, thus framing the face; or extend forwards to the point at which it would meet the natural line of the moustache. These sideburns appear to have been kept trimmed and groomed, not grown into the 'mutton chops' style of later periods.

[**See also:** 30. Corporal; 50. Barber; 80. Petty equipment; 134. Military justice.]

## 74. Tattoos and jewellery

One area not investigated by Bardin (because it was not the subject of a regulation or instruction) was the fashion of wearing tattoos and earrings. Although tattoos had been known since ancient times, the practice underwent something of a revival in the latter half of the 18th century. The principal reason for this was the interaction between Europeans and natives of the New World who sported tribal tattoos, particularly in the Pacific region, which was opened up by the British explorer James Cook in the 1770s. Generally speaking, in French society tattoos were seen as something associated with 'low people' such as criminals and 'public women' (particularly those who had served a custodial sentence). Given their association with 'savage' natives, tattoos were seen as somewhat pagan and were frowned upon by the church. Sailors journeying to the South Pacific often returned home with tattoos, and there was apparently a custom in some of France's maritime departments of tattooing children so they would be recognised by the father after a long sea voyage. In terms of soldiers, the habit of being tattooed appears to have been well established by the time of the Revolution. Tattoos were made by the soldiers (every company probably had its own 'artist') using small needles and an 'ink' made from gunpowder. The artist would first mark out the design on the body and then begin piercing the epidermis. Colours could be applied if dyes like indigo or vermillion were available. The dye appears to have been mixed with saliva, and new tattoos were cleaned using spit. It was not until the latter half of the 19th century people began to suspect the practices associated with tattooing were a means of transmitting disease.

Few contemporary texts address the subject matter, but a dictionary of medical science from 1820 noted old soldiers could be seen with tattoos on their arms and chests, with the names of famous generals, their mistresses, and their brothers-in-arms. Another account on tattooing from 1811 claimed the French had been influenced by Hessian soldiers returning from the Americas or India with their girlfriend's names tattooed on their arms. Out of 'imitation and idleness', French soldiers would have tattoos of their name, coats of arms, the portraits of their girlfriends and other images. One ex-serviceman recalled having a tattoo of a heart pierced by an arrow on his left forearm simply because he thought it looked nice (see the memoirs of Médard Bonnart). In 1823 Louis-Gabriel Montigny published an anecdote entitled 'history of a tattooed invalid' in which the author claimed he was given his first tattoo at the age of ten, while serving as an 'honorary drummer' in an infantry regiment. Having been taught to drink brandy by the drum major, he was encouraged to have a liberty bonnet tattooed on his chest. The procedure was performed by two grenadiers. While a prisoner on the hulks in England a master-at-arms tattooed an imperial eagle on his left arm. After the fall of Napoleon in 1814, he returned to his regiment and was chastised by his colonel after revealing his politically associated tattoos when the whole regiment stripped naked to take a bath in a river. His sub-lieutenant advised him to have a fleur-de-lis tattooed on his right arm to complete the set, after which he was admitted into the Hôtel des Invalides. A final point: the author of this story claimed he felt stigmatised for having tattoos, and made a point of being the last man to undress in his bedchamber at night. Another veteran of the Empire, with twelve campaigns and fifteen wounds to his name was given a medical examination and was found to have VIVE LE ROI (long live the king) tattooed on his right forearm. For political expediency, the veteran quickly had this tattoo amended to read VIVE LE RÔTI (long live roast meat). On a similar vein there is also the well known example of Jean-Baptiste Bernadotte, a former sergeant elevated to the rank of marshal and made the King of Sweden in 1810. On his death bed doctors ironically found the words 'MORT AUX ROIS' (death to kings) tattooed across his chest along with the image of a Phrygian cap.

Earrings were another common adornment sported by soldiers, particularly those of elite status. Long associated with funerary rites (the earrings symbolically paid the ferryman's fee across the River Styx), they had several other useful purposes. Gold earrings were an easily transferable source of emergency credit, and they might one day serve as a wedding ring for a sweetheart. It is said earrings were a soldier's first purchase on entry to the Imperial Guard (see Hippolyte de Mauduit's 1854 *Histoire des derniers jours de la Grande Armée*). New arrivals would have their ears pierced by the company tattoo artist and a lead band would be inserted until gold rings the size of a five *franc* écu (37 mm diameter) could be afforded. In order to purchase gold earrings, men would have to forgo many a night in the regimental canteen, unless of course they came into a windfall of booty. Although it is claimed by Mauduit that wearing of earrings was observed by everyone from 'Marshals of the Empire to fifers', and that during the Bourbon Restoration one did not see a veteran without his earrings, it is likely earrings were worn mainly by established soldiers, particularly those on high pay, rather than the average conscript fresh off the farm.

[**See also:** 37. Drummer; 47. Master-at-arms; 120. Entry to the Imperial Guard; 122. Les Invalides.]

An unusual sketch by Beyer showing three soldiers in a mixture of civilian and military garments. The central figure is wearing a smock-frock (*sarrau*), a garment worn while performing fatigue duties.

# Chapter 10

# Equipment

## 75. Introduction

There is a great deal of speculation about what items of uniform and equipment a French Napoleonic soldier was issued with, and even greater speculation at what they actually used. Even Bardin is inconsistent in his infantry manual. In truth then, we might only conclude what a soldier *ought* to have, or what he *might* have had; the truth being dependent on the state of the supply system at the time and the level of supervision within the regiment for inspecting the contents of soldiers' pack. Equipment was described as being *grand équipement* or *petite équipement*, the former being objects paid for directly by the government and provided to each corps (including weapons, cartridge pouches, tents, utensils and tools); and the latter being objects which were purchased by the soldier himself through deductions to his wages.

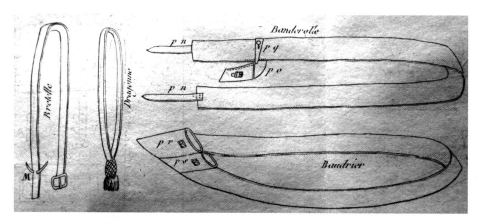

Musket sling (*bretelle*), decorative sabre wrist strap (*dragonne*), cartridge pouch belt (*banderolle*) with bayonet holder, sabre baldric (*baudrier*). From Bardin's infantry manual.

## 76. Cartridge pouch (*giberne*)

The cartridge pouch was made of blackened cow hide and held thirty-five cartridges in a wooden box contained inside it. The dimensions of this block were 230 mm long by 67mm wide; its height was 81mm. The box was divided into three sections. The central section was made of a block pierced by six circular holes in the middle, five of which held a cartridge each, with the sixth containing a

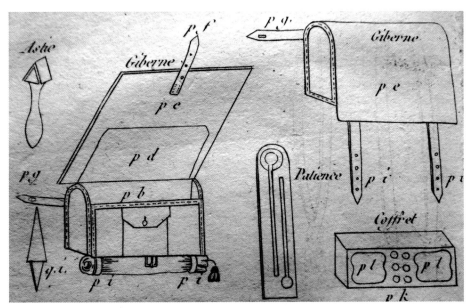

Two views of the cartridge pouch. Note forage cap rolled underneath; the wooden box (*coffret*) insert. Also shown are the button stick *(patience)*, the *astic*, below which appears to be a scraper *(curette)*. From Bardin's infantry manual.

white metal phial of oil. The two lateral compartments each held a paper package containing fifteen cartridges.

On the outside of the inner case was a pocket made of leather which held the turn-screw *(tourne-vis)*, ball extractor *(tire-balle)*, spare flints and leads, an oiled rag and a wooden or horn practice flint. The pocket was sealed by means of a toggle button made from rolled leather.

The wooden box and interior pocket were protected by a thick leather flap called the *patelette*. It was common for grenadiers and voltigeurs to fix a brass grenade or hunting horn device to the exterior of this flap. There were no standard designs for these devices because the practice was not ordered by a ministerial decision and was therefore up to the whim of the colonel. This outer flap was sealed by a buckle underneath the box. Some regiments also issued their men with a cartridge pouch cover *(couvre-giberne)* which might have some device or at least the company, battalion and regimental numbers; however these were not universally adopted.

The cartridge pouch was worn on a leather shoulder belt *(banderolle)* and was held in place over the right buttock by a leather strap called a *martingale*. This strap attached to a button on the rear of the soldier's coat or greatcoat. His belt might also carry the bayonet scabbard. Following an instruction of *4 Brumaire X* (26 October 1801) two leather belts were added on the underside of the pouch in order to hold the soldier's rolled up fatigue cap. Sergeants carried a smaller cartridge pouch which held two packets of cartridges without the central slots.

[**See also:** 77. Gun tools; 89. Ammunition; 208. Polishing the cartridge pouch; 209. Varnishing cartridge pouches.]

## 77. Gun tools

The ball extractor (*tire-balle* or *tire-bourre*), was a steel device which screwed into the end of the ramrod. It comprised of a solid body pierced at its axis with a screw threaded hole (the end of the ramrod was similarly threaded), with two spiral branches terminating with sharp points, which dug into the wadding. In the middle of the spiral was a spike which pierced the ball. As the ramrod was withdrawn, it pulled the wadding and ball out of the barrel. The device could also be used for inserting a piece of cleaning cloth into the barrel. Another indispensable tool was the turn-screw (*tourne-vis*). There were various forms of this, but essentially it was a three pronged tool which could be used to remove the various screws and to tighten the jaws holding the flint. Soldiers were also issued with a vent pick (*épinglette*), a metal pin which was used for clearing the touchhole if it became fouled by powder residue and cartridge paper debris. The vent pick was sometimes kept in the right side of the cartridge pouch, sandwiched between the wooden box

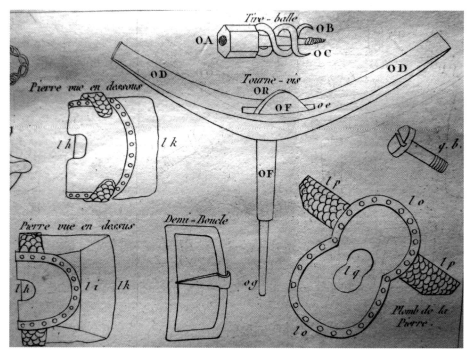

Ball extractor (*tire-balle*), turn screw (*tourne-vis*), flints and leads.

Imperial Guard grenadier and officer.
Note the grenadier wears earrings.
Both men wear the Legion of Honour
decoration on a red ribbon.

and the leather pouch. Some regiments kept it under the cross belt in a small case level with the chest. During the Revolution it became common for soldiers to suspend the pick from a lapel button by means of a chain. This practice was frowned upon because the chain would become rusty with use and then badly stain the coat's white lapels. For this reason brass chains were preferred. In addition to these gun tools, corporals would carry a spring mounting tool (*monte-ressort* or *démonte ressort*) which enabled soldiers to take the lock apart.

[**See also:** 76. Cartridge pouch; 210. Maintaining the musket; 233. Duties of sub-officers in battle.]

## 78. Flints (*silex*)

The firing mechanism of the Napoleonic musket relied on the sparks created by a sharpened flint striking a metal strike plate, or frizzen. Flints took the form of an irregular trapezoid when viewed in profile, approximately 35mm in length and 15mm thick. The flint was originally held in place in the jaws of the lock with strips of paper or cloth. By the beginning of the 19th century the French used a lead envelope or a piece of leather. The regulation of 24 June 1792 wisely advised the edges of the flint to be rounded off so soldiers did not slice their thumbs open while opening the pan during priming. A well made flint would provide forty or fifty shots. Sometimes the life of the flint could be extended by knapping it with a knife or turn-screw. Apparently the profession of flint knapper (*tailleur de pierres à feu*) was extremely unhealthy. Bardin recorded the majority of men employed in this trade were often sent to the grave from lung disease by the age of thirty-five or forty.

[**See also:** 56. Weight of arms and equipment; 76. Cartridge pouch; 77. Gun tools; 86. Musket; 229. Outpost duty; 232. Role of officers in battle; 233. Duties of sub-officers in battle.]

## 79. Haversack (*havresac*)

The haversack held the bulk of a soldier's equipment, either inside it, or strapped to the outside. The word haversack is believed to originate from the German for oat (*hafer*) and bag (*sack*). The object was also known to soldiers as a *sac à peau* (hide bag) because the French model was manufactured from hide (usually calf, but earlier models used goat, or sometimes even dog), the hair side facing outwards and providing waterproofing for the contents. It was carried by means of a pair of looping leather belts worn over the top of the epaulettes or shoulder straps and under each arm. The flap of the haversack was fastened by means of three buckled straps.

The design of the haversack carried in the 1790s and early empire differed very little from the regulation design of 25 April 1767. On *4 Brumaire X* (26 October 1801) it was described as being 1 foot deep and 17 inches wide. It contained a linen lining divided into several compartments to segregate items such as spare shoes and brushes from the bread and other 'booty' (*butin*), as soldiers colloquially referred to their personal effects and garments. The bag was a rounded rectangle in shape, with the outer flap being closed by three straps and buckles. There were additional leather fittings on the top of the pack which allowed a greatcoat and other items of equipment to be strapped to it.

In 1812 the design of the haversack changed, and a squarer model was adopted based on a Dutch pattern. This new design was flatter and facilitated packing. The new design also made marching in closed ranks easier, not to mention making it easier to move into the cross bayonets position and to load the weapon. On the down side, the haversack sat higher on the back, passing above the line of the shoulders, making it even more difficult for the rear rank to fire if the front rank did not kneel. The movement of the elbows could be obstructed by it; the upper arms were, in Bardin's opinion, 'murdered' by the weight of fully laden packs during long marches, and this was blamed for an increase in chest infections and diseases.

After the Revolution it became common for soldiers in garrison to wear their packs when on guard duty and at parades. Wearing the pack therefore became synonymous with being on duty. However, when in garrison, the pack was more often than not stuffed with hay to bulk it out and give the appearance of being full; the soldier's effects being kept in his barrack room on the shelves provided. During the Napoleonic wars only Russia maintained the old tradition of soldiers removing their packs before battle. The provisional regulation of 5 April 1792 specifically forbade removing packs on days of action. There were pros and cons to this of course. If the packs were removed before combat, the ranks could press closer together and all three ranks could have fired while standing. However, the French did not like the idea of being separated from their equipment, and were very mindful of the long lines of Russian packs discovered after Austerlitz in 1805, when the Russians had been forced to retreat without having the chance to recover them. During reviews the inspector could ask for the ranks to be opened and for men to ground and open their packs for inspection. On a day to day basis it was the corporal who taught recruits what and how to pack.

Officers did not carry a haversack and instead carried their spare clothing, equipment and petty effects in a portmantle (*portmanteau*) or case (*valise*) which was usually transported with the regimental baggage. In their most common form, portmantles were sausage-shaped and made of soft leather, buttoned or secured with straps and carried on the back of a saddle. No specific descriptions are given of an infantry officer's case, although Bardin reckoned the most practical for packing were those long and square in design.

[**See also:** 56. Weight of arms and equipment; 59. Greatcoat; 82. Packing the haversack; 83. Utensils and tools; 182. Lodgings and the arrangements of the bedchamber; 232. Role of officers in battle; 253. Medical treatment in garrison.]

## 80. Petty equipment

In his 1813 edition of the infantry manual Bardin believed the following items of petty equipment were required for each man: three linen shirts (*chemises*), one black collar (*col*), three white collars (rarely used by 1813), two pairs of thread or cotton stockings (*bas*), one pair of woollen stockings, two pairs of shoes, two pocket handkerchiefs (*mouchoirs*), two night caps – variously called a *bonnet de nuit* or a *serre-tête* (headband). Bardin also recorded each soldier ought to have two *rabats*. These were an archaic adornment which attached to the collar and covered the throat and part of the chest. Although described as necessary in the regulation of 2 September 1775, the *rabat* had been generally replaced in general fashion by the cravat which was introduced to France by Croatian mercenaries during the reign of Louis XIV (cravat is said to have been derived from the word Croat). We must therefore assume Bardin is referring to cravats and not being pedantic.

Petty equipment also included a distribution sack (*sac à distribution*), which was a hemp bag 4 feet 10 inches by 28 inches in size and was also used as a form of sleeping bag; two cockades (one of which was worn on the hat); a smock frock (*sarrau*) which was worn for fatigue duties (normally only several per squad); one pompom (or plume on the earlier pattern shakos); one pair of black gaiters; one pair of grey gaiters; and a water canteen – (*petit bidon*) a squarish white metal flask with a spout on top holding a pint (French) of water. The canteen was concave so it rested comfortably against the body. A wicker covered bottle (*bouteille clissée*) was more common in the later period. Both types of canteen were carried on a leather strap worn over the right shoulder and suspended on the left side of the body. Sergeants had an additional canteen which contained their section's vinegar supply.

By 1813 'waxed' (actually oiled) linen shako covers (*couvre schako*) were in general use with all regiments. These covered the whole hat and had a flap which could be lowered to protect the nape of the neck. Lock covers (*couvre-platine*) were used to protect the musket's firing mechanism from rain and damp. These were often made of leather, but there was no official model. Some regiments employed cartridge pouch covers as well, but again, there was no standard pattern for these either.

Generally speaking, gloves were not issued to infantrymen. Officers might wear leather gloves on active service, and the field regulations of 1788 described mittens as an article of winter equipment. In 1793 the Army of the North was issued with woollen, fingerless gloves (*poignets de mitaine*) made from knitted *tricot*, so it is entirely possible men acquired similar articles as necessity dictated.

Smaller pieces of equipment included a comb. In the regiments which retained the queue, the men would also have a bag of powder, a powder puff and a queue ribbon. Between each squad two *martinets* would be carried. These were a sort of wooden handled whip made from strips of hide and were used for beating clothes. Each man would carry three brushes – one each for leather, coat and shoes; a button stick (*patience*) – a device for polishing uniform buttons, consisting of a wooden board about six inches long which was pierced by a slot with an opening at one end wide enough for a large uniform button to pass through. Each man would have a supply of scrapers (*curettes*) – these were pieces of softwood which were used in to rub abrasive materials when polishing metalwork; a repair kit (*trousse garnie*) containing needle, threads, spare buttons, pieces of leather and latterly a razor; an awl for punching holes through leather; a button pull (*tire-bouton*) – a hooked implement for pulling buttons on gaiters, etc. through button holes; and, most importantly, an account book (*livret de compte*) in which pay and deductions would be recorded.

In addition to their uniform, arms, equipment and shared camping equipment, soldiers would also carry a number of consumables including rations and cleaning products and materials. Of the latter group the following items appear to have been essential: an *astic* – a triangular wooden tool mounted on a handle and used for applying wax to the cartridge pouches; a *copper brush* used for abrasive cleaning; *Tripoli* – a fine powder used as an abrasive for cleaning metals; a bag of wire wool or emery; Spanish whitener (*blanc d'Espagne*) – a fine white powder; pipe clay (*terre de pipe*), a fine white clay which forms a ductile paste with water; a brush (*vergette*) for applying whitener, and a polishing cloth – either a linen *tampon* or piece of material.

[**See also:** 51. Worker; 53. Uniform – general description (introduction); 55. Lifespan of uniforms; 56. Weight of arms and equipment; 62. Gaiters; 68. Shako; 81. Non-regulation equipment; 82. Packing the haversack; 110. Pay; 191. Rations & supplies (introduction); 206. Cleaning the uniform; 208. Polishing the cartridge pouch; 207. Whitening leather belts; 210. Maintaining the musket.]

## 81. Non-regulation equipment

Soldiers carried a number of pieces of equipment which were everyday essentials but which were not provided by the government or described in the regulations. For example, Bardin makes mention of soldiers having a spoon when calculating the weight of equipment carried, but eating utensils are nowhere else described. An item such as a pocket or sheath knife would have been absolutely indispensable to soldiers. Equally, there are no references to cups or beakers – but how else would a wine or brandy ration have been distributed fairly? An adjutant without a pocket watch would have been a very poor adjutant indeed, and a senior light infantry officer without a spyglass might have found his career filled with unpleasant surprises.

Money would have been carried in a leather purse or a belt. Coins were also hidden in the lining of the coat or jacket as a precaution against being robbed when taken prisoner. Although soldiers were officially prohibited from gambling, they could play card games like *la drogue* (lit. 'the dope') for forfeits. The game was played between two pairs of players, the partners sitting opposite one another, forming a cross. The rules were complex, and involved an obscure vocabulary (the rules were not written down until 1836). The loser was obliged to have his nose pinched by a wooden peg; sometimes the ears too. To play such games, soldiers required playing cards. Of course, following the decree of *1 Brumaire II* (22 October 1793) all symbols of royalty and feudalism were outlawed, so card manufacturers had to replace the traditional kings, queens and *valets* (not to mention any references to crucifixes, crowns, and fleurs-de-lis) with symbols such as Phrygian caps, and allegorical figures representing republican virtues such as fraternity and bravery. Under the Directorate traditional card designs began to return.

Smoking was *de rigeur* among soldiers and smokers would have required a pipe and a tobacco pouch (sometimes carried in the shako). Soldiers in Spain may have used cigarillos, but the cigarette was not introduced to France properly until the 1830s. Snuff taking was extremely common in the 18th century, but fell out of favour after the Revolution as a symbol of elitism and aristocracy. However, Napoleon was an avid user of snuff (*tabac à priser*) and one imagines its use was common among French officers, which means they would have carried snuff boxes (*tabatières*). Everyone would have required access to a metal fire striker (*briquet*), but again no official mention of these is made.

Officers would have packed their *portmanteau* with a 'necessary' (*nécessaire de campagne* or *necessaire de toilet*), a compact case made from leather or wood with all toiletry necessities including a comb, razor, shaving brush, mirror, glass phials or tins. Others might have included scissors, nail files, an ear pick and, more rarely, toothbrushes. The most common method of cleaning the teeth was to use a wooden pick or goose quill for removing food debris. Even chewing bread would have helped keep teeth clean and with a low sugar diet, some of the causes of tooth decay experienced in modern times would have been avoided. Napoleon was an avid user of toothbrushes and had one made from the hair of wild boar set in a gilded metal handle. It is therefore likely some officers would have had similar, albeit less ornate, toiletry objects to take on campaign. (Incidentally, toilet paper in the modern sense was not invented until the 1870s – prior to this the custom was to use anything from sticks, leaves, moss, rags, sponges and papers torn from books or pamphlets.) Some of the more elaborate necessaries carried by an officer may have included a small beaker for drinking drams, and perhaps writing accoutrements. To while away the hours of boredom, there are also references in memoirs of officers packing items of recreation such as books, flutes and sheet music. None of these items were mentioned in the various statutes, but they were found indispensable.

[See also: 40. Cantineer; 74. Tattoos and jewellery; 79. Haversack; 132. General disciplinary measures.]

## 82. Packing the haversack

The following instruction is provided by Bardin for the 1812 pattern haversacks worn in the last years of empire. The first items to be inserted into the haversack were the soldier's two spare shirts. These were rolled as tightly as possible and inserted into the main internal compartment. They were placed side by side at the bottom of the pack because they would only ever be required when the soldier was at rest. To the side of the shirts were placed his socks rolled together, handkerchiefs and spare collars. Above the shirts, the soldier would place either his woollen breeches or linen pantaloons, depending on which pair he was wearing. Soldiers carrying a clothes whip (*martinet*) would roll it up in their spare trousers in order not to hurt their back. The spare pair of gaiters would be turned inside out and folded, the straps inside, and placed on top of the breeches, either side of them. The repair kit (*trousse*) was placed in one of the corners of the bag and the dirty linen was placed in the front compartment. In the side pocket would be placed the copper brush, scrapers, *astic*, and button stick. The double pocket of the flap contained the shoes; a small bag of wire wool or emery; the shoe brushes (wrapped in paper or linen); a box of grease; wax for the cartridge pouch; a small bag containing whitener; pipe clay; *Tripoli*; and a tampon or piece of material.

Soldiers would be issued with two loaves of bread (enough for four days), but there was only room inside the haversack for one loaf, which was placed in the front compartment. The other loaf would be carried outside, having a piece of string put through it which was hung from the greatcoat straps. This practice was inconvenient because the bread was dried out by the sun, soaked by rain, made dirty by dust and was easily lost, or stolen. However, there was no real alternative as 'bread bags' were not issued. If raw, meat was divided by squad, into pieces weighing two or three pounds and shared out between the soldiers of the squad. The meat was wrapped in a handkerchief or in a piece of linen and hung from the haversack. If the meat was cooked, it was divided between each man, who wrapped their portions in some paper, and placed them in the bread compartment of the haversack. The haversack might also be used for storing packages of cartridges, so it would be common to hold up to thirty rounds of ammunition.

The linen distribution sack was also placed inside the haversack, folded in half and rolled as tightly as possible. Many carried this sack outside the haversack, rolled up and stored above or below the greatcoat, but this had its inconveniences. It was less pleasing to the eye because uniformity was difficult to obtain. Moreover, in the event of stormy weather, the soldier would require too much time to unstrap the greatcoat, put it on, and then have to strap the linen bag back to the haversack. The linen bag would then become so soaked with rain it would become heavy and useless for sleeping in.

If the regiment was marching in its greatcoats, the coat was sometimes removed, turned inside out, rolled up and placed in the haversack. If this was the case, there would not be space to include the linen bag. In this case there was no alternative but to roll up the linen bag and strap it to the exterior of the haversack where the greatcoat was normally carried.

In addition to the items described, a number of mess utensils had to be carried. The cooking pots (*marmites*) would be placed in a linen bag and attached to the haversack carefully so as not to impede or damage the cartridge pouch. The mess pans (*gamelles*) would be attached to the haversack by means of a wire ring, the bottom of the mess pan facing outwards. Drummers were exempt from carrying pots and mess pans because they carried their drums over the top of their haversacks when on the march.

[**See also:** 56. Weight of arms and equipment; 59. Greatcoat; 69. Bearskin cap; 80. Petty equipment.]

## 83. Utensils and tools

The *marmite* was a cooking vessel used for cooking meat and obtaining a broth. They were typically large enough for either eight or sixteen men. Those taken on campaign were not cylindrical but were flattened on one side and slightly concave (some say like a haricot bean) to facilitate transport. The lid (*couvercle*) of the *marmite* was designed to serve as a small saucepan (*casserole*) in its own right. The whole thing was covered in a cloth bag although these were quickly lost on campaign. It is interesting to note the concave model was specifically associated with being on campaign, not in barracks. In his dictionary, Bardin speaks of *marmites de casernes* which took the form of cauldrons and followed local designs. The better ones were made of copper which was lighter, more durable and transferred heat more readily. In addition to the main cooking vessel there would often be a smaller cauldron used for boiling water. These smaller vessels were apparently also very useful for making stock from bones.

Food was eaten from a communal metal mess pan called a *gamelle*. This pan was carried on the haversack by means of a wire ring. The water can (*grand bidon*) was a long cylindrical bucket. In addition to cooking equipment, soldiers needed sufficient equipment for them to collect wood, straw and to dig trenches for latrines

Infantryman (probably a sergeant) with cooking pot (*marmite*) strapped to haversack, and a cup suspended from buckle strap. The officer has a cape with a fur lined collar. The sleeping figure is a drummer. (Beyer)

or drainage channels, and picks to break up hard ground. Therefore, every eight men were issued a pick (*pioche*), shovel (*pelle*), billhook (*serpe*), hatchet (*hachette*) and scythe (*faulx*).

[**See also:** 28. Sergeant; 82. Packing the haversack; 84. Tents; 199. Food preparation (introduction); 200. Preparing soup; 227. Duties in camp.]

## 84. Tents

At the beginning of the wars there were two models of tent. The 'old' model, also known as a gunner's tent (*tente des canonniers*), was 3.55 metres long, 2.60 metres wide and housed eight men. The tent had an entrance at one end and a semi-circular lamp pit (*cul de lampe*) at the other. The 'new' model was 5.85 metres long by 3.90 metres wide (2x3 *toises*) and was described as a sixteen man tent, but in fact only accommodated fifteen. This model had a circular lamp pit at both ends, with the entrance to the tent set in the middle of one of the long sides. The men slept with their feet to the centre of the tent. The 'new' model had in fact been around for some time and had been used by the cavalry, the greater size being required for eight men and thcir saddlcs.

Officers would have the larger model tents (lieutenants and sub-lieutenants shared one between them), with an additional old model tent for their orderlies; the colonel would have a marquee in which he could hold meetings of the council of administration and other assemblies; the quartermaster treasurer and his secretaries would have a separate tent for an office. Old style tents were issued to the laundresses and a new model tent would serve as a temporary guardhouse. The stacks of arms would have a small cover called a *manteau* which held up to forty muskets.

At the beginning of the war of the Revolution, the army of General Dumouriez was issued with tents and these were used in the campaigns of 1792 and 1793. Tents were also used at diverse training camps. However it soon proved impossible to procure enough cloth and equipment to provide tents for the hundreds of thousands of levies called to arms, not to mention sufficient pack animals to transport them. Tents were also extremely unpopular. When exposed to an unfavourable climate they quickly became sodden and filthy. French soldiers much preferred to bivouac, which is to say to either make rudimentary shelters from straw and timber, or to sleep unprotected from the elements, with their feet warmed by a campfire. In the autumn of 1793 the commander of the Army of the Moselle, General Lazare Hoche convinced his soldiers it was 'more soldierly, more republican, and more glorious' to go without tents. His troops agreed with him, and soon after, all of France's armies had abandoned their tents. Once made, this decision had a critical advantage. Armies without tents enjoyed greater mobility because the men did not have to spend hours making and breaking camp each day. On the downside, it was far more difficult to enforce discipline if the men were not confined to tents each night.

Out of practicality it is true generals and senior officers required tents in order to read and consult maps, although most would far sooner have commandeered a house or barn than pitched a tent for the purpose. Another advantage of abandoning tents was to make it far more difficult for the enemy to spy the numbers of troops in a camp. It was far easier to count neat rows of tents than to gauge the number of small fires around which soldiers were resting. If the army ever remained in one place long enough to require a proper camp, the men would generally build wooden huts as occurred in the camps around Boulogne in 1804/05 and in Poland and Prussia after the Peace of Tilsit in 1807.

Despite them no longer being used, several administrative documents were issued with references to tents, which perhaps gave the false impression they were still taken on campaign. Even Bardin's infantry manual contains sections on forming and dressing a camp – simply because the regulations had not been repealed, and the process of forming a camp could be applied to building a camp from wooden huts.

[**See also:** 40. Cantineer; 83. Utensils and tools; 85. Wagons and horses; 112. Deductions and funds; 226. Arrival at camp; 243. After the battle; 249. Bivouacs.]

## 85. Wagons and horses (*fourgons et chevaux*)

The provisional field service regulation of 5 April 1792 allowed each regiment a number of wagons and horses. The colonel and the surgeon major were each allowed a two or four-wheeled carriage which could also be used to carry wounded officers if necessary. Each regiment of two battalions was allowed two, four-horse wagons to carry the tents, equipment, and spare items such as shirts and shoes. All of the regimental vehicles would be marked with the number of the regiment, to whom they belonged, and their intended use. The lead wagon would contain the regiment's pay chest and papers.

Each regiment was also allowed one four-wheeled sutler's wagon drawn by four horses. All other sutlers would make do with bat horses. There would only be four of these horses per battalion, including the horses of the laundresses. The sutler's wagon would have a tin plaque with the name of the proprietor, the number of the regiment and the sutler's patent number. Originally each regiment was also allowed a four-wheeled wagon drawn by four horses for a butcher and a baker who would provide for the regiment. However, these trades were very quickly absorbed into the army headquarters establishment and did not feature at regimental level. The overall weight was not to exceed the following:

- Four horse wagon: 750 kg or 1,532 pounds, or ten to twelve convalescing men.
- Three horse wagon: 600 kg or 1,226 pounds, or eight to nine men.
- Two horse wagon: 450 kg or 920 pounds, or five to seven men.
- One horse wagon: 260 kg or 512 pounds, or two to four men.

If a wagon broke, its baggage would be redistributed and the wagon thrown from the road. Everything which could not be reloaded or carried would be burned.

In terms of horses, in 1792 the following allowances were made for officers and their orderlies: colonels, six horses; battalion commanders, four horses; captains, three horses; lieutenants and sub-lieutenants, three horses between them; quartermaster, three horses; surgeon major, three horses; adjutant majors were given an allowance of three horses between two of them. There was an allowance of four spare horses for the wagons.

A new edition of the 1792 provisional field service instruction was issued on 9 June 1809. This stated every line or light infantry regiment would have three ammunition caissons for the regimental artillery, a campaign forge, an 'ambulance' caisson containing field hospital equipment, and one caisson for the regimental papers. In addition, each battalion would have a caisson for infantry cartridges and one for transporting bread. A decree of 22 February 1813 made the following allowances for infantry regiments in terms of horses and wagons, which are given in Table 8.

**Table 8:** Allocation of wagons and horses.

| Rank | Saddled horses | Wagons | Draught horses | Bat Horses |
|---|---|---|---|---|
| Colonels and majors | 3 | 1 | 2 | 3 |
| Battalion commanders | 2 | 0 | 0 | 1 |
| Quartermaster treasurer | 1 | 0 | 0 | 1 |
| Adjutant majors | 1 | 0 | 0 | 1 |
| Captains (over 50 years old) | 1 | 0 | 0 | 1 |
| Lieutenants and sub-lieuts. (over 50) | 1 | 0 | 0 | 1 |

In addition to these allowances, there would be four mules or bat horses per battalion for transporting the officers' baggage. The wagons would have an inscription on the left hand side stating the owner and registration number of the vehicle. If this was not done on first inspection by the Army Corps, the owner would be fined 100 *francs*. If an unauthorised vehicle was found on the march, it would be burned.

[**See also:** 4. Regimental artillery, 23. Baggage master; 40. Cantineer; 84. Tents; 224. Duties of the baggage master; 248. Forced marches.]

A senior infantry officer wearing high riding boots, rather than turndown boots *à l'anglaise*. Note the bread ration strapped to the haversack of the seated figure.

# Chapter 11

# Weapons & Ammunition

## 86. Musket (*fusil d'infanterie*)

The flintlock musket (*fusil*) was the primary weapon of French infantry. In English the word 'musket' is a generic term for a long, smoothbore, muzzle-loading firearm. However, in French the word *mousquet* refers specifically to the matchlock firearms of the 17th century. The term *fusil* was therefore specific to the flintlock muskets – hence the difference between a musketeer and a fusilier.

The model of musket carried by the majority of Napoleon's infantry regiments was a variation of the 1777 model, which was known as the *modèle de 1777 corrigé en l'an IX* (lit. the 1777 model adjusted in Year IX). Without a bayonet, the Year IX model was 1.515 metres long and weighed 4.375 kg. Some troops such as voltigeurs used the dragoon pattern musket which was essentially the same weapon, but was shorter at 1.463 metres, and somewhat lighter at 4.267 kg. Both had a calibre of 17.5 mm. When firing at will, using ball cartridge and properly ramming the ball home, the normal maximum rate of fire was three or four shots a minute.

In summary the weapon functioned as follows: a small priming charge was added to a pan above the trigger guard, and then the lid of this pan was closed. The butt of the musket was then placed on the floor and a charge of gunpowder poured down the barrel. After this a lead ball was inserted along with the cartridge paper which enclosed it (this served as wadding), and rammed to the bottom of the barrel using a detachable ramrod which was stored in a channel under the barrel. With the musket loaded, the lock was pulled back into the 'full cock' position. When the trigger was pulled, springs forced the lock mechanism to drive a sharpened flint against a metal scraper thus creating sparks. The scraper was attached to the lid of the pan. As the flint struck the scraper, the pan would open, allowing the sparks to fire the priming charge, which then ignited the main charge in the barrel via a touchhole. There would be a deflagration and the expanding gases would force the ball and wadding out of the barrel.

The standard infantry muskets were smoothbore, which is to say there was nothing in the barrel to cause the lead ball projectile to spin. This lack of rifling was one of the many reasons the weapon had limited range and accuracy. The range of an infantry musket fired on a level trajectory with an ordinary charge was approximately 120 fathoms (234 metres). The maximum range of a musket (500 fathoms or 974 metres) could be achieved by firing the weapon at a trajectory of 43°. An instruction of 19 June 1806 regarded shots over 234 metres as unlikely to strike a target. After 300 metres the ball would be spent, and unlikely to achieve a kill even if it struck a target. The most effective range for musketry was therefore considered as 70 fathoms (136 metres) and so infantry officers were advised to learn the art of estimating distances in order to achieve the best results.

If the target came within effective range, accuracy now came into play. On the battlefield soldiers were often not aiming at individual targets, but at a dense mass of soldiers, packed shoulder to shoulder. One would think these large formations would be shot to pieces, but the evidence shows this was often not the case. Indeed, it was believed as few as one in five hundred musket balls struck an enemy soldier, and it was generally supposed each enemy soldier killed on the battlefield cost his own weight in lead.

There were a host of other factors which had a negative impact upon accuracy. Firstly there was the manner in which the musket was held, particularly the manner of supporting the butt in the shoulder and the placement of the left hand along the stock beneath the barrel. To a degree, this was a matter of practice, of how the musket was bought to the *en-joue* position (i.e. to the cheek), in other words, how it was levelled to the aiming position after being prepared for firing.

Muskets had a formidable recoil when discharged, and if they were incorrectly held, the firer might be struck in the face by the lock and given a bloodied nose or lip. This might make the user reluctant to hold the musket near to his face and therefore leave him unable to aim correctly. Soldiers were not always taught to close their left eye while taking aim. Volley firing was also a cause of poor aim; with soldiers shielding their faces and closing their eyes as all the muskets around them fired.

Accuracy could also be diminished by the disparity of ground, the fineness and dose of powder, and the atmosphere, which could modify the burning characteristics of the powder and therefore alter the range of the weapon. The heating of the barrel also had an impact, precipitating the deflagration of the powder and increasing the impulse of the ball. The different pressures created by ramming the charge, ball and wadding home also had an impact, as did the calibration of the ball and the thickness of the cartridge paper surrounding it. All these factors stood in the way of a marksman trying to achieve a hit.

Observation of troops in the field concluded troops would fire horizontally out of habit, even if they were at the foot of a mountain or on the bank of a rampart. By holding their muskets horizontally, the bullets would either strike the ground after a few paces, or go too high. Bardin's infantry manual cautioned men against blindly aiming at the cross straps of the opposing forces. Although the junction of the cross straps marked a convenient 'X' target across the chest of a soldier, if the barrel was inclined slightly to point at this mark, the shot would almost certainly fall short, unless fired at relatively short range.

With smoothbore weapons there was a significant difference between the line of sight along the length of the barrel towards the target and the actual trajectory of the ball in flight. For a start, the barrel of the musket was not a straight tube along which to aim. The barrel was much thicker at the breech end (where the deflagration of gunpowder took place) than at the mouth of the barrel. A rudimentary sight was placed near the mouth of the barrel to attempt to correct this imbalance. Secondly, it was recognised musket balls, as well as any missile, could only travel through a space by describing a curve. In perfect test conditions the ball would only travel 4.2 meters from the barrel along the line of sight, but then the heaviness of the ball (or rather the effect of gravity) would then make it fall.

Of course, these faults were only an issue if the musket actually fired. Misfires were commonplace and could be attributed to a range of causes. The quality of the flint was of vital importance. Was it sharp, or had it been blunted by repeated firings, or was it liable to shatter on impact? Had the flint been placed securely in the lock? The flint was held in place by an envelope made of lead or leather. If the flint had not been securely enclosed, it would move slightly, and this would prevent the creation of sparks. Of equal importance was the condition of the strike plate against which the flint struck, and the lock mechanism itself. The springs inside the lock were sometimes removed for cleaning and if they had not been remounted properly, or were dirty, or had lost their tension, this could also cause misfires. It was established there would be one failure for every seven shots due to a poor spring. If the spring's tension was correctly adjusted, the misfire rate fell to one in twenty-six. Atmospheric conditions played an important part in misfires. If the firing mechanism or priming charge became damp through humidity or precipitation it was very difficult to make the weapon work. The musket would also become fouled with repeated use by unburnt powder residue and cartridge paper. All things considered, Bardin still considered the French flintlock musket superior to all others in Europe at the time.

[**See also:** 77. Gun tools; 89. Ammunition; 90. Bayonet; 93. Weapon markings; 154. Manual exercise; 167. Musketry (introduction); 168. Loading procedure; 210. Maintaining the musket; 211. Storage of weapons; 216. Target practice.]

## 87. Carbine (*carabine*)

The carbine was a shortened firearm typically carried by light cavalry. A version also existed which had a rifled barrel and was used by various infantrymen. Although the concept of a rifled barrel had been around since the late 1500s, the extremely slow rate of fire of these weapons meant they were not adopted in any significant number by the French Army in the Napoleonic era. The Austrians were acknowledged as masters of the rifled weapons and countered the slow rate of firing by having two musket-armed soldiers for every rifle armed soldier – the first two being quick firing, the third being able to take aimed shots over greater distance. The French conducted some experiments with rifled carbines in the late 1780s, and some Belgian troops in French service at the beginning of the war also used carbines. However, they were not universally adopted.

During the Consular period, carbines began to be manufactured, notably by the Versailles armament factory. In Year XII Bonaparte wanted voltigeur officers, sergeants and quartermaster corporals to be armed with the weapon. The Versailles carbine was 1.025m in length and weighed 3.450 kg. It had a calibre of 13.5 mm, but the ball was 14.4 mm. This disparity can be explained by the loading procedure of the weapon.

Loading a rifled carbine was extremely difficult, and generally took four times as long as a standard musket. First a powder charge would be poured down the barrel and then a piece of greased wadding called a *calpin* would be inserted. The ball followed and was hammered home by hitting the weapon's iron ramrod with a mallet. As the ball was forced down the barrel it would lose its spherical shape and instead take on the shape of the interior of the barrel, rotating around the axis of the cylinder. It was this deforming process which caused the ball to spin as it passed along the barrel, and this gave the carbine an accuracy over distances which could not be matched by a musket. However, if the ball was not driven right down onto the powder charge, an air pocket could be created in the barrel which could cause it to burst on ignition of the charge. The barrel also had to be clean to hammer the ball home and the weapon was therefore prone to fouling.

Where the carbine was not the primary weapon, it was generally worn slung over the shoulder, with the barrel pointing downwards. The Versailles carbine was not compatible with a bayonet.

[**See also:** 35. Carabineer; 36. Voltigeur; 56. Weight of arms and equipment; 210. Maintaining the musket.]

## 88. Pistol (*pistolet*)

Flintlock pistols were predominantly a cavalry weapon and, generally speaking, were only utilised by mounted infantry officers who carried so-called saddle pistols (*pistolets d'arçon*). They were also used for close defence by the eagle guard and some officers carried them for protection, particularly in Spain. The most common model during the Napoleonic era was the *pistolet modèle An XIII*, which came into service from 1806. It was 352 mm in length, weighed 1.27 kg and had a 17.1 mm calibre. It had an effective range of five to ten metres. Senior officers might purchase better quality pistols, perhaps even with rifled barrels. Pistols were often the weapon of choice in duels.

[**See also:** 17. Second and third eagle bearers; 137. Duelling.]

## 89. Ammunition (*munitions*)

The cartridges for infantry muskets (*cartouches à fusils*) were made from paper formed into a cylinder-shaped receptacle containing the ball and gunpowder. Cartridge paper was formed from a sheet 35 cm x 43 cm, which was folded and cut in such a way as to provide a dozen trapezium shapes each measuring 14.43 cm x 11.5 cm x 5.86 cm. To form the cartridge, the paper would be rolled around a wooden 'mandarin' which was 18.95 cm long and 1.52 cm in diameter. One end of the mandarin was rounded and the other end formed a dimple deep enough to insert one third of a musket ball. To form the cartridge, a musket ball was placed in the dimple and the paper rolled around the mandarin. The ball end of the cartridge was sealed by compressing the paper against a dimpled former (or the dimpled end of another mandarin). A charge of gunpowder was then inserted, and the open end of the cartridge pinched shut and folded over. The charge inserted into the cartridge was one fortieth of a pound of gunpowder for live ammunition, or one sixtieth of a pound for blank practice cartridges (musket balls were weighed 16 to 20 per pound (half kilo) and the quantity of gunpowder was ordinarily equal to half the weight of the ball). Once assembled, the cartridges would be formed into packages of fifteen rounds, each wrapped in paper and then tied with string. Two of the packages could then be inserted into the wooden box inside the cartridge pouch.

[**See also:** 76. Cartridge pouch; 82. Packing the haversack; 85. Wagons and horses; 86. Musket; 216. Target practice;]

### 90. Bayonet (*baïonnette*)

One of the drawbacks of adopting muskets was that the slow rate of fire made the user vulnerable to cavalry attack. Initially it was necessary for musketeers to be protected by pikemen (*piquiers*) and at the turn of the 18th century one third of infantrymen were still armed with pikes and halberds, weapons which gave excellent defence against cavalry and were useful in 'shock' attacks. In 1671 the plug bayonet was invented; a simple spike which plugged into the barrel of the

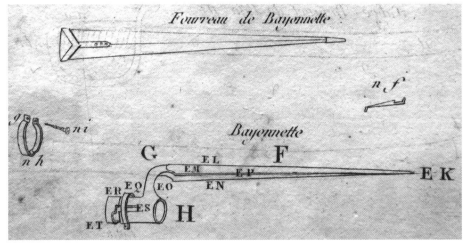

Bayonet and scabbard. Note the slot (ES) which fixed onto the musket barrel, and the band which locked the bayonet in place (EQ).From Bardin's infantry manual.

musket, providing musketeers with a means of defence. It took another thirty years to develop a socket attachment so the musket might fire while the bayonet was attached. It meant muskets combined all the advantages of a firearm with those of a bladed weapon. With this invention pole arms were phased out in 1703 (although officers and sub-officers retained the spontoon). In essence the bayonet changed very little over the course of the century. The Year IX bayonet used in the Napoleonic wars was 465 to 500 mm in length, including a triangular blade 400–407 mm long. When not attached to the musket it was carried in a leather scabbard which was attached to the baldric if infantry sabres were carried, or to the cartridge pouch belt when not.

[**See also:** 86. Musket; 154. The manual exercise; 165. Infantry squares; 166. Bayonet charges.]

## 91. Infantry sabre (*sabre briquet*)

The infantry sabre was initially worn by all grenadiers and light infantry, but was later limited to sub-officers, grenadiers, carabineers and drummers by the imperial decree of 7 October 1807. The Napoleonic infantry sabre was 75 cm, approximately 59 cm of which was made up of the blade, which was just over 2 cm wide at its broadest and had a point for piercing and a blade for slashing or cutting. The sabre weighed 1.498 kg with its scabbard. The sabre was carried on a baldric (*baudrier*) worn over the right shoulder, which also had a bayonet scabbard attached to it. For full dress, the sabre was decorated with a tasselled wrist strap called a *dragonne*.

The term *sabre briquet* has an amusing origin. Since 1747 the infantry short sword had been known as the *sabre de grenadier*. This changed with the introduction

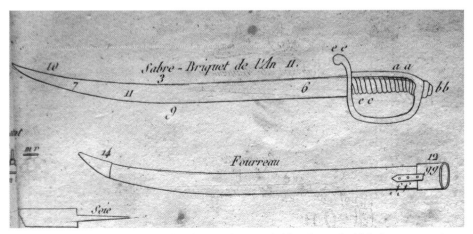

The Year XI *sabre briquet* and scabbard. Note the rounded hand guard which drew comparisons with a tinder striker.

of a new model in Year IX. In modern French a *briquet* refers to a cigarette lighter, and before that, in the Napoleonic era it referred to a metal blade which was struck against flints for lighting fires. The most common type of fire strikers had some form of circular hand guard which was used to grip the blade while striking the flint. The Year XI model infantry sabre also had a circular handguard, which led to cavalrymen mocking their infantry counterparts that their swords were so short they looked like fire strikers. The name *briquet* therefore caught on as a derisory term for the infantry short sword. The bureaucrats at the ministry of war heard the weapon described as a *briquet* and so made the term official in an instruction of 19 June 1806.

[**See also:** 22. Master craftsmen; 28. Sergeant; 34. Grenadier; 36. Voltigeur; 71. Plumes; 93. Weapon markings; 211. Storage of weapons.]


## 92. Officer's épée

In the 18th century the principle weapon of senior officers was the spontoon (*esponton*) until 1738, and company level officers were armed with muskets until as late as 1786. The épées carried by officers were therefore originally just a side arm which was both honorific (swords being associated with the nobility) and ornamental. Described in the regulation of 21 February 1779, the officer's *épée* was a light weapon, with a long, flat, narrow blade 26 French inches long (approximately 70 cm). This blade was not designed for cutting or parrying, and was therefore principally a thrusting weapon. During the 1790s many light infantry officers adopted the sabre which had a broader, curved blade which was designed for slashing, but this was more likely out of a desire to imitate light cavalry officers than for any practical considerations.

There was a tradition that on the death of an officer his sword would be auctioned and the proceeds would either pay off the dead man's debts, or go to the major. On *5 Brumaire XIII* (27 October 1804) the *épée* was declared to be part of the man's estate and would be returned to the family as part of their inheritance.

[**See also:** 119. Awards and national recognition; 139. Honouring dignitaries; 140. Honours to religious parades and services; 141. Funerary honours. 154. The manual exercise.]


## 93. Weapon markings

In addition to the manufacturer's stamp, during the 1790s weapons produced in the national armouries were stamped with the letters 'RF' (as in *République Française*) to signify they were government issue and not to be sold. The RF was on the top of the barrel half an inch above the touch hole. The French Army also imitated the Roman custom of marking weapons with the name of the soldier and his troop. The main purpose for this was so soldiers might recognise their own weapons and give them an incentive to take proper care of them. The regulation of accounting (*comptabilité*) dated *8 Floréal VIII* (28 April 1800) stated all muskets, bayonets and sabres should be marked with the letter assigned to the company, and the number of the soldier in the company (this would be a number between one and the effective strength of the company – not the soldier's number in the regimental rolls). An instruction of 19 June 1806 standardised the marks using the company and soldier's number. The marks were to be carried on the ramrod, barrel, bayonet blade, lock and stock.

[**See also:** 86. Musket; 90. Bayonet 91. Infantry sabre.]

Line infantry sergeant major at the time of the French Revolution. This rank is designated by two strips of gold or silver braid worn on the forearms. Also note the musket is carried at 'advance arms', a position reserved for sub-officers.

*Chapter 12*

# Flags

## 94. Flags and eagles (*drapeaux / aigles*)

Since 1776 all French infantry battalions had been equipped with a single flag (two had been common before this date). The standards came in a multitude of colours representing various provinces or other identifying traits. They often took the form of crosses, cantons or quarters, often with warlike or religious devices added (flags were then blessed by the clergy). The standards carried by each battalion served as a rallying point in times of crisis, but more pragmatically, their most common purpose was to help preserve the alignment of a line and to indicate the direction of march. When a battalion was ordered to march, at the caution 'forward' (*en avant*) the colour guard would advance six paces ahead of the battalion so the general guides on the wings could see it. Only when this had occurred would the order to march be given. The trouble was, after a few days exposed to the elements, the flag would be sodden and likely in tatters from becoming blown on bayonets by the wind, not to mention shot to pieces in action. Taking a pragmatic view of things, the colour guard would attempt to preserve the flag by wrapping it tightly round the pole and encasing it in a sheaf. On most occasions then, the flag appeared as nothing more than a pole with a pike head on it.

On 30 June 1791 the army of Louis XVI adopted a new flag in the new national colours. The flag was white and was divided into four white quadrants by a symmetric white cross. The royal fleur-de-lis emblem was located at the extremity of each point on the cross. The upper left quarter contained a canton of three horizontal bands, blue at the top, white in the middle and red at the bottom. The remaining quadrants were bordered with red and blue bands, except on the lower left quadrant, where the side touching the pole was white. The regimental number was given in gold lettering, centred in the middle of the cross. On the top vertical branch of the cross was the word 'DISCIPLINE'; on the horizontal branch in two halves 'OBEISSANCE À LA' (obedience to the); and on the lower branch of the cross, the word 'LOI' (law). The dimensions of the flag's 'silk' was approximately 1.5 x 1.6 metres and the reverse of the flag was identical. The flag staff was surmounted by a gilded pike head which had a hollow centre in the shape of a fleur-de-lis, and decorative tricolour cravats. These flags were also issued to the battalions of National Guard Volunteers and to the light infantry battalions, although Bardin indicates they never received them, the Ministry of War being against encumbering fast-moving light infantry with a bulky flag. In addition, each second battalion in the line infantry regiments received a colour in the distinctive colour of the regiment. This flag had the same dimensions and inscription as the first battalion's standard.

After the fall of the monarchy in September 1792, political expediency saw the removal of the fleur-de-lis symbols, either by covering with patches or by painting them over. New flags were issued to the line infantry half-brigades in 1794. These were 162 cm square, mounted on a staff approximately 3 metres long surmounted by a gilded pike head. There was no standard pattern for the flags issued to the 1st and 3rd battalions, which had all manner of tricolour geometric designs and republican devices displayed on them. However, the second battalion flags were all made to a standard pattern, which was very similar to 1791 pattern, but without the white cross and fleur-de-lis symbols. This was replaced by a laurel wreath and a *faisceau de licteur* (a Roman style bundle of sticks bound around an axe) with spear surmounted by a red liberty cap. The number of the half-brigade was written in the four corners of the flag. The front of the flag had the words REPUBLIQUE FRANCAISE, the lettering above and below the *faisceau*; the reverse had the motto DISCIPLINE ET SOUMISSION / AUX LOIS MILITAIRES (discipline and submission to military laws) in the same style.

After the peace of Leoben in the summer of 1797, General Bonaparte issued various corps in his Army of Italy with new flags which contained battle honours of their campaigns together. This was somewhat embarrassing for the government because Bonaparte had in effect usurped one of the prerogatives of a sovereign state. Having an army general issue flags to his soldiers raised the question of their collective loyalty. The Directory eventually reacted on *3 Thermidor VI* (21 July 1798) by forbidding units from carrying flags with inscriptions on them. Those which had been issued were to be handed over to the councils of administration to be stored with their archives. This motion in effect censured Bonaparte's decision to adapt the legal form of a flag and personalise them in his favour.

The last official issue of flags before the imperial period came with the law of *21 Prairial X* (10 June 1802) which gave flags to all the light infantry half-brigades. These were distributed on the anniversary of 14 July that year. The only previous issue of flags under the republic had been in April 1798 to those light half-brigades going to Egypt, and on *15 Prairial X* (4 June 1802) to the 'Incomparable' 9th Light Infantry, which was awarded a special set of flags in recognition of its performance at Marengo on 14 June 1800.

On 5 December 1804, Napoleon issued an entirely new design of standard. By adopting the Roman eagle as the new national emblem, Napoleon transferred the importance from the flag to the pike head. The Napoleonic eagle standard was a gilded bronze eagle, with its wings outstretched and with its right talon on a 'spindle of Jupiter' (i.e. a thunderbolt). The regimental number was displayed on the front and back of the plinth, which was 40 mm high and 120 mm wide. With plinth, the eagle measured 310 mm in height and 255 mm from wing tip to wing tip. The base of the plinth had a socket which allowed it to be mounted onto a blue wooden staff. In all, the eagle weighed 1.85 kg. The accompanying flag measured 810 mm square, approximately half the size of the previous model. The tricolour

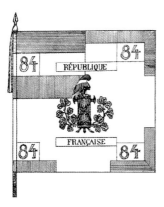

84th Half-brigade, 2nd Battalion, 1794.

84th Half-brigade, 1st and 3rd Battalions, 1794.

32nd Half-brigade, 1794.

32nd Half-brigade, 1796.

9th Light Infantry, 1802.

32nd Line, 1804.

flag was made of oiled silk and consisted of a central white lozenge with the corner triangles alternately red and blue. The lozenge was charged with golden lettering, 'L'EMPEREUR DES FRANÇAIS AU [regiment] on one side and 'VALEUR ET DISCIPLINE' with the number of the battalion on the other. The corners of the flag had golden wreaths containing the regimental number.

There were a number of important changes to the eagles before Napoleon's abdication in 1814. On 26 March 1807, Napoleon issued an order for all regiments of light infantry to return their eagles to the depots. The fears of previous administrations about embarrassing light infantry with flags proved correct when the 2nd Battalion of the 9th Light lost its standard to the Russians at Mohrungen on 25 January 1807. The battalion had been skirmishing at the time the eagle was lost and there had not been sufficient men to defend it. In the regulation of 18 February 1808 Napoleon reduced all infantry regiments to having just one eagle, which would be located wherever the colonel was. On 25 December 1811 there was a further decree concerning the eagles which resulted in the 1812 issue flag. The flag attached to the eagle was changed and it came to resemble the modern French tricolour of blue, white and red in equal vertical bands with elaborate gold embroidery. On one side of the flag were the words L'EMPEREUR NAPOLÉON AU [regiment]; and on the other side a series of battle honours. These had to have been gained in action with the *Grande Armée* and in 1811 included the battles of Ulm, Austerlitz, Jena, Eylau, Friedland, Eckmull, Essling and Wagram. The battle honours gained under the republic were not recognised (including Marengo); nor were those fought in Spain. The flag would be replaced every two years by the Ministry of War.

After Napoleon's abdication in 1814 the majority of eagles were melted down by order of Louis XVIII. When Napoleon returned to Paris in 1815, he ordered the creation of new emblems for his army. The 1815 eagle differed slightly in design to the 1804 model and slightly lighter at 1.45 kg. The new tricolour flags were much larger at 120 cm square, but were much less ornate than the 1812 pattern flags in particular.

[**See also:** 13. Eagle bearer; 17. Second and third eagle bearers; 27. Sergeant major; 119. Awards and national recognition; 138. Salutes; 141. Funerary honours; 146. Placement of the colour guard; 164. Battalion formations and manoeuvres.]

## 95. Ensigns (*ensigne*)

The decree of 18 February 1808 was particularly interesting, because it effectively removed the principal of each battalion having a standard which would help guide it on the march. This must have been a concern because the imperial decree of 25 December 1811 introduced a new type of flag called the ensign or more commonly (and confusingly) a pennant (*fanion*). Assuming the eagle was with the 1st Battalion, the remaining battalions each received an ensign. They were made of woollen cloth and garnished around the outer edge by a strip of wool in the same colour. Each ensign was 813 mm (30 inches) square, with no fringe, cravat, nor any type of adornment, supported on a staff measuring 2 metres 60 (8 feet) terminated by an iron or steel point. The 2nd Battalion had a white ensign; 3rd Battalion, red; 4th Battalion, blue; 5th Battalion, green; 6th Battalion, yellow. The ensigns were issued to the battalion by the colonel and were carried by a sergeant major chosen by the colonel, in the same manner as the colour guards prior to

1808. The decree of 25 December 1811 was at pains to state no importance was to be attached to the ensign; that no honours would be given to it, and it was not to carry any inscription. Of course, because the issuing of the ensign was the colonel's prerogative, all manner of abuses probably resulted, with regimental titles, perhaps even battle honours embroidered on them.

[**See also:** 27. Sergeant major; 45. Ensign bearer; 96. Pennants; 146. Placement of the colour guard; 164. Battalion formations and manoeuvres.]

## 96. Pennants (*fanions*)

In the Royal Army every company had its own pennant which was in the company's particular colour. When the regiment arrived at an overnight halt, the sergeant major or quartermaster corporal would leave this pennant flying outside the captain's quarters. The ordinance of 12 August 1788 recognised three such pennants per battalion, which were located with the guides (*jalonneurs*) on the wings and centre and used to maintain the alignment of the battalion in exercises. These same pennants could be used in the process of tracing out a camp. In the majority of cases the pennant was mounted on a pole thin enough to be inserted into the barrel of a musket. During the wars of the Revolution and Napoleonic wars, some of the more disciplined corps maintained this tradition at the whim of the commanding officer.

[**See also:** 95. Ensigns; 145. Assembling the battalion; 164. Battalion formations and manoeuvres; 226. Arrival at camp.]

## 97. Flags as signals

Flags could also be used as a means of communication. Although there was no regulation for this, the following signals were recognised across Europe by combatants of the Napoleonic era.

- *White flag*: since the Middle Ages a white flag had been associated with surrender or requesting a parley.
- *Black flag*: this was a sinister symbol of all-out war (*guerre à outrance*); victory or death, or in a siege no quarter would be sought or given. It might also be raised in time of epidemic to warn people away from an infected area. A witness to the fall of Paris in 1814 (Underwood) described how black flags were hung from hospitals so they would not be targeted by Allied artillery.
- *Red flag*: this might be raised by the civil authorities at times of revolt. The law of 20 October 1789 wanted them deployed as a warning a proclamation of martial law was imminent.

[**See also:** 37. Drummer; 229. Outpost duty; 235. Prisoners of war.]

*Part III*

# Recruitment & Administration

## Chapter 13

# Recruitment & Conscription

## 98. Introduction

Before the Revolution in 1789, France's armies had drawn their infantrymen from three primary sources. The bulk of the regular army was formed of volunteers. Some of these were honest adventurers, or came from families with a military tradition; but in the popular consciousness they were often labelled as vagabonds, drunkards, and bankrupts. Many volunteers had been recruited by agents operating in the major towns. These agents were known as a *raccoleurs* from the Italian verb *raccogliere* – to pick up or assemble, and in fact the word *raccoleur* might be better translated into modern English as 'a tout'. These *raccoleurs* were well known for employing all manner of tricks, debauchery, and even violence in order to fulfil their quotas. Needless to say the harvest of recruits was not always the best. In wartime the army was reinforced by a militia which was raised by a form of conscription by lottery, which was extremely unpopular among the peasantry and was a common source of complaint at the time of the Revolution. Great use was also made of foreign mercenaries, notably Irishmen, Swedes, Walloons, Germans and Swiss, with up to twenty-six thousand mercenaries permitted on the army's books. This reliance on foreigners probably reinforced the negative stereotypes of military service – a career in which the chances of advancement for commoners were slim, and discipline was brutally strict.

Although the call up of National Guardsmen was initially successful, as hostilities commenced and the list of France's enemies expanded, there was a further clamour for recruits. The decree of 25 February 1793 put all Frenchmen between the ages of 18 and 40 in a state of 'permanent requisition'. This law was followed by a mass levy of 300,000 men. A second decree followed on 23 August 1793 which called up all remaining unmarried males, or childless widowers between the ages of 18 and 25. Although these levies were effective as a short term response to an immediate crisis, they were not considered a sustainable system of recruitment.

General Jean-Baptiste Jourdan was put at the head of a military commission set up to investigate ways of providing an effective, sustainable flow of recruits for the army. The result of this was the law of *19 Fructidor VI* (5 September 1798) which enshrined the principal of all Frenchmen being responsible for the defence of the *patrie* (fatherland) and therefore liable to service in the army through either voluntary enlistment or military conscription. This formed the basis of recruitment during Napoleon's leadership of France and remained enshrined in the country's laws until 2001. In the period of the First Empire alone, this system summoned something in the region of 2.4 million men for military service.

A word should be said about the status of foreign soldiers as a source of recruits. As territories were annexed into the French Empire they were subjected to the conscription law and became a source of recruits for the existing French regiments. In this way native Dutch, German and Italian speaking conscripts found themselves serving alongside Frenchmen in French regiments. During the 1790s and throughout the First Empire, France continued with the practice of using foreign auxiliaries, and a host of foreign regiments (*régiments étrangers*) were formed from Swiss, Croat, Illyrian, German, Italian, Irish and Polish soldiers. These regiments were part of the French Army establishment and followed the French system, but with regional distinctions outside the scope of this work. Lastly Napoleon's armies contained numerous contingents provided by various states allied with France, such as Bavaria, Westphalia, Saxony, and the Kingdom of Italy.

## 99. Voluntary enlistment

According to the recruitment law of 1798, Frenchmen aged from 18 to 30 years of age were able to enlist in the army voluntarily. Ever eager for recruits, in the circular of 27 November 1806 Napoleon lowered the age to 16 years old if the recruit had the consent of his parents or tutor. Before this, only the official regimental children had been able to enlist at this age. Former soldiers up to the age of 40 were also allowed to enlist if they had previously served for four years or more. The period of engagement for volunteers was four years in peacetime or until such time as circumstances allowed in wartime (usually the end of hostilities). After four years, a volunteer could renew his engagement for periods of two years until he qualified for retirement pay (i.e. after thirty years' service, or on a medical discharge).

Unlike in the old Royal Army, there was no bounty for volunteering; but volunteers received a 'high pay' of 1 *franc* per month for the first four years of service, 2 *francs* per month for the next four years, and 3 *francs* after that. This high pay would cease if the soldier was promoted into the officer corps. Volunteers could also choose which branch of the army they wished to serve in, provided they had the correct height and met any other necessary qualifications the service required.

Volunteers had to be in possession of a certificate of good conduct signed by their local municipal agent, a justice of the peace from their canton or municipal administration, and by a justice of the peace from their commune. If these endorsements were forthcoming, the volunteer would enter his name on a register held by the municipal authorities. This register would indicate his name, forename, age, height, place of abode, and a physical description recording eye colour, shape of the face, chin and nose, hair and eyebrow colour plus any distinguishing marks which would ease the task of the *gendarmerie* in their search for absconders.

The municipal administration would notify the minister of war about the volunteers, and the local war commissary. Once confirmation was made, a travel itinerary (*feuille de route*) would be issued from the volunteer's place of residence to the residence of the local war commissary who would then send him on his way to the corps he had applied to join. The itinerary document granted the volunteer the right to free food and accommodation on the way, but if he failed to arrive at his destination he would be pursued and punished as a deserter.

On arrival at the regiment, a sergeant major would place the recruit in the weakest squad and introduce his corporal and sergeant, as well as his instructor. The sergeant major would then take the recruit to the surgeon major who would sign his admission papers. The sergeant major or quartermaster corporal would enrol the man's name onto the relevant registers and go about procuring him a uniform, arms and equipment. The recruit would be measured by the master tailor and then issued with a uniform as swiftly as possible. When recruits were assigned to a squad, the corporal would inform them about the importance of obeying and respecting their officers and sub-officers, and warn them against deserting. Once this process was completed, the recruit would be presented to the captain and the other company officers.

As an aside, during the Wars of the Revolution the old practice of soldiers adopting a *nom de guerre* fell out of favour. Unlike the soldiers of the *ancien régime*, some of whom had good reason to conceal their true identities, the soldiers of the French Revolution enjoyed a higher status in society as citizens and their legal status became important in terms of obtaining a pension and supporting their families.

[**See also:** 2. Line infantry regiments; 98. Recruitment & conscription (introduction).]

## 100. Military conscription

Under the law of *19 Fructidor*, all French males aged from twenty to twenty-five were eligible for conscription. Known as defender-conscripts (*défenseurs conscrits*), these conscripts were divided into five classes based on age. The first class composed of Frenchmen who on *1 Vendémiaire* (22 September) had attained their twentieth birthday. The second class was formed of those aged twenty-one on this date, the third aged twenty-two, the fourth aged twenty-three, and the fifth aged twenty-four. Men who had attained their twenty-fifth year were no longer liable for conscription. If the country was at peace, conscripts aged over twenty-five would be discharged from the army; however, in wartime their service was prolonged indefinitely.

Once conscripted, men were not allowed to volunteer and earn the privileges of a volunteer. Unlike volunteers who could choose which branch of the armed forces they would join, conscripts were liable for service in any branch of the army depending on their height and skills. Conscripts could not be promoted to the officer corps unless they had served for a minimum of three years, or performed some outstanding feat of bravery on the battlefield. However, at the end of their conscripted service, they could choose to enrol voluntarily.

There were exemptions, including those who had already volunteered for service; those who had married on or before the previous *23 Nivôse* (11 January), widowers or divorcees who were caring for children, and also men who had been honourably discharged from the army before the age of twenty-five. Certain groups and individuals were exempted from the conscription process. Seafarers, rivermen, and those in similar or associated trades in France's maritime departments were not permitted to join the army if they had already been listed in the *inscription maritime*, a register of men liable for service in the navy. An instruction of 1 November 1811 clarified other exemptions: prize winning students of painting, sculpture, architecture, engraving or musical composition were also exempt. Following a decree of 7 March 1806 clergymen were exempt from conscription and service in the National Guard, as were students who were taking ecclesiastical studies. Engravers in the war depot (*dépôt de guerre*) named by the Minister of War, and men engaged by armament factories did not serve; nor did adjuncts to war commissaries, medical officers, or veterinary artists drawn from the schools of Lyon, Turin or Alfort. Conscripts who had permission to serve with foreign corps were exempt, along with pupils of the special military or naval schools, students of the *Prytanée Militaire* (a military prep school), students of the Polytechnic School, of schools of application or language studies; normal school pupils; authorised students at the schools of arts, and pageboys of the emperor. Conscripts of the departments united to France who were married before the conscription law applied to their departments were exempt, as were the sons of refugees from the colonies who were receiving government aid.

A decree of 4 April 1792 had granted citizenship to all Frenchmen regardless of colour, and the decree of *16 Pluviôse II* (4 February 1794) abolished slavery. However the instruction of 1 November 1811 stated 'men of colour' were exempt from conscription levies and the maritime inscription, even if they had acquired residency in France. The instruction did not elaborate on the reasons for this. Men of the Jewish faith had been granted citizenship status in 1790 and were expected to fulfil their duties as citizens. In fact, Napoleon saw military service as an important means of integrating Jews into mainstream society. Therefore the decree of 17 March 1806 urged rabbis to encourage 'Israelites' to see military service as a sacred duty and to exempt Jews from any inconvenient religious observances during their period of military service. One inequality was Jewish conscripts were initially not allowed to purchase a replacement; but this condition was relaxed in July 1812.

There was an element of compassion in the process and although not made exempt from the process, some potential conscripts were placed at the back of the queue because of family circumstances (this was termed being placed in the *fin du dépôt*). They included men with a brother who had been conscripted or had volunteered and was in service or had been killed in the line of duty, or discharged from wounds or infirmities contracted in service. The eldest sons of widows were given this same protection, as were orphans who had several younger brothers and sisters to support. It also extended to a conscript whose father was aged 71 before the day fixed for departure.

Those young men of military age who did not possess papers explaining why they were not in service would lose their rights as citizens, and be barred from any public function.

[**See also:** 2. Line infantry regiments; 14. Surgeon major; 43. Recruitment captain; 98. Recruitment & conscription (introduction); 101. Recruitment council; 102. Replacements; 103. Objectors; 104. Reserve battalions; 105. Velites; 115. Leave; 117. Promotion; 134. Military justice.]

## 101. Recruitment council (*conseil de recrutement*)

Each year an assessment was made by the government to determine the number of 'defender conscripts' the army would require for the following year. The youngest in each class were the first to be called up. Those in the second class were not called until all those in the first class were in active service. The municipal administration of each commune and canton would form a register with the names of all men eligible for conscription. This register contained their personal details including their profession and place of abode. There was a degree of reliance on men coming forward, but those who refused to register their names would, on reaching the age of twenty years and one day, be placed at the head of the list of those destined to march out first. The selection was made by lottery with the draw made by each canton. Those who drew a low number were called up first. For example, if the canton had to supply fifteen men out of a total of thirty eligible men, those drawing the numbers 1–15 would be selected. The remainder were not free until the first fifteen men had been declared fit by a recruitment council.

This council was responsible for overseeing the conscription levy and deciding on exemptions, exceptions, suspensions of departure, discharges, adjournments, substitutions and replacements. The body legislated on individuals absent from the lottery, or who proved incapable of serving. Each department had its own council which was chaired by the prefect. The other members were made up of the superior officer or general commanding the department, and a major designated by the minister of war whose principal goal was ensure the conscripts selected were actually fit to serve and measured over the height of 1.542 metres. The council was also attended by a recruitment captain from one of the infantry regiments who led a team of officers and sub-officers responsible for escorting conscripts to the depots. The recruitment captain assisted at the council sessions and could make any observations he judged necessary, but he was not allowed to vote.

Discharges were considered as part of the second phase of the council's deliberation. Those with infirmities who were deemed unable to support 'the fatigues of war' were discharged and ordered to pay a 50 *franc* indemnity. Acceptable infirmities included a total loss of sight, being mute, the total loss of a limb, or a hand or foot. Other infirmities disqualified conscripts from infantry service, including the loss of the right eye (for aiming), the loss of the incisor, or canine teeth (or anything else which prevented the man from biting a cartridge open), or the loss of the right thumb or index finger. Those conscripts measuring under 1.488 metres were immediately discharged. Conscripts measuring over 1.488m but under 1.542m would be adjourned and held in a reserve if the required number of conscripts was not reached. Numerous infirmities were recognised, although the council could insist a conscript who was ill could be sent to hospital for a month, after which, if he showed signs of improvement he could be sent to a regiment. Doctors, medical officers, civil servants, army officers and sub-officers convicted of attesting false infirmities or other incapacities would receive a prison sentence of between one and two years, plus a fine of 300 to 1,000 *francs*. Anyone found guilty of forging recruitment documents would get five years in irons. Those suspected of self-mutilation, and who could not provide a satisfactory excuse for an injury, or those who feigned injury, would be arrested and sent under escort of gendarmes to a pioneer company for five years hard labour. Conscripts summoned by law who did not travel to their corps would be pursued and punished as a deserter by the gendarmerie. Once the quota was filled, a departure date would be nominated upon which the conscripts would gather in the department capital and be escorted to the various depots by the recruitment party.

[See also: 43. Recruitment captain; 98. Recruitment & conscription (introduction); 100. Military conscription; 102. Replacements; 103. Objectors; 104. Reserve battalions.]

## 102. Replacements (*remplacements*)

The national citizen army created by the French Revolution was not entirely classless. When the law of 24 February 1793 raised a levy of 300,000 men, the legislation made provision for requisitioned men to avoid service if they provided a substitute. This decision was reversed in the law of 23 August 1793; nor did the law of *19 Fructidor VI* (5 September 1798) initially allow replacements. This stance was relaxed in the law of *17 Ventôse VIII* (8 March 1800), which allowed those who could not support the fatigues of war or wished to continue their careers or studies to be replaced by a substitute, at least 1,651 mm tall, a Frenchman, of strong constitution, robust health and not already subject to conscription. The sub-prefect, having taken the advice of the mayor, would decide if the replacement was acceptable. Requests to be replaced were put in writing to the sub-prefect of the district along with the details of the substitute. The replaced man was also required to pay 100 *francs* towards the uniform of the replacement. Once a replacement had been hired, the hiring party was not completely free of obligations and remained on the conscription list until the death of the replacement, his medical discharge, or if he was released from service after five years. There were risks in the process. The decree of *8 Fructidor XIII* (26 August 1805) stated that if the replacement deserted he had to be replaced in turn, or the original conscript would have to serve. For this reason the contract with the replacement often stipulated the sum would be paid in instalments.

The law also allowed men in service, coming to the end of their own engagement, to put themselves up as replacements by informing their council of administration. This came about after the law of *8 Brumaire X* (30 October 1801) which permitted one eighth of sub-officers and men to be honourably discharged if they had been replaced by new conscripts. Those deserving of such recognition were recommended by the captain, overseen by an inspector of reviews. However, many men who had fought during the wars of the Revolution knew no other life outside soldiering. They had valuable experience and were still relatively young in age. On *8 Floréal X* (28 April 1802) a new law allowed these old soldiers to forego their discharge by acting as a substitute for a conscript. Those volunteering as substitutes agreed to serve the conscript's full five year term of service, or to remain with the colours for the duration of a war. The party being substituted would deposit 400 *francs* in the regimental chest, which would provide a new uniform for the replacement. The remainder of the money would serve as a form of high pay, at the rate of 10 *centimes* a day until his service expired.

[**See also:** 100. Military conscription; 101. Recruitment council.]

## 103. Objectors (*réfractaires*)

Despite the colourfully worded bulletins, and France's impressive martial feats, not everyone was in such a clamour to submit to the conscription process. The numbers of objectors who did not willingly show up for the conscription process was significant, so much so the law of *19 Vendémiaire XII* (4 October 1803) created eleven special military depots for them. At these depots the objectors were subjected to a military regime. Groups of 160 objectors were formed into companies, each commanded by a captain, one lieutenant, two sub-lieutenants, a sergeant major, and eight sergeants. The objectors were divided into sixteen squads each commanded by a corporal drawn from their own number. They were treated like soldiers, with pay and rations, but were always confined to barracks unless taking part in working parties or fatigues. Their day was taken up with drill sessions, or manual labour, working (without pay) in the arsenals or repairing fortifications. Their movements were constantly watched by *gendarmes* to ensure no one escaped. They were only allowed to wear fatigue caps and their hair was to be kept cut short. They were not allowed bayonets with their muskets. Twice a year the depots were visited by a general who would inspect the men and decide which ones were ready to submit to active military service.

[**See also:** 100. Military conscription; 134. Military justice.]

## 104. Reserve battalions (*bataillons de réserve*)

The law of *28 Floréal X* (18 May 1802) made a provision for 30,000 reservists to be formed from the surplus of conscripts who had drawn one of the higher numbers, but had not been required by the army at the time. Each department formed a 'reserve battalion' which was divided into a number of companies, each formed of men from the same district. Each company was subdivided into a number of platoons, each being formed of men from the same canton.

The reserve battalions were led by officers and sub-officers from the recruitment party attached to the department. Each company would be commanded by a lieutenant or sub-lieutenant, and each platoon by a sergeant or corporal. The captain of recruitment would command the battalion, and if there were several regiments recruiting in the same department, the command would fall to the captain who was located at the departmental capital.

One Sunday each month, the reserve would gather locally in each municipality for a drill session. Once a year the company would assemble for up to five days at a time when there was the least agricultural work. The men would receive the first principles of discipline and training for which they would be paid 20 *centimes* per day, with an additional 20 *centimes* in place of receiving a bread ration. If men failed to turn up for these reunions they would be punished with fifteen days to a month's detention in the guardhouse (*salle de discipline*). If they missed three consecutive reunions, they would be treated as a deserter.

[**See also:** 43. Recruitment captain; 98. Recruitment & conscription (introduction); 101. Recruitment council.]


## 105. Velites (*vélites*)

There was another pathway open to conscripts and volunteers alike, albeit only those with certain physical and financial qualifications. On *30 Nivôse XII* (21 January 1804) two corps of Foot Velites (*velites à pied*) were raised; each 800 strong, one attached to the grenadiers the other to the chasseurs of the Imperial Guard. Named after a type of Roman light infantry, velites had to be 1.67 to 1.73 metres tall, well constituted and assured of an income of 800 *francs* paid as a quarterly advance from their own purse or that of their parents. In addition to the usual infantry training, they were provided with masters of writing, arithmetic, drawing and gymnastics. After three years of intense instruction, the best were able to serve in the senior guard regiments and were exempted from the usual entry requirements in terms of age and the number of campaigns they had fought. Others were able to transfer into the line and take sub-officer positions and sometimes sub-lieutenancies.

[**See also:** 100. Military conscription; 120. Entry to the Imperial Guard; 218. Gymnastic and fitness exercises.]

# Chapter 14

# Administration & Pay

## 106. Introduction

For administrative purposes each battalion was divided into nine companies (six after 18 February 1808). Each company was divided into eight squads (*escouades*), each of which was led by a corporal. Each squad, more or less, formed an ordinary (*ordinaire*) by which it pooled its monies to purchase foodstuffs and necessary supplies. Two squads formed a subdivision, each of which was watched over by a sergeant. Two subdivisions formed a section, or half company, one of which was assigned to the lieutenant, the other to the sub-lieutenant. Above this structure sat the captain, who delegated day-to-day administration to his sergeant major. The sergeant major oversaw the book keeping, although much of it was performed by the company quartermaster corporal. At regimental level, the administrative lynchpin of a regiment was its quartermaster treasurer, the officer who oversaw all financial management, and acted as secretary to the regiment's council of administration, the executive body for administrative matters. Without this administrative backbone the regiment would quickly find itself unpaid, unfed, and unclothed.

**Table 9**: Company administrative structure.

| Captain | | | | | | | |
|---|---|---|---|---|---|---|---|
| Lieutenant<br>First Section | | | | Sub-lieutenant<br>Second Section | | | |
| Sergeant major<br>Quartermaster corporal | | | | | | | |
| 1st Sergeant<br>1st Subdivision | | 3rd Sergeant<br>3rd Subdivision | | 2nd Sergeant<br>2nd Subdivision | | 4th Sergeant<br>4th Subdivision | |
| 1st Squad | 5th Squad | 2nd Squad | 6th Squad | 3rd Squad | 7th Squad | 4th Squad | 8th Squad |
| 1st Corp. + drum | 5th Corp. | 2nd Corp. | 6th Corp. | 3rd Corp. + drum | 7th Corp. | 4th Corp. | 8th Corp. |

## 107. Council of administration (*conseil d'administration*)

As its name suggests, the council of administration was in charge of all non-operational matters relating to the regiment, i.e. the administration and financial management of the regiment's affairs and its personnel. Councils met at the home of the chairman weekly or extraordinarily if required. Each member sat to right and left of the chairman in order of rank, with the secretary sitting opposite him. The main duties of the council included the nomination of adjutants, drummers, the drum major, the master craftsmen, the price of repairs with the master armourer, granting soldiers the right to marry, the proposals for promotion, the enrolment of musicians, the choice of secretaries to the treasurer, overseeing the company accounts, the nomination of a baggage master, and authorising leave. The council would hold a number of registers, including a record of their deliberations, of the contents of the regimental chest, a journal of receipts and expenses of the quartermaster treasurer, registers detailing all the various funds (*masses*), the annual regimental rolls, and a record of travel expenses. The council did not deliberate on matters relating to the policing, discipline, instruction and operational command of the regiment. These remained the prerogative of the colonel.

Like so much else of Napoleon's army, the origins of these councils can be traced to the reforms after the Seven Years War. Captains had been traditionally responsible for the management of their own companies, but in 1762 the regimental administration was centralised and placed under the supervision of a major. The first councils consisted of a triumvirate including the colonel, the major and the treasurer, but eventually evolved into a body of five members. The colonel was the chairman, the treasurer was the secretary, and the major acted as clerk of the council (*rapporteur*). The latter post was an advisory one, with the clerk of the council responsible for ensuring the judgements and deliberations of the council were made within the confines of military statute. Two senior captains made up the remaining members, deliberating and voting on matters arising.

After the Revolution the size of the council swelled to reflect the democratic ideals of the day. The law of *19 Ventôse II* (9 March 1794) set the council at twenty three members. The brigade commander (*chef de brigade*) was chairman; the most senior battalion commander also attended, along with six officers, six sub-officers and nine soldiers representing the interests of the other ranks. The membership was drastically pared down by the law of *25 Fructidor V* (10 September 1797) which set the composition of the council as the brigade commander, four officers, a sub-officer, and a corporal or volunteer. Napoleon streamlined the council further on 21 December 1808 so it comprised of the colonel (chairman), the two most senior battalion commanders, the most senior captain, and one sub-officer. If the colonel was absent the major would act as chairman. Otherwise the major would act as clerk of council while the quartermaster treasurer acted as secretary. The next three senior captains could attend meetings and join in the debate, but they were not permitted to vote.

Under the Napoleonic model, each company put forward a sub-officer candidate for the place on the council. The ultimate decision was made by the officers of the council (but not the colonel) who elected the representative and nominated two substitutes. The sub-officer was elected for a period of one year and was free to run for election again at the end of his term.

When a battalion was detached more than three days march away from the corps, a contingent council (*conseil éventuel*) was formed. The battalion commander acted as chairman; the three senior captains and a sub-officer made up the remainder of the council. A lieutenant or sub-lieutenant stood in for the quartermaster treasurer. When the regiment was on active service the depot battalion would also have its own council, composed of the major, three captains (not the clothing officer) and a sub-officer. If the quartermaster treasurer was absent from the depot a lieutenant or sub-lieutenant again deputised.

[**See also:** 5. Colonel; 6. Major; 9. Adjutant major; 10. Quartermaster treasurer; 18. Drum major; 22. Master craftsmen; 40. Cantineer; 42. Clothing officer; 49. Secretary; 84. Tents; 102. Replacements; 106. Administration & Pay (introduction); 109. The regimental chest; 113. Credit and debt; 115. Leave; 116. Military postal service; 117. Promotion; 124. Marriages; 126. Registering deaths; 128. Assistance for wives and orphans; 129. Pensionable pay; 219. General education.]

## 108. The Ordinary

For the purpose of purchasing foodstuffs, cooking meals and other sundries, groups of 14 to 16 men were formed into an 'ordinary' (*ordinaire*). Although this term has fallen out of common usage in English today, in Georgian times, the word 'ordinary' also described an eating house, or establishment, or the price of a meal. The ordinary was not necessarily the same thing as a squad. If numbers were low, different squads might be mixed together to achieve the required number of fellows. The captain would then appoint a chief (*chef d'ordinaire*), often the corporal, but perhaps a trusted soldier possessing a certain flair or enthusiasm for organising the catering and supplies (the corporal always remained in charge of discipline). This chief was also required to be literate and *au fait* with the newly introduced metric system lest he be cheated by unscrupulous merchants.

Each ordinary possessed a register where all its expenses were detailed: everything from groceries, to the upkeep of property and laundry expenses (to the value of one shirt per man, per week). The chief would write his expenses in this register and sign it, noting the names of the men who had accompanied him shopping (the chiefs were paid by the quartermaster corporals). Every fifteen days the company commander had to assure himself of fair play and his charges were not spending their mess money on drink, or not paying their debts. On behalf of the captain, the sergeant major would visit the bakers, butchers and other providers of supplies checking there were no monies due from the ordinary chiefs and all accounts had been settled satisfactorily.

[**See also:** 28. Sergeant; 106. Administration & pay (introduction); 112. Deductions and funds; 133. Regimental prisons; 183. The daily routine; 191. Rations & supplies (introduction); 199. Food preparation (introduction); 207. Whitening leather belts.]

## 109. The regimental chest (*la caisse*)

The regiment's cash was held in a chest deposited at the colonel's quarters. The chest was approximately one metre long and half a metre high (see the regulation of 1 January 1792). It had a lock which required three keys to open it. One key was held by the commander, one by the quartermaster treasurer and the other by one of the senior members of the council of administration. The chest was usually opened every eight days to provide the treasurer with the appropriate funds.

[**See also:** 10. Quartermaster treasurer; 85. Wagons and horses; 224. Duties of the baggage master.]

## 110. Pay

Soldiers were awarded a salary, the value of which was linked to the soldier's rank, his station, and activity status. In all cases, wages were subject to a number of deductions for various communal funds (*masses*) and a form of pocket money called *prêt*, which is usually translated as 'money loaned', but which is perhaps best understood in this case as 'an advance'. The purpose of the advance was officially to allow the soldier to pay fines, repair bills for damages, to purchase items of petty equipment (e.g. cleaning products).

Essentially there were two types of pay – one for being present, and one for being absent. In both cases the rate of pay varied considerably, depending on various factors. For example a bonus was given for 'Paris pay' – life in the capital being much more costly than elsewhere in France, and there was an augmented 'high pay' for soldiers who wore stripes (e.g. sergeants, corporals, veterans), and served in the elite companies. Soldiers who were on campaign with full rations received a lower wage than those on a peace footing, who only received bread and had to pay for other foodstuffs. Equally, soldiers on the march travelling in peacetime from one place to the next, were only entitled to receive a bread ration, and were paid correspondingly more than their counterparts residing in barracks. Men absent from the regiment continued to receive pay, but the rate for this varied. Those travelling singly on the road would receive an indemnity of 30 *centimes*, plus an allowance of 15 *centimes* for every half *myriametre* (5 km) travelled over the distance of 35 kilometres. Those on leave would receive 15 *centimes*, while the men in hospital received 10 *centimes*. Soldiers held as prisoners of war by the enemy would be paid their normal rate up to a maximum value of two month's pay. (They would normally expect their captors to provide them with pay for their food and clothing while held in captivity). As one might imagine, these sliding scales made accounting for wages hellishly bureaucratic. The treasurer had to know every soldier's whereabouts and movements every day in order to calculate the correct level of pay they were entitled to. The treasurer then had to factor in the various deductions for food, heating, uniform items, and the advances already paid to the man before issuing final payment.

The advance (*prêt*) was paid every five days. There was no formal regulation for this, but long held practice was for the duty officer to deliver the money to the head of each bedchamber on the 1st, 6th, 11th, 16th, 21st, and 26th of each month in the presence of the sergeant major, or quartermaster corporal. The head of the bedchamber then distributed the advance at the rate of five *centimes* per day at the time of morning soup. All other monies due to soldiers were paid quarterly at the last distribution of *prêt* of that quarter.

Prior to the Revolution soldiers' pay had not changed for almost two centuries, having been set by Henri IV (reigned 1589 to 1610). It was commonly believed a soldier required a daily expenditure of 6 *sous* 4 *deniers*, of which the soldier only saw tuppence paid in pocket money. This really was a pittance; rations were poor and the uniform coat was deemed to last six years (it was reduced to three years in 1779). The soldier was even required to pay for his own hat. One thing that must be said in Napoleon's favour was the amount of money spent on a soldier did increase in real terms, although the rise from 6s 4d to the equivalent of 9 *sous* (45 *centimes*) may appear modest. The Napoleonic infantryman of 1807 was no longer required to pay for items such as hair powder and pomade, and the amount spent on his food more than trebled, which is somewhat ironic considering the number of French soldiers who complained in their memoirs of being near starved to death on campaign. Tables 10–12 illustrate how a soldier's salary was allocated over the 1780s, 1790s and 1800s:

**Table 10:** Pay and deductions of an infantryman before the Revolution.

| | | |
|---|---|---|
| Linen and shoes | – | 8d |
| Hat | – | 2d |
| Laundry and barber | – | 4d |
| Queue ribbon, powder, tallow or pomade, black for canvas gaiters, oil for shoes and musket, combs, brushes, petty equipment, thread, needles, uniform repairs | 1s | – |
| Supply bread | 2s | – |
| Bread for soup, meat, vegetables, fat, salt, brushes, candles, pipe clay, bran, cartridge pouch polish | 2s | – |
| Pocket money | – | 2d |
| Total pay | 6s | 4d |

**Table 11:** Pay and deductions of an infantryman *23 Floréal V.*

| | |
|---|---|
| Linen and shoes | 5c |
| Hat (provided by the state) | – |
| Laundry and barber | |
| Queue ribbon, powder, tallow or pomade, black. oil for shoes and muskets, uniform repairs | |
| Supply bread (provided by government) | 20c |
| White bread, meat, vegetables, fat, salt, brushes, candles, pipe clay, bran, cartridge pouch polish | |
| Pocket money | 5c |
| Total pay | 30c |

(The exchange rate had been set at 1 *franc* to 1 *livre*, 3 *deniers*)

**Table 12:** Pay and deductions of an infantryman under Napoleon (circa 1807).

| | |
|---|---|
| Linen and shoes | 5c |
| Hat (provided by the uniform fund) | – |
| Laundry and barber (provided by company funds) | – |
| Queue ribbon, powder, tallow or pomade (abolished) | – |
| Oil for shoes and muskets, etc. | 3c |
| Uniform repairs (either uniform or company funds) | – |
| Supply bread (provided by government) | – |
| White bread, meat, vegetables, fat, salt, brushes, candles | 32c |
| Pipe clay, bran, etc. (provided by company funds) | – |
| Pocket money | 5c |
| Total pay | 45c* |

* This was the equivalent to 9 sous under old money.

Officers were paid monthly on the first or second day of the month. Colonels received a supplement of 1,800 *francs* per year, paid in monthly instalments on top of their salary. Officers about to go abroad on government service were authorised to delegate up to a quarter of their salary to their wives, children or others. Members of the Legion of Honour could delegate all or part of their income from the Legion to their dependants.

**Table 13:** Daily 'presence pay' (circa 1810).

| Officers | On campaign with rations | | In station with bread | | On the march with bread | |
|---|---|---|---|---|---|---|
| | Fr. | c. | Fr | c. | Fr | c. |
| Colonel | 13 | 88.8 | 13 | 88.8 | 18 | 88.8 |
| Colonel in 2nd | 13 | 33.3 | 13 | 33.3 | 18 | 33.3 |
| Major | 11 | 94.4 | 11 | 94.4 | 16 | 44.4 |
| Major in 2nd | 11 | 11.1 | 11 | 11.1 | 15 | 61.1 |
| Batt. commander | 10 | 00.0 | 10 | 00.0 | 14 | 00.0 |
| Adjutant major | 5 | 55.5 | 5 | 55.5 | 8 | 55.5 |
| Quartermaster Treas. | 3 | 33.3 | 3 | 33.3 | 5 | 83.3 |
| Paymaster officer | 3 | 33.3 | 3 | 33.3 | 5 | 83.3 |
| Eagle bearer | 6 | 47.2 | 3 | 47.2 | 5 | 97.2 |
| Captain 1st class | 6 | 66.6 | 6 | 66.6 | 9 | 66.6 |
| Captain 2nd class | 5 | 55.6 | 5 | 55.6 | 8 | 55.5 |
| Captain 3rd class | 5 | 00.0 | 5 | 00.0 | 8 | 00.0 |
| Lieutenant 1st class | 3 | 47.2 | 3 | 47.2 | 5 | 97.2 |
| Lieutenant 2nd class | 3 | 05.5 | 3 | 05.5 | 5 | 55.5 |
| Sub-lieutenant | 2 | 77.7 | 2 | 77.7 | 5 | 27.7 |

| Petty staff | On campaign with rations | | In station with bread | | On the march with bread | |
|---|---|---|---|---|---|---|
| | Fr. | c. | Fr. | c. | Fr. | c. |
| Adjutant sub-officer | 1 | 60 | 1 | 75 | 2 | 60 |
| Baggage master* | 1 | 66 | – | – | – | – |
| 2nd & 3rd eagle bearer | 0 | 80 | 0 | 95 | 1 | 20 |
| Drum major | 0 | 80 | 0 | 95 | 1 | 20 |
| Drum corporal | 0 | 55 | 0 | 70 | 0 | 80 |
| Musician | 0 | 55 | 0 | 70 | 0 | 80 |
| Master craftsman | 0 | 30 | 0 | 45 | 0 | 55 |

*wartime only.

| Elite companies | On campaign with rations | | In station with bread | | On the march with bread | |
|---|---|---|---|---|---|---|
| | Fr. | c. | Fr. | c. | Fr. | c. |
| Sergeant major | 0 | 85 | 1 | 00 | 1 | 25 |
| Sergeant | 0 | 72 | 0 | 87 | 1 | 07 |
| Quartermaster corp. | 0 | 72 | 0 | 87 | 1 | 07 |
| Corporal | 0 | 50 | 0 | 65 | 0 | 75 |
| Grenadier / Volt. | 0 | 35 | 0 | 50 | 0 | 60 |
| Drummer / cornetist | 0 | 45 | 0 | 60 | 0 | 70 |

| Centre companies | On campaign with rations | | In station with bread | | On the march with bread | |
|---|---|---|---|---|---|---|
| | Fr. | c. | Fr. | c. | Fr. | c. |
| Sergeant major | 0 | 80 | 0 | 95 | 1 | 20 |
| Sergeant | 0 | 62 | 0 | 77 | 0 | 97 |
| Quartermaster corp. | 0 | 62 | 0 | 77 | 0 | 97 |
| Corporal | 0 | 45 | 0 | 60 | 0 | 70 |
| Fusilier | 0 | 30 | 0 | 45 | 0 | 55 |
| Drummer | 0 | 40 | 0 | 55 | 0 | 65 |
| Child | 0 | 40 | 0 | 55 | 0 | 65 |

[**See also:** 10. Quartermaster treasurer; 11. Paymaster officer; 27. Sergeant major; 109. The regimental chest; 111. High Pay; 112. Deductions and funds; 114. Auditing and reviews; 119. Awards and national recognition; 129. Pensionable pay; 183. The daily routine.]

## 111. High Pay (*Haute paye*)

Soldiers serving in the elite companies were paid at a higher rate than those serving in the centre companies. For example, a grenadier received 35 *centimes* a day on campaign against 30 *centimes* for a fusilier. Sub–officers and soldiers temporarily transferred to make up numbers in an elite battalion (i.e. those formed from grenadier and voltigeur companies) also received a high pay of 5 *centimes* per day. A high pay of 1 *franc* per month was also awarded to sub–officers and soldiers who reenlisted after ten years unbroken service. After fifteen years this rose to 1.5 *francs*, and then 2 *francs* after twenty years' service.

[**See also:** 21. Musicians; 31. Chosen man; 34. Grenadier; 35. Carabineer; 36. Voltigeur; 99. Voluntary enlistment; 102. Replacements; 110. Pay; 119. Awards and national recognition.]

## 112. Deductions and funds

The financial administration of French regiments was managed through a series of funds (*masses*) which were either financed directly by the ministry of war, or from deductions from soldiers' pay. The practice of deducting soldier's wages in order to meet communal expenses apparently dated back to the ancient Greeks. Before the French Army was centrally regulated by the government, the rate of these deductions was entirely up to the captain, the sole arbiter of administration. In 1762 the administration of companies was centralised and came under the king's accounts. Two years later in 1764 the practice of paying into the funds was regulated for the first time. Soldiers referred to these funds which swallowed up their wages as the *grenouille* (literally 'the frog'). During the latter half of the First Empire the most important funds included:

- **Bakery fund** (*masse de boulanger*)
This was to provide one ration of supply bread (i.e. half a loaf) for every sub-officer and soldier per day. The fund was fixed at 51 *francs* per man per year at 1810 prices.

- **Ordinary fund** (*masse d'ordinaire*)
It had long been the case men of the same bedchamber would pool a sum of money for common expenses and originally this money came from the soldier's advance pay. However in the Napoleonic period this fund was made from a direct deduction. The decree of 12 March 1806 clarified the purpose of this fund, which was to provide soldiers with abundant nourishment, to preserve their health and contribute to fortifying their constitutions. Each ordinary was to procure three ounces of white bread per man, per day, for thickening soup; half a pound of meat (250 grams) and the necessary vegetables. The ordinary fund was not to be used for any other purchases, and surplus funds were not to be distributed among its members. By 1810 the ordinary fund was set at 17.5 *centimes* a day.

- **Heating fund** (*masse de chauffage*)
This was to provide men with fuel for heating and for cooking. Adjutants, sergeant majors, quartermaster corporals and master craftsmen received a double ration. The fund was to the value of 10 *francs* per year per man distributed every month in advance.

- **Clothing fund** (*masse d'habillement*)
This fund incorporated the earlier 'general fund' (*masse générale*). The decree of 25 April 1806 set this fund at 48 *francs* 29 *centimes* per man per year in the line infantry, or 49 *francs* 53 *centimes* for light infantry (by comparison a hussar was 80fr 41c). This fund provided for the manufacture of uniforms and for sundry items such as adjutants' epaulettes, sub-officers' stripes, long service stripes, musicians' braid, plumes and pompoms. It also covered general repairs to uniform, arms and equipment which were not the result of negligence by the owner. The fund also included the first full issue of uniform and equipment on a soldier's arrival at the corps, including two shirts, a black collar, a pair of cotton socks, a pair of woollen socks, two pairs of shoes, one pair of grey canvas gaiters, one pair of black gaiters, a linen sack, a hide haversack, two cockades, not to mention petty equipment such as a vent pick and turn-screw. Following the order of *9 Frimaire XI* (30 November 1802), soldiers promoted to the rank of sub-lieutenant would receive their first officer's uniform free of charge from this fund, if they had served for five years. In the line infantry the value of the officer's uniform was set at 250 *francs*, in the light infantry 270 *francs*.

- **Linen and shoe fund** (*masse de linge et chaussure*)
The linen and shoe fund supplemented the articles provided by the clothing fund with various items of petty kit. These included a third shirt, three white collars, an extra pair of cotton socks, a pair of white canvas gaiters, two handkerchiefs, and the necessary cleaning equipment. The fund was made up of deductions at the rate of 12 *centimes* per day for sub-officers and 7 *centimes* for the men.

• **The company fund** (*masse de compagnie*)
This fund was used for various sundry items purchased with the captain's authorisation, including polish for cartridge pouches, whitener, the laundry bill and salary of the company barber and tailor. The company fund was raised by selling the effects of dead men and deserters, and a levy against those men who were on leave. This amounted to a daily rate of 10 *centimes* for a sergeant, 5 *centimes* for a corporal and 2½ *centimes* for men and drummers.

There were numerous additional funds which were managed by the government directly. This included the fund for lodgings and barracks (*masse de lodgement et casernement*), which provided beds, utensils, overcoats for sentries; and wood and lighters for the guardhouse and candles or oil for the lamps. The fund was set at 3 *francs* per year per man. There was also an encampment fund (*masse de campement*) which was set at 1.50 *francs* per man, per year and was used to provide tents and camping equipment, such as shovels and axes. There were also funds for travel expenses, hospitals and medical supplies and equipment, a fund for horse forage as well as for harness, horse shoeing, and remounts.

There were also so-called 'secret funds' (*masses secretes*) which were forbidden but which occurred nonetheless (see the memoirs of Fezensac). Such large numbers of men passed through the infantry regiments that senior officers could make various economies from their purchases without significantly harming the interests of the soldiers. If administered with a degree of probity, these secret funds were considered a precious resource; for example, Fezensac gives an example of a bonus being paid to officers who survived the 1812 retreat from Moscow (200 *francs* to superior officers, 100 *francs* to the other officers). Many regiments also required officers to pay into a music fund which paid for additional hireling musicians.

[**See also:** 10. Quartermaster treasurer; 21. Musicians; 22. Master craftsmen; 50. Barber; 107. Council of administration; 108. The Ordinary; 110. Pay; 114. Auditing and reviews; 183. The daily routine.]

## 113. Credit and debt

Soldiers were only permitted to obtain credit on behalf of the regiment by means of a bill made by an officer and signed by the commander or the council of administration. Ordinances dating back to 1673 had tried to prevent soldiers from falling into debt by such preventative measures as outlawing gambling and forbidding merchants and innkeepers from giving credit to soldiers. Indeed, when a regiment arrived in a new garrison one of the first duties of the adjutants was to make a tour of neighbouring establishments reminding proprietors of this requirement. If for some reason an officer or soldier did sign a 'letter of exchange' or make other written obligations to a creditor, the debt had to be cleared within two months or they might face punishment, including dismissal from the regiment. They could also be pursued by civil magistrates.

Unofficially, it was a fairly easy matter to obtain credit, the most common way being to borrow money from cash rich individuals such as cantineers. On campaign, when soldiers were limited in their options for procuring brandy, cantineers could quickly amass large sums of money and therefore ran the risk of being robbed. By loaning money at a modest rate of interest, they could make an investment and reduce the amount of cash they carried on their person. At the end of the campaign the debts would be called in. There was of course a risk the debtor might be killed before settling, but this risk was on balance smaller than the one of being robbed or otherwise separated from ones assets. The other 'cash rich' individuals were those engaged in victualing and supply, such as the army's commissaries. Financial abuse was endemic and loaning money to officers for the duration of a campaign was viewed as a relatively safe means of laundering illegally obtained gains.

[See also: 40. Cantineer; 74. Tattoos and jewellery; 114. Auditing and review; 123. Civil matters (introduction); 132. General disciplinary measures; 92. Officer's épée; 108. The Ordinary; 186. Making the rounds.]

## 114. Auditing and reviews

With so much money changing hands the opportunities for embezzlement were all too available. Therefore a strong system of auditing was required to ensure fair play. At the lowest level the sergeant majors and quartermaster corporals would audit the ordinaries and ensure funds had not been diverted for nefarious purposes. The quartermaster treasurers would in turn scrutinise the sergeant majors and quartermaster corporals. To ensure the quartermaster treasurer and colonel were not committing fraud, the ministry of war employed review inspectors (*inspecteurs aux revues*) and commissaries (*commissaire des guerres*) to monitor the various aspects of regimental administration.

The inspectors generally held the rank of brigadier general and were charged with reviewing conscription, organisation, the amalgamation of different units (*embrigadement*), incorporations, levies, the disbanding of units, the pay and accounting of regiments, the maintenance of regimental rolls and the formation of reviews. Commissary officers were responsible for the surveillance of provisions when the army was in garrison; the raising of contributions in enemy countries, the monitoring of travel expenses and military convoys; the vehicles delivering rations, artillery and ambulance vehicles; hospitals, prisons, guardhouses and other military establishments; the distribution of rations, forage, heating fuel, uniform and equipment, the verification of expenses resulting from these expenditures, and all other expenses, except pay.

[See also: 10. Quartermaster treasurer; 27. Sergeant major; 29. Quartermaster corporal; 107. Council of administration; 108. The Ordinary; 112. Deductions and funds; 113. Credit and debt.]

## 115. Leave

It was possible for soldiers to request a period of leave (*congé*) to attend to personal affairs, although it is true to say it is unlikely such a request would be granted if the regiment was in the presence of the enemy. The soldier would apply to his captain, who would in turn make an appeal to the colonel, setting out the duration of the period of leave, where the soldier would travel to and the reason for it. If leave was granted, permission would be given in writing. The document was known colloquially as a *cartouche*, a reference to the note being handwritten on a piece of cartridge paper. The *permissionnaire* (i.e. the soldier granted leave) would also receive a travel itinerary (*feuille de route*) which would hopefully keep him fed and quartered on the way, and prevent the *gendarmes* from arresting him as a deserter. When an officer required leave for personal affairs, the council of administration or the colonel had to agree and put the request to the ministry of war. Before the request was sent to the ministry it would go past the general commanding the division in the army or military administrative division to ensure they could spare the officer.

Before the wars of the Revolution, when the officer corps was almost entirely staffed by nobles, during peacetime there were generally two officers for every position. The senior was known as being *en premier;* the deputy *en seconde*. It was common practice for these officers to take turns at being on service; one being on duty and the other returning home for a period of six months. This type of extended leave was known as the *congé de semestre*. In the period of peace following the Treaty of Amiens (25 March 1802) a similar type of leave was reintroduced. The law of *21 Messidor IX* (9 July 1795) stated officers could return home for the winter (approximately 1 October to 1 May) if they had the approval of the commander of the division, and at least one officer per company remained on duty. Colonels wishing to take advantage of this leave needed to obtain permission from the government. This privilege was also extended to sub-officers and the men, the choice being made by the colonel on the advice of the captains. In Year X (1801–1802) a quarter of sub-officers, and one eighth of the men had to remain with the regiment, but the rest were free to apply for leave and were issued with a travel itinerary and written permission (the *cartouche*).

Officers and men alike might be granted a leave of convalescence after suffering serious illnesses or wounds. To obtain this required a medical certificate signed by two surgeons. Absolute leave (*congé absolut*) could be granted to soldiers and conscripts reaching the end of their term of service, and those retiring from service through old age or as a result of medical discharge (*réforme*). When granting absolute leave, the medical officer would certify they had made an examination. The council of administration would verify this, attach the man's service record (*état de service*) and record if the man had married while in service. The papers would be countersigned by an inspector general or the general commanding a division. This precious document was absolutely vital for the man to avoid accusations of deserting and to enable him to claim a pension, if one was due.

[**See also:** 14. Surgeon major; 24. Captain; 27. Sergeant major; 71. Plumes; 101. Recruitment council; 107. Council of administration; 110. Pay; 134. Military justice; 183. The daily routine; 205. Cleaning & maintenance (introduction).]

## 116. Military postal service

With men serving from the Baltic coast to the Adriatic and from the Pas de Calais to Portugal, an effective postal system was vital for the army. Whether it was colonels writing to track their missing accoutrements, or (more likely) ill-paid and homesick soldiers begging their parents for money, the postal system was vital for morale. Prior to the introduction of postage stamps (*timbre postal*) in 1849, the cost of postage was normally met by the addressee. Soldiers were required to pay the cost of postage within France, but were exempted from the cost of transporting the letter through foreign lands. Rather than using plain paper, soldiers might purchase a cantineer letter (*letter de cantinière*) from their sutler. These letters usually had a portrait of the emperor and empress, with a hand coloured drawing of a soldier in the uniform of the regiment.

The arrangements for the postal service were thoroughly detailed in an ordinance of 31 August 1809. At a regimental level, the baggage master was responsible for receiving, logging and distributing post. With a great deal of money being sent hither and thither, the postal system was naturally open to abuse, so a great deal of regulation was put upon the humble baggage master to ensure fair play and punctuality. The baggage master would be assigned a certificate by the regiment's council of administration, authorising him to collect post on behalf of the regiment. The baggage master was then required to set up a register of all the post he received and despatched. This register was examined by an officer every Monday. The same officer would also investigate any complaints from soldiers relating to their letters or the money attached to them. When post arrived the baggage master would sort it by company and hand the post to the relevant sergeant major to distribute to the men.

With regiments constantly on the move in wartime, officers were instructed to remind their men to inform their parents and other correspondents of the number of their company, battalion, regiment, the arm of service, and which army they were serving with, along with the name of the general they were serving under.

In the event of them being killed, wounded, detached, missing, deserted, or otherwise misplaced, the soldiers were advised to instruct their correspondents to include their own address, the name and address of the nearest post office and the name of their regional department. In this way, undelivered post and money might be returned to the sender. The baggage master would also return post for men who were absent for whatever reason, had died, or were unknown in the corps. When returning a letter to the post office, the baggage master would write the reason for returning on the letter itself.

It should be remembered the French postal service was subject to censorship. The *cabinet noir* of the *ancien régime* was maintained during the Revolution and Empire. For this reason, soldiers often took whatever opportunities they could to send mail home by hand, particularly when a comrade in arms returned to the depot, or went on leave.

[**See also:** 23. Baggage master; 40. Cantineer.]

# Chapter 15

# Promotion & Rewards

## 117. Promotion (*avancement*)

The army had no shortage of brave and patriotic soldiers, but the key to obtaining promotion was for the candidate to be literate. The law of *27 Pluviôse II* (15 February 1794) forbade the promotion of anyone between the rank of corporal and commander-in-chief if they could not read and write. Even at the lowest level of command, literacy was absolutely vital. Some might argue a general might get away with poor standards of literacy if he were a 'lucky general', but a corporal who was unable to read or write would be unable to perform the most basic administrative tasks for his squad. A corporal who had yet to master basic arithmetic would have quickly found himself cheated and hoodwinked by merchants and other unscrupulous types, not to mention castigated by his sergeant, the quartermaster corporal, sergeant major and quartermaster treasurer to whom his accounts were routinely presented.

The law of *14 Germinal III* (3 April 1795) stated corporals were always nominated by election; but the candidates had to be from the company with a vacancy, and the voters had to be volunteers, not requisitioned men or conscripts, and literate. The volunteers would assemble at the battalion commander's quarters and scrutinise a list of candidates, choosing the six most suitable men. There would then be up to three rounds of voting. In the first round the candidate required an absolute majority to pass. If a second round was required, the candidate would still require fifty per cent of the vote. If there was still no absolute majority, a third round would be declared, and the winner would be the one with a simple majority.

Sergeants were either elected or promoted through seniority (the process alternated). All the corporals in the battalion were considered, with a list of six drawn up by the corporals themselves. The sergeants would reduce this list to three, and then pass it to the sub-lieutenants who would vote on their choice. Quartermaster corporals were chosen in a company from among the corporals. The sergeants and sergeant major would draw up a short list of three and the captain would decide. Sergeant majors were selected by the captain from all the sergeants available in the battalion. Adjutant sub-officers were promoted by the decision of the council of administration. In all cases, when someone was promoted to a sub-officer post he was formally presented at the head of the company. A decree of 2 August 1811 stated that before being considered for promotion prospective corporals had to have two years' service, quartermaster corporals two and a half years, and sergeants four years.

[**See also:** 17. Second and third eagle bearers; 31. Chosen man; 34. Grenadier; 39. Regimental children; 118. Promotion to the officer corps.]

## 118. Promotion to the officer corps

Before the Revolution, entry to the rank of sub-lieutenant was mostly restricted to those who had passed through military school and, following the stipulations of the ordinance of Ségur (22 May 1781), were able to demonstrate 'four quarters' of nobility (in other words, their father, grandfather, and great-grandfather held a noble title). This was not purely an act of snobbery on the part of the aristocracy. In feudal times the eldest son inherited the whole estate, and many young nobles were therefore obliged to seek an income from the military, or join the clergy. Some noble families had a long tradition of military service and the Ségur ordinance was seen as a way of protecting their careers from the sons of the upwardly-mobile bourgeois. Even then, a small minority of commoners were raised to the officer corps through merit, or long service, and these men were known as officers of fortune (*fortune* in this case referring to fate, or good luck, rather than financial worth). After the Revolution, noble prerogatives were swept away and the rank of officer was theoretically open to everyone. The emigration of significant numbers of nobles in the early 1790s paved the way ahead for rapid promotion; as did the creation of the battalions of the National Guard Volunteers, who elected their own officers.

The law of *14 Germinal III* (3 April 1795) established three modes of promotion:

* One third would be by seniority of grade.
* One third by election where candidates had to receive a two-thirds majority.
* One third at the choice of the government.

For example, if there were three vacancies, the first would go to the most senior candidate; the second would be elected and the third chosen by the government from a list of nominees provided by the regiment. Napoleon was not a great supporter of the election system and considered it unjust and discouraging. All too often good, steady officers were overlooked for promotion in favour of fast-talking demagogues. Equally, the process of nomination to the government was open to abuse, particularly if the colonel had a favourite he wished to advance.

Napoleon limited the scope for abuse, stipulating the candidates must have served for at least four years in their present grade before being considered. This put a halt to the sort of rapid promotions which had occurred in the 1790s. If the colonel could not find a suitable candidate the emperor would choose another candidate from a regiment in the same arm with the required experience. In turn, sub-lieutenancies would only be awarded to sub-officers of at least six years' service, four of which was in their current grade (this was raised to eight years in 1811), or to graduates of military school. They would remain sub-lieutenants for at least four years. Candidates for the rank of captain would require eight years' service, including four as lieutenant; battalion commanders would require eight years' service as captains. Officers proposed for the rank of major or colonel would only receive their brevets after having commanded parade manoeuvres in front of the emperor.

Newly appointed officers received a brevet which was a formal commission of employment. Under Louis XV the brevet only applied to the likes of an aide major, chaplain and major. Lieutenants and sub-lieutenants received *lettres* and captains and senior officers received *commissions* (generals received a *patente*). These documents were issued as a certificate in gothic script, but after the Revolution came on simple paper. The date on the brevet was used to determine seniority between officers of an equal rank. As a sign they had received the brevet, officers wore a gilded gorget (*hausse col*) when they were on duty – a symbolic representation of the armour previously worn by knights.

There was another route for promotion open to officers, particularly those who were highly educated, or came from a family of influence. This was to secure an attachment to the staff of a general as an adjunct (*adjoint*) or ordinance officer (*officier d'ordonnance*), running messages, carrying out office duties, transcribing orders, and generally being useful. Very often these positions were secured, directly or not, through nepotistic means. Initially the officer might be retained on the books of his parent regiment (a so called supernumerary, or *officier à la suite*); but some were then made full time aide de camp to a general. From that point onwards, the officer would enjoy better conditions, would move in higher circles and, if he proved himself useful (and lucky), his general would ensure he was mentioned in despatches and secure what promotion he could.

All soldiers might also be promoted on the battlefield. This practice was enshrined in the law of *14 Germinal III* (3 April 1795) which stated 'when a soldier distinguishes himself in war by a stunning action, the general-in-chief can, if he judges the action important enough, raise him on the spot to the grade immediately superior to that in which he had fought.'

[**See also:** 25. Lieutenant; 26. Sub-lieutenant; 99. Voluntary enlistment; 100. Military conscription; 112. Deductions and funds; 117. Promotion.]

## 119. Awards and national recognition

During the French Revolution all decorations and chivalric orders such as the *Order of Saint Louis* were abolished. In 1793 even the medals worn by the *Victors of the Bastille* were forbidden (one of the awards was in the shape of a crown). This left soldiers with no symbolic reward for feats of bravery and other meritorious acts. In 1796 the Directory government began the practice of awarding flags, or ornate weapons to deserving soldiers or units. In 1797, at the end of his first Italian campaign, General Bonaparte commissioned one hundred sabres which were given to the heroes of his army. He followed a similar practice when in Egypt and, as First Consul, formally created the national award of the Weapons of Honour (*armes d'honneur*) on *4 Nivôse VIII* (25 December 1799). For infantrymen the rewards took the form of sabres for officers and soldiers who had exhibited extraordinary bravery; muskets for infantrymen, and drum sticks for drummers. There were also financial rewards. Those who merited a first class distinction (i.e. a sabre) were given double pay. Second class recipients received a high pay of 5 *centimes* per day.

The decree of *29 Floréal X* (19 May 1802) established the institution of the Legion of Honour. Admission was granted by right to those already in receipt of Weapons of Honour. Henceforth it would be granted to servicemen who rendered important services to the state in the war of liberty, and to civilians who, by their knowledge, talents and virtues, made a significant contribution to the French republic. There were different levels within the Legion, each of which received a different level of pay. At the top, grand-officers received 5,000 *francs* per year; commanders, 2,000 *francs*; officers, 1,000 *francs*; and legionnaires, 250 *francs*. At the end of each campaign a number of places would be announced and colonels would put forward the names of those they felt deserving of recognition. In peacetime, men who served more than 25 years would be nominated for the award by right. On *22 Messidor XII* (11 July 1804) a decree announced the issuing of a decoration to be worn by members of the Legion. This was known as the star of the Legion (*etoile de la l*égion) and was worn on the coat suspended from a red ribbon.

On 15 August 1809 Napoleon decreed the formation of the Order of the Three Golden Fleeces (*ordre des trois Toisons d'or*), the idea being to create a chivalric order linking France, the recently vanquished Austria, and Spain (then ruled by Joseph Bonaparte). The emperor styled himself as grand master of the order, which would be composed of one hundred grand knights (*chevaliers*), four hundred commanders, and one thousand *chevaliers*. Membership could only be awarded in wartime, and was reserved for the elite of the imperial nobility and marshals. Each regiment would nominate its bravest officers for the award of commander. The bravest soldier or sub-officer in the battalion would be nominated as a *chevalier*. Soldiers who had been wounded three times, or had been distinguished in the defence of their eagle, were first into a breach, the first to cross a bridge under fire, or had performed some other stunning feat of arms (and survived to tell the tale), would be admitted into the order. The eagles of regiments which had fought at the grand battles of the empire would also be awarded the order. Alas, this project came to nought. There was opposition from those who thought it would devalue the Legion of Honour, which was open to all citizens, not just soldiers. Napoleon finally relinquished the project on 27 September 1813. By then it was clear the majority of Austrians and Spaniards did not share Napoleon's vision of European unity.

[**See also:** 94. Flags and eagles; 110. Pay; 128. Assistance for wives and orphans; 234. After the battle.]

Napoleon awards the Legion of Honour to a distinguished sergeant major. (after Raffet)

## 120. Entry to the Imperial Guard

Formed from the Guard of the Consuls on *28 Floréal XII* (18 May 1804), the Imperial Guard was the elite of Napoleon's army. At its peak, it formed an army within itself, with an establishment of over 100,000 men by 1814. The infantry component of the Guard was formed into two distinct branches representing the line and light infantry – grenadiers and chasseurs. Within each branch was a senior regiment (known as the Old Guard); then came the so-called Middle Guard – the Fusilier (Grenadiers) and Fusilier (Chasseurs) formed from the Velite corps in 1806. The last tier was formed from 1809 and was known as the Young Guard – this comprised of a number of units, the best known of which were the regiments of Tirailleurs and those of Voltigeurs. Soldiers aspired to join the Guard for the better conditions of service and the sheer prestige of belonging to it. Arguably it robbed the line regiments of its veterans (Bardin wrote it 'devoured the best troops'); but the Guard could also act as a nursery for sub-officers and officers in the regular regiments.

Admission to the Consular Guard was granted in reward for bravery and irreproachable conduct, to serving soldiers who had undertaken four campaigns, to those who had received a reward for bravery, or to those who had been wounded. Grenadiers had to measure 1.8 metres; chasseurs 1.7 metres tall. The decree of *10 Thermidor XII* (29 July 1804) stipulated grenadiers had to measure over

1.76 metres tall and to have had five years' service, plus seen action in at least two campaigns. In the later Imperial epoch, entry into the Old Guard required twelve years of active service.

[**See also:** 74. Tattoos and jewellery; 105. Velites; 119. Awards and national recognition.]

## 121. National veterans (*veterans nationaux*)

What then of soldiers long in year, but still mentally alert and ready to serve their country? The law of 16 May 1792 created a corps of 5,000 National Veterans. Members had to have served 24 years in the military. The soldiers who made up this corps were considered as being on active service. They were organised into one hundred companies of fifty men each. Twelve companies were composed of artillerymen, and eighty-eight from soldiers of all arms. The latter were based in the departmental capitals while gunners were located along the coast and at ports. Each entrant served in the company attached to the department of his birth.

The law of *19 Frimaire V* (9 December 1796) authorised the formation of two hundred new companies of veterans for wounded invalids. This raised the number to three hundred companies, thirteen of which were gunners. On *16 Fructidor V* (2 September 1797) a captain, lieutenant, and sub-lieutenant were attached to each company. By 1799 there were fourteen thousand veterans, all drawing pay. On *4 Germinal VIII* (25 March 1800) they were reorganised into ten half-brigades, each with three battalions, with each battalion composed of six companies. Retired generals took the role of brigade commander and the battalion commanders were retired adjutant generals or brigade commanders. The captains were former battalion commanders. The effective strength of the companies was raised to seventy-seven men each soldier receiving 30 *centimes* a day; sergeants double.

The decree of *27 Floréal XIII* (17 May 1805) rebranded the force as Imperial Veterans (*vétérans impériaux*), 12,533 men strong in one hundred companies, seventy five of which were one hundred and twenty men strong. The remaining twenty-five companies were formed of gunners, each one hundred strong. Of the first category, fifteen companies formed a garrison regiment in Paris, while the sixty others occupied forts, posts and castles in the interior, with particular orders to prevent fortifications becoming dilapidated, and to ensure drawbridges were in good order. The gunners remained on the coasts. In 1808 there were 13,950 Imperial Veterans. The figure rose again on 8 March 1810 with the creation of a battalion of 'Roman Veterans' from Italians in French service.

Although these institutions were a good way of rewarding veterans and releasing younger troops for frontline service, their cost was prohibitive. On 10 June 1810 ten half-brigades were disbanded, and a number of metropolitan units were reformed. By 1 June 1815 there were just over eight thousand members. The institution outlived the First Empire.

[**See also:** 2. Line infantry regiments; 65. Distinctive markings; 122. Les Invalides.]

A veteran pensioner
at Les Invalides.

## 122. Les Invalides

Each year a number of servicemen were allowed to enter the *Hôtel National des Invalides* in Paris. This institution was founded in 1670 by Louis XVI as a way of providing assistance to invalided servicemen. Up to three thousand men could be admitted. Qualification was the loss of a limb or sight, or thirty years or more of service, and aged over sixty years old. Two thirds of the available places went to active soldiers eligible for retirement, one third to national veterans or pensioners.

[**See also:** 115. Leave; 121. National veterans; 129. Pensionable pay.]

*Chapter 16*

# Civil Matters

## 123. Introduction

One of the lasting impacts of the French Revolution was the recognition French soldiers were citizens and had the rights of free citizens, albeit with the necessary caveats about being bound by the penalties set out in law with regards to military discipline. In 1804 Napoleon introduced a civil code (henceforth known as the *Code Napoléon*) which is widely regarded as his greatest achievement as ruler of France. When a regiment operated outside the borders of France, officers had to replicate the various functions of civil servants with regard to civil matters such as registering births, marriages, wills and deaths. There was guidance on the settling of debts, on pensions and the rights of orphans and widows, all of which are described in this chapter.

## 124. Marriages

The civil laws of marriage also applied to soldiers. In order to marry, males had to be have reached their eighteenth year and females the age of fifteen. If the male was under the age of twenty-five and the female under the age of twenty-one, they would need parental consent. Marriage was prohibited between brothers and sisters, legitimate or not, and (unless the emperor personally decreed otherwise in exceptional cases), between uncles and nieces, or aunts and nephews. The respective rights of spouses were described in traditional terms. Both parties were to offer one another mutual faithfulness, succours and assistance. The husband's duty was to protect the wife, and the wife to obey her husband. The wife was obliged to live with the husband and to follow him wherever he judged it proper to reside.

Following the decree of 16 June 1808, officers could not marry without first gaining the permission of their colonel (or the senior commanding officer if the colonel was absent). The colonel would then make enquiries into the family, reputation and fortune of the persons involved before advising the minister or war of his recommendation. If the minister of war authorised the marriage, the match could go ahead. If the match went ahead without authorisation, the officer would be dismissed with the loss of all rights. Sub-officers and soldiers had to gain the permission of the regiment's council of administration.

If the marriage took place within the boundaries of the French empire, the wedding banns were published on two consecutive Sundays. If there was no objection, the marriage might go ahead three days after the second publishing of the banns. To guard against bigamy, if the soldier was away from home, the wedding banns would be published in the soldier's last place of residence twenty-five days before the celebration was due to take place. The wedding ceremony was presided over by an officer of the registry office and attended by four witnesses. However, in lieu of a registrar the service could be performed by an officer, normally the quartermaster treasurer.

When a Frenchman married outside the boundaries of the empire, this had to be recorded on the French public register of marriages within three months of the couple's arrival in the territory of the empire. Some documentary evidence of this foreign marriage was required.

Marriages could only be dissolved by the death of one of the spouses; by a legally pronounced divorce; or if one of the spouses was sentenced to death by a court. The wife could only ask for a divorce if the husband was convicted of a crime, if he was proved insane, or he openly lived with his mistress under the same roof. In the event of a marriage being dissolved for any reason, the wife was not allowed to remarry for ten months; a precaution to ensure there was no question over the parentage of any child born subsequent to the dissolution.

[**See also:** 6. Major; 10. Quartermaster treasurer; 40. Cantineer; 244. Sexual health.]

## 125. Births

When the regiment was outside the boundaries of the empire, the quartermaster treasurer or captain commanding the company performed the functions of the civil registrar. Births had to be registered within ten days of the delivery, with the child presented to the officer charged with holding the register. A report would be sent to the registrar at the last residence of the father, with a copy sent to the minister of war. When the regiment returned to the territory of the empire, the officer would deposit the register in the war archives.

[**See also:** 6. Major; 10. Quartermaster treasurer; 39. Regimental children.]

## 126. Registering deaths

Deaths were registered by the quartermaster treasurer within ten days and sent to the registrar at the deceased man's last place of abode. If the man died in hospital it was for the director of the hospital to notify the quartermaster treasurer. The cause of death also had to be recorded, albeit briefly. The usual categories given were: killed on the battlefield; died of wounds received in combat; died of a malady caused by the fatigues of war; died of ordinary sickness. In the case of being killed in action, there was no requirement to record the circumstances of a death.

When a soldier died, his possessions were auctioned and the proceeds given to the regimental council of administration to hold in trust for the next of kin. When there was evidence of a violent death (including duels and suicide, but excluding battlefield combat), or any suspicious circumstances, an officer of police and a surgeon or doctor would examine the body and make a report on its condition.

[**See also:** 6. Major; 10. Quartermaster treasurer; 127. Wills; 128. Assistance for wives and orphans; 141. Funerary honours; 253. Medical treatment in garrison; 254. Military hospitals.]

## 127. Wills

On drawing up a last will and testament, a soldier would present it to his battalion commander or another senior officer in the presence of two witnesses. They could also present it to two war commissaries, or a war commissary and two witnesses. If the testator was ill or wounded at the time of making the will, it could be received by the chief medical officer assisted by the military commander in charge of policing the hospice.

The will could not be made in favour of those on a military expedition, or in quarters or a garrison outside the territory of the empire, or to prisoners held by the enemy, within a besieged place or a locked citadel with which communications were interrupted by hostilities. Nor could a will be made to benefit the doctors of medicine, surgeons, medical officers and pharmacists who were treating the testator. The same applied to 'ministers of cults'.

[**See also:** 92. Officer's épée; 112. Deductions and funds; 128. Assistance for wives and orphans.]

## 128. Assistance for wives and orphans

The law of *14 Fructidor VI* (31 August 1798) made a provision for the spouses of soldiers who died on the battlefield or from wounds sustained in combat; or died of sickness, or from a wound, or an accident sustained while carrying out their duties. The widows of officers and adjutants would receive a quarter of the maximum pension due to the man up to the value of 400 *francs*. The widows of sub-officers and soldiers would receive a third of the maximum pension. The value of this pension would not be less than 100 *francs* or greater than 200 *francs*. The sum might be increased if the soldier had won an award such as a weapon of honour, or had been admitted to the Legion of Honour. If the wife no longer survived, the pension could be claimed by the children until the youngest reached the age of twenty-one years.

In order to claim a pension the widow had to prove she was married before the fatality or wound occurred, and to present the following documents:

1. A certificate provided by the council of administration or the commander of the corps, certifying the man was dead, where he died and the manner and time of his death, along with his length of service.
2. A legal copy of the civil act of marriage.
3. A 'certificate of inheritance', provided by the municipal administrations of the place of the residence of the petitioner setting out their financial assets, land and taxable contributions.
4. A copy of the birth records of children establishing their parentage.

[**See also:** 39. Regimental children; 100. Military conscription; 129. Pensionable pay.]

## 129. Pensionable pay (*solde de retraite*)

The law of *28 Fructidor VII* (14 September 1799) made all citizens serving in the army eligible for a pension after thirty years' service, or if they were wounded or otherwise incapacitated by military service. The level of award ranged from 100 to 6,000 *francs* per annum depending on various factors. Soldiers who had to retire before thirty years' service were given a pension relative to the nature and length of service and the type of wound or infirmity they were afflicted by.

When counting a soldier's length of service, each year overseas from Europe counted as eighteen months. In wartime, each year of campaigning counted for two years. When a soldier made five campaigns, each additional year would be classed as three years. The qualification for a campaign was for the regiment to be on a war footing and assembled with an Army Corps, hence each year in attendance at the camp of Boulogne in 1804/05 qualified as a campaign even through the expedition to England never sailed. In some cases, such as the 1805 campaigns against Austria and Russia, Napoleon decreed the Ulm and Austerlitz campaigns counted as two separate events, despite them being only a matter of weeks apart. As another qualification, if a soldier did not see out the entire campaign because he was wounded, he would still receive the full pensionable allowance for having served. Regardless of the length of service and the augmentations for overseas or campaign service, there was a cap at fifty years' service or the equivalent.

Pensions would also take into account the severity of wounds, particularly the loss of limbs. The regiment's medical officer was required to write a report on the injury and the council of administration had to confirm the injuries were the result of wartime service. When awarded a pension for an injury suffered in the course of duty the pensioner was required to present himself to the local authorities annually, bearing a certificate signed by two medical officers confirming he was still afflicted by the injury which caused his retirement.

To give some examples of the level of pension awarded, a captain with 30 years' service would receive a basic pension of 600 *francs*. This would be supplemented by his campaign service. Each additional year would provide him a bonus to the value of one twentieth his pension (30 *fr*) up to a total of fifty years maximum

(1,200 *fr*). By contrast, a sergeant would receive 136.87 *fr*, plus increments of 6 *fr* 84.35 *centimes* up to a total of 273 *fr* 75 *c*.

For pensions due to wounds a captain would receive 1,800 *fr* for the loss of two limbs; 1,500 *fr* for the loss of one limb. A sergeant with the same afflictions would receive 410 *fr* 62.5 *c*, or 342 *fr* 18.5 *c* respectively. When the pension was awarded due to an infirmity caused by military service rather than an actual wound, a captain would receive one quarter the maximum (300 *fr*) after twenty years' service, for each campaign an additional 30 *fr* up to fifty years maximum (1,200 *fr*). A sergeant would receive a basic of 68 *fr* 43 rising in increments up to a maximum of 273 *fr* 75.

[**See also:** 99. Voluntary enlistment; 115. Leave; 122. Les Invalides; 128. Assistance for wives and orphans.]

Soldiers of the Imperial Guard circa 1813. Note the chasseur (second left) still wears his hair in a 'queue'. Also note the mess pan carried by the infantryman on the right of the group.

*Part IV*

# Discipline & Honours

*Chapter 17*

# Discipline & Military Justice

## 130. Introduction

Discipline was the bedrock of the army. It was discipline (and honour) that held the ranks together under showers of shot and shell, and discipline which deterred soldiers from running amok. When discipline broke down, soldiers could expect to be punished. In essence there were two types of punishment. Those inflicted for minor disciplinary offences and criminal sentences by the equivalent of a court martial.

Before the Revolution there were all manner of corporal and capital punishments inflicted on soldiers; at best humiliating, these punishments ranged from being struck by the flat of a sword, to being broken on a wheel. The Revolution put a stop to corporal punishment and henceforth soldiers would either receive custodial sentences (sometimes with hard labour added), or were executed militarily (i.e. shot by a firing squad). The only exception made to this was in the face of revolt and sedition, which could be dealt with by all means, including summary execution.

French infantrymen fighting during the Cairo revolt of October 1798.

## 131. The hierarchy of command

From the highest grade to the lowest, discipline in the army was managed through a hierarchy of gradual subordination. There were three distinct levels of seniority. At the top were officers, divided into the superior officers who made up the regiment's staff, and company level officers. Next were the sub-officers (*sous-officiers*). Known as low-officers (*bas-officiers*) before the Revolution, in the French Army this designation traditionally applied only to those holding the rank of sergeant and above, not the corporals, who were classed as 'men of the ranks'. However, in the spirit of egalitarianism after 1791, corporals were designated as sub-officers too, albeit perhaps not quite of the same status. The class of sub-officers also included a number of specialists, such as the drum major and the regimental craftsmen, all of whom formed part of the regiment's 'petty staff' (*petit état-major*). The third level were the men; some simply classed as men of the ranks (*hommes des rangs*), others drummers, or even elite soldiers. Within each of these classes was a strict hierarchy in which everyone knew their place and function.

A corporal was responsible for what occurred within his squad; the sergeant was responsible for his sub-division. The sergeant major was directly responsible to the captain for the discipline, service and administration of the company, with a particular emphasis on diligent accounting and book keeping, the execution of which was entrusted to the quartermaster corporal. The lieutenant and sub-lieutenant were technically responsible for half the company each, but on a weekly basis shared the role of duty officer. The real power was entrusted to the captain, who was responsible to the superior officers for the police, discipline, service, dress, instruction and accounts of his company. Following the chain to its zenith, captains were commanded by their battalion commanders who in turn gave way to the colonel, the ultimate arbiter in all matters pertaining to the regiment.

In the event of one of these stalwarts being absent, responsibility was delegated to the next most senior man in line. There were three exceptions to this general rule:

1. When a corporal was absent, the company commander would nominate the deputy, length of service sometimes proving an unreliable measure of competence.
2. In the absence of a battalion commander, the most senior captain would deputise, not the adjutant major whose many tasks made him far too important to neglect his own duties, even for an instant.
3. If the depot commander was absent, the quartermaster treasurer was not allowed to command in his stead. A circular of 24 June 1807 confirmed this, stating the quartermaster treasurer was disqualified because he did not possess a 'purely military character'.

[**See also:** 5. Colonel; 9. Adjutant major; 10. Quartermaster treasurer.]

## 132. General disciplinary measures

Although the colonel was ultimately responsible for any misdemeanour within his regiment, day to day control was very much delegated to the corps of sub-officers. The latter were required to be firm and honest with their subordinates; never drinking with them, and never asking for gifts. Sub-officers were to study their men, learn their character, their inclinations and needs, and, as required, employ kindness or firmness toward them. If they saw a man from their regiment in the street, in bad company, committing violence, or otherwise engaged in reprehensible behaviour, the sub-officers were to employ all means in their power punish the fault.

Commanders were to employ all means to watch out for and prevent quarrels, brawls and 'batteries' within the regiment, or with soldiers of another regiment, or the inhabitants of the town. If the quarrel was between soldiers in the same regiment the colonel would order frequent roll calls, confining men to their quarters, reinforcing the guard or the frequency of patrols. If it were with another regiment, the senior officers would consult one another and come to a solution, or with the municipal authorities if the matter involved civilians. All 'games of chance' (*jeux de hasard*) were severely forbidden even if only small sums of money were gambled. Officers who ran into debt had to be watched to ensure they paid their account at the local inn at the end of each month.

Minor disciplinary infringements included being drunk, improperly dressed, quarrelling, fighting, missing roll call, and so on. Small faults of uniform were usually punished with being confined to quarters. These men would remove one gaiter. Sub-officers confined to quarters wore their coat and fatigue cap, but not their sword. They would also join the instruction platoon with the recruits. Other minor faults were punished with bedchamber fatigues, or general fatigues around the quarters. As the fault increased, so did the punishment, from being confined to quarters for two months, confined to the guardhouse for one month, sentenced to prison for fifteen days, or prison with the reduction of diet to bread and water. In camp ordinary faults were punished with fatigue duties. Officers had the right to sentence soldiers to prison; colonels the right to confine to cells. Sub-officers could only be confined to prison by their captain, and only confined to a cell by the colonel. If sub-officers committed an offence three times, they were stripped of their rank – busted (*cassé*). He would then be placed at back of the queue in seniority, and possibly transferred to another company.

When a soldier felt he had been unjustly punished, he might ask for the decision to be reviewed. This was undertaken by a regimental council of discipline (*conseil de discipline*) which was formed of the three most senior officers, the first three captains and the first lieutenants. The colonel assumed the role of chairman and each member had a deliberative voice. Each member would give their verdicts in reverse order of superiority, the most junior man first, in order to prevent members being swayed by the opinion of their superiors. The duty adjutant major would act as secretary to the council, recording the decision in a register which each of the council members would sign.

[**See also:** 133. Regimental prisons; 138. Salutes; 184. Police.]

## 133. Regimental prisons

A garrison would contain two types of prison for miscreant officers and soldiers: a regular 'police chamber', and a cell (*cachot* – a word derived from the verb *chacher* 'hidden'). Generally speaking five rooms would be assigned in the barracks: a chamber for officers, a police chamber and cell for sub-officers, and the same number for soldiers. These were to be located away from the bedchambers. The prison chamber for officers was provided with a bed and furniture, consisting of a table, chair, chandelier, a pair of snuffers, and one chamber pot per officer. The bed sheets were replaced frequently and exchanged before the arrival of a new officer. The chamber was also provided with a shovel, tweezers, a wash basin, a pot of water and tongs. Sub-officers were provided with a wooden double bed and straw mattress, a washbasin and a jug of water. The straw would be replaced as necessary. If a sub-officer was sent to the cell he would be issued with twelve pounds of straw which would be replaced every fifteen days, or upon the change of a prisoner. There would be no bed. Prison chambers for the men would contain no bed or mattress, just straw which was replaced every fifteen days. Each prison chamber or cell would be provided with a washbasin and jug of water. Soldiers and sub-officers were not permitted candles or firewood; nor were they allowed to smoke. If possible, soldiers and sub-officers would be provided with an old coat out of stores while in prison. Food for corporals would be provided by their ordinary. Their meal would consist of a double ration of bread while their portion of the soup was enjoyed by the remainder of the ordinary. Soldiers in the hall of discipline were exercised regularly at two in the morning and two in the afternoon, summer or winter. When the weather was bad this exercise would take place in a hall or shed.

[**See also:** 16. Adjutant; 53. Uniform – general description (introduction); 132. General disciplinary measures; 183. The daily routine; 188. Duties of the corporal of the guard; 243. Sanitation of bedding.]

## 134. Military justice

Some offences were deemed serious enough to be classed as criminal acts, and as such were dealt with by a formal system of justice. A succession of laws were passed in the 1790s which formed the military penal code. It must be remembered at the time many of these laws were passed the French Republic was fighting for its very existence, and faced treachery, civil war and the occasional threat of famine.

From reading them in succession one obtains a fair reflection of the government's concerns about its armies. For example, the *code militaire* issued on 16 October 1791 came after a wave of mutinies and acts of disobedience the year before. Under the code those who committed passive disobedience would be sentenced to two years in irons if they did not obey their commanders on the third summons. Ringleaders of such revolts would receive five years in irons. Subordinates who struck a superior would be sentenced to death. Anyone who insulted a sentinel would receive one month of arrest; six weeks if the sentinel was a sub-officer, and three months if he was an officer. If the insult was made with the threat of a weapon, the sentence was death.

As France headed towards the abyss of war and revolutionary terror, the rate of noble emigration increased. On 17 May 1792, anyone of any rank absent from camp, garrison or quarters without leave was labelled a deserter. Deserters who crossed over to the enemy would be punished by death. Suspicion was everywhere. Papers authorising leave for soldiers had to be signed by their captain and the commander of their regiment or battalion. Officers had to have the signature of the commander of their regiment and the commander of their division. Any 'chief' preaching desertion would be punished with death, even if no desertion actually took place.

In 1793 the laws were aimed at penalising theft and waste. On 28 March 1793 the sale of arms issued to soldiers of the Republic was forbidden. Sellers would receive a fine up to 3,000 *livres*. The decree of 12 May 1793 saw the formal issuing of a penal code in which anyone found selling their rations or forage to civilians was dismissed and imprisoned for a year. Those stealing money from the ordinary were punished with six years in irons; anyone selling uniform or equipment issued by the republic would receive five years in irons. Those who stole the furnishings from barracks got three years in irons. Anyone attached to the army selling gunpowder, musket balls or other munitions would get three years in irons. Soldiers who stole from the homes they were lodged in were sentenced to ten years in irons. Any soldier or individual attached to the army who fraudulently took, or did not pay for food and drink from an inhabitant would receive three months in prison; six if the act was accompanied by menaces; and two years in irons if there was actual assault. If the attack was classed as an assassination, the culprit would be sentenced to death.

In the penal code of 1793 anyone disobeying an order would receive one year in irons; if this disobedience was made in face of the enemy, the sentence was death. The ringleaders behind revolts were to be executed, their accomplices receiving ten years in irons. If an assembly did not disperse in the name of the law, an officer was authorised to employ all means required to restore order. To reinforce the message, the code had to be read to each company every eight days, or the commander of the corps would be imprisoned for a month, rising to dismissal on the third offence.

The penal code of *21 Brumaire V* (11 November 1796) listed a host of crimes. Deserters who crossed over to the enemy were sentenced to death; as were those who left a besieged place without permission, or abandoned an advanced post in the presence of the enemy. The death penalty was extended to anyone found guilty of treason, communicating with the enemy, or committing espionage. Anyone found making drawings or plans of military encampments, arsenals, magazines and other military installations would also be executed. Those convicted of pillage, ravage or arson, would be sentenced to death. Rapists would receive eight years in irons; if the rape was accompanied by violence or the aid of an accomplice, the sentence was extended to twelve years. If the victim died as a result of the attack, the sentence would be death.

Officers away from their posts while 'in the presence of the enemy' would be declared incapable of service, relieved of their duties, and be sentenced to three months in prison. Soldiers caught robbing a corpse on the battlefield would receive five years in irons; sutlers would get ten years for the same offence. Marauding for food in someone's private garden or farm was punished by being paraded twice round the camp with their coat turned inside out with the word 'marauder' written on the back in large letters. The offender would then be 'exposed' (i.e. publically humiliated) for three hours in the middle of the camp. If he had climbed a wall or forced a door, there would be three walks around camp and four hours of exposure. Sub-officers caught marauding would be busted. Sutlers received five years in irons and were forced to repay double the value of the item taken. Officers who ignored marauding were to be dismissed and imprisoned for three months; but of course there are innumerable examples of where such laws were not enforced because the army was unable to provide rations to its troops on campaign.

There were four potential penalties for soldiers convicted of desertion, ranging from a fine, to being sentenced to public works (i.e. hard labour), 'the bullet' (i.e. chained to a cannonball), and lastly, death. The fine for deserting was set in the law of *17 Ventôse VIII* (8 March 1800) at 1,500 *francs*. Those sentenced to 'the bullet' (*boulet*) would be attached to an eight pound cannonball by an iron chain measuring two and a half metres in length. They would then carry out public works (road building, etc.) for eight hours a day between October and the end of March, then ten hours a day for the rest of the year. In addition, they would always work away from other labourers. They were dressed in unmilitary garments and would only have wooden clogs rather than shoes. They were forbidden from shaving their beards, but would have their heads and moustaches shaved every eight days. Men sentenced to public works without the bullet, would retain their shoes and a military style outfit, albeit different colours to those worn by the army and those sentenced to the bullet. They were not allowed to shave their beards or moustaches, but their hair would be shaved every eight days. Deserters could be sentenced to death for the following infringements:

- Deserting to the enemy.
- Deserting while on guard duty.
- Being the leader in a plot to desert.
- Deserting with arms.

[**See also:** 135. Councils of war; 136. Military executions.]

## 135. Councils of war

The decree of *3 Pluviôse II* (22 January 1794) established military tribunals for judging crimes by soldiers. These bodies were suppressed on *2nd complimentary day III* (18 September 1795) and then replaced by the law of *13 Brumaire V* (3 November 1796) with a permanent council of war (*conseil de guerre*) set up in each division of the army and the interior. This body was composed of seven judges: a colonel who chaired the sessions, a battalion commander, two captains, a lieutenant, a sub-lieutenant, and a sub-officer. By custom, each of the seven judges was over twenty-five years old and none could be related to, or in any way allied with, the accused. Another captain would perform the duties of 'reporter', and would conduct the investigation against the accused, collecting evidence and witness statements. Before the trial, the reporter would build a case against the accused then visit them and read out the accusations. The reporter would then take a signed statement from the accused outlining their defence. With the evidence collected, the reporter would notify the council of war and a date for the judgement would be set.

Councils of war were open to the public, but to deter unruly behaviour the number of spectators was limited to three times the size of the council and its attendants. Trials would begin with the clerk of the court (*greffier*) placing a copy of the law of *13 Brumaire V* (3 November 1796) on the bench. This was an important protocol as this law set the procedure of the court. The reporter then began by reading out the statements for and against the accused. Having heard the case, the chairman would summon the accused into the chamber unchained. The accused was also allowed an advocate to help in their defence. In theory the advocate could be a civilian, but was most commonly a fellow soldier either asked for, or appointed by the reporter. The accused would be asked to confirm their name, age, profession and place of birth. With the identity of the accused established, the reporter would sum up the prosecution's case. In turn the accused and their advocate would be asked if they had anything to add to the accused's earlier statement.

After the evidence, came the deliberation. The chairman would ask for the accused to be returned to prison by their escort and for the public to be cleared from the chamber. The reporter and clerk of the court were also required to withdraw. Other than the seven judges only one man was permitted to remain behind. This was a captain who performed the functions of executive commissar (called the imperial commissar in the empire), who was appointed by the general commanding the division to independently ensure the judges acted legally and applied the correct sentencing. The chairman would ask the other judges if they found the accused guilty of the crime(s) as charged. Votes were cast in reverse order of rank, commencing with the sub-officer and ending with the chairman. In order to find the man guilty a simple majority was required.

After establishing the accused man's guilt, the imperial commissioner would read out the punishment required by law. A second vote then took place to ensure the judges endorsed this sentence with a majority of five out of seven votes required to pass it. With the judgement passed the doors were reopened and the reporter and clerk of the court returned to hear the verdict. The chairman would announce the verdict publicly. Meanwhile the reporter went to the prison and read the judgement to the accused in the presence of a guard under arms.

There was an appeal process. The law of *18 Vendémiaire VI* (9 October 1797) allowed for a council of appeal (*conseil de révision*) to be established in every division of the army or troops of the interior. The purpose of this council was to review the judgements made by the councils of war. They had to be convened within twenty-four hours of the original judgement and be provided with all the relevant paperwork from the case in question. The council would not rest until a judgement on the sentence was made. Each council would comprise of a general officer who chaired the council, a colonel, one battalion commander, two captains and a clerk of court appointed at the choice of the chairman. The reporter would be taken from among the council at its own choice. In addition, there was an executive commissar (later imperial commissar), a position filled by an ordinance officer (*commissaire ordonnateur*) or a war commissary first class. Each member had to aged over thirty or to have made three campaigns in front of the enemy. The council could choose to uphold the original decision, annul the decision, or refer the case to a second trial by a different council of war.

[**See also:** 134. Military justice; 136. Military executions.]

## 136. Military executions

Military executions were by firing squad within forty-eight hours of the sentence being passed. The troops from the garrison or division would assemble without weapons at the place of execution and form three sides of a square, the open face allowing the passage of balls. The corps of the condemned man would take the place of honour on the right and everyone would face inwards to witness the unhappy spectacle. One of the members of the council who delivered the sentence would also be present.

The condemned man would arrive with an escort of fifty soldiers and be led before the regiment with his arms bound. First he would be degraded (ceremonially expunged of his military identity) before being handed over to the executioners. His uniform buttons and distinctive colours were removed and a musket was symbolically reversed by one of the sergeants to indicate the withdrawal of weapons from the condemned man. In some corps the condemned man was also symbolically stripped of his cartridge pouch, which was allowed to fall on the floor. The condemned man would then be made to kneel and a blindfold administered.

The firing squad would be composed of four sergeants, four corporals and four of the longest serving fusiliers (this duty would be rotated). The twelve soldiers would be formed in two ranks, muskets loaded and ready to fire when the signal was given by the adjutant. It was sometimes the case the condemned man would refuse the blindfold, and perhaps even ask to utter the words of command himself.

The condemned man would often beseech his former brothers in arms not to miss; but the emotion of executing one of their own might sometimes prove too much, and the men might fire wide, accidentally or not. In truth a clean kill was the best outcome for everyone. The regulations said nothing about administering a *coup de grâce* but Bardin states the victim was clubbed to death with the butt of a musket, while Blaze mentions a reserve platoon being available if required. (There was no mention of a sub-officer firing point blank into the victim's ear, as later detailed, for example in the decree of 25 October 1874). Once the victim had expired the assembled troops would parade before the corpse, the victim's former regiment leading the procession.

[**See also:** 34. Grenadier; 37. Drummer; 130. Discipline & military justice (introduction); 134. Military justice.]

## 137. Duelling

'Affairs of honour' between men were an extra-judicial means of settling disputes. In the Revolution and Empire, duelling was not explicitly banned. In 1792 there was merely an edict that the drawing of swords was not permitted within the walls of a fortress. This implied it *was* acceptable to fight outside the walls of the garrison or encampment. The causes of a duel might be any manner of insult in which the offended party felt his personal honour, or that of his corps, had been besmirched. A man might also be forced into fighting a duel if his comrades or commanders considered an insult had been inflicted, even if the 'injured' party did not. To not act in the defence of one's honour would be to risk being ostracised. The offended party might instigate the duel by administering a symbolic slap to his intended opponent, or by making a verbal challenge.

There were certain etiquettes to duelling. After the challenge had been made, the details would be arranged between the two parties by means of 'seconds'. These seconds would agree the time and place of the duel, and in some cases, act as mediators if one party attempted reconciliation. The choice of weapon would also be negotiated by the seconds. Swords were an obvious option, although if for any reason one party had a marked disadvantage in using swords (for example an injury), then pistols were an obvious option. When pistols were chosen, the two men would start from a specified distance and advanced towards each other. After an agreed number of paces, the men were allowed to fire. The outcome of the duel was seen as an act of God. In the more extreme cases, even if a man was wounded, his comrades might not consider the wound sufficiently severe enough for honour to been seen to be satisfied. A second duel might therefore ensue once the injured party had recovered.

[**See also:** 47. Master-at-arms; 88. Pistol; 126. Registering deaths.]

## Chapter 18

# Rendering Military Honours

## 138. Salutes

In their original form, salutes were a form of polite greeting, such as removing one's hat, or bowing. Over time salutes between soldiers became an act of hierarchical deference and discipline; a means of rendering honour. By the Napoleonic period there were numerous ways of making a salute, with or without weapons, by firing, or with flags. Individuals could be saluted, as could flags; in an extreme case French soldiers apparently once saluted the ruins of Karnac in Egypt, they were so impressed by the ancient monument.

A salute by firing (sometimes called a *feu de joie*) was most often (but not exclusively) made by artillery fire. It was also common to fire muskets at military funerals to mark the passing of a comrade in arms. On a more ordinary level, soldiers could shoulder or present arms depending on the rank of the personage before them (presenting arms was typically reserved for the emperor, princes, ministers, grand dignitaries, marshal of the empire, and the holy sacrament). Officers would salute with their swords. When a soldier was without arms, a salute could be made with a gesture of the hand, or with the removal of the hat.

The etiquette of saluting without weapons (i.e. with the hand) was given in the provisional interior service regulations of 1 July 1788. When the regulation was finalised on 24 June 1792, the section on saluting was omitted, presumably for political expediency. However, Bardin included a reminder of the 1788 rules in his infantry manual. If a sergeant, corporal or soldier encountered a superior officer, or the captain of their company, they would stand to attention. The soldiers would salute with their hand, while the sub-officers removed their hat, holding it by the right hand side of the body, and facing the personage without inclining their head or bowing. The hand salute was described in 1788 as bringing the right hand flat to the side of the hat. Bardin described it as having the fingers in the air with the palm facing outwards. He also clarified sub-officers wearing shakos should also salute with their hands, rather than remove their hat. When an officer called a man to speak to him, the fellow would advance to within two or three paces of the officer. Sub-officers would remove their hats and soldiers salute, holding this pose until after the officer had finished talking to them. On the subject of officers other than those already described, war commissaries, adjutants and sub-officers: they would make a salute with the hand, but were not required to stop if they were walking. Officers would salute one another, the superior returning the salute of the inferior grade.

On a similar subject, when a soldier addressed an officer he would call him 'my lieutenant' (*mon lieutenant*), for example; or if he was not sure of the grade 'my officer' (*mon officier*). Officers would often address men by their rank, as would sub-officers. Sub-officers and officers of more or less equal grades would address one another as *monsieur*.

[**See also:** 131. The hierarchy of command; 139. Honouring dignitaries; 140. Honours to religious parades and services; 154. The manual exercise.]

## 139. Honouring dignitaries

The 1790s were set against a backdrop of egalitarianism, where everyone was to be addressed as 'citizen', and people deliberately broke convention by using the familiar 'thou' (*tu*) rather than the formal 'you' (*vous*). With Catholic worship forbidden, the conventions of military church parades and paying honour to the holy sacrament were discontinued (as presumably was the practice of avoiding meat on Fridays). In contrast, Napoleonic France was extremely hierarchical with Napoleon atop a great tree of princes, grand dignitaries, cardinals, ministers, grand-

A drummer salutes the Emperor. Interestingly he salutes with his left hand because he is holding his sticks with the right hand. The regulations on saluting were quite vague.

officers of the empire, senators, councillors of state, grand-officers of the legion of honour, prefects, members of the judiciary, generals, police commissioners, mayors and so on. The decree of *24 Messidor XII* (13 July 1804) set out this hierarchy and the honours due to each tier of the new imperial elite.

To give some examples, when the emperor visited a fortress, half of the infantry within it would form up on the glacis, right and left of the gate of entry. As the emperor approached, the men would present arms, the drummers beat *aux champs*, and the officers salute with their épées. The emperor (he only) would then be presented with the keys to the city by the governor or the commander of arms. If the emperor's visit was expected in a camp, all the soldiers would form in line along the front of their tents, or the piles of arms. If he arrived without warning, the guards and pickets would present arms. The remainder of the soldiers would form up as quickly as possible, without arms, and then wait for his majesty's orders.

If the emperor passed in front of a line of troops, the infantry would present arms; the officers would salute, along with the standard bearers. Meanwhile the drummers would beat *aux champs*. If the troops were on the march when the emperor passed them, they would halt, form into line and then perform the honours previously described. A similar procedure would occur if the emperor happened to pass a guard post or picket. Things became somewhat more complicated if the emperor made a halt at a garrison or camp. Even when travelling with his guard, the emperor would often require additional detachments for guard duty. Each infantry regiment would provide one battalion commanded by its colonel, with its standard. The first spell of guard duty would fall to the most senior regiment (i.e. lowest regimental number first). While providing guard duty, the colonel would have the honour of taking orders directly from the Grand Marshal of the Court. While in residence the emperor would issue the password (*mot d'ordre*). Also, to prevent Paris or other cities from coming to a complete standstill, when the emperor was in residence and forty-eight hours before his arrival or departure no honours would be given to anyone else.

There then followed a sliding scale of honours due to various dignitaries of empire. The empress received the same honours as her husband, but was not presented the keys to the city, nor trusted with issuing the password. When a prince or grand dignitary passed, quarter of the infantry would turn out to meet him at the gates. He would then be assigned a guard of one hundred men, commanded by a captain, lieutenant, sub-lieutenant and a flag. If a minister arrived, he would be honoured by having the route lined by the garrison. A guard of sixty men, a flag, a captain and a lieutenant would be provided (the minister of war was allowed eighty grenadiers and three officers). Marshals also merited the route being lined with soldiers, and received a guard of fifty men. Grand officers of the empire and inspector generals warranted the same treatment as marshals, but the troops did not present arms as they went by. Generals of division were allowed to have grenadiers guarding their quarters. Generals of brigade were only allowed fusiliers. Colonels merited the presenting of arms and were granted one sentry at their lodgings when present with the regiment. Sentries would also present arms to majors and battalion commanders, but only port arms to company officers. Foreign ambassadors were not to be granted any honours at all without formal notice of the minister of war.

[See also: 13. Eagle bearer; 37. Drummer; 94. Flags and eagles; 138. Salutes; 154. The manual exercise.]

## 140. Honours to religious parades and services

Before the revolutionary government forbade it, soldiers would observe worship. Regiments had their own chaplains, and soldiers would have attended church service or evening prayer on a regular basis, observed religious festivals, and even followed dietary restrictions such as abstaining from meat on a Friday. An important part of church services was the act of genuflection before the altar in order to receive the holy sacrament (the wine and bread representing the blood and body of Christ). In the regulations of 1 August 1791, this important religious observance was rendered into a military act, with officers and men presenting arms, kneeling on their right knee and removing their hats, placing them on the left knee, while the drummers beat *aux champs*.

In the Napoleonic period (Catholic worship was restored in 1801), when religious processions passed in view of a military guard or post, the soldiers would present arms, place their right knee on the ground and incline their heads, raising their right hand to their hats, as if in salute. Drummers would beat *aux champs*; the officers would salute with their épées, raising their left hands to their hats, but keeping their heads covered. Standard bearers would also salute. In addition, the first post encountered would provide a military guard of two fusiliers to accompany the procession. When troops lined the route along which the procession would pass, the first place of honour was to the right of the church door by which the procession would leave. The senior regiment was placed there, with the second formed against the left side of the door. The other regiments would take their place right and left alternatively. The cavalry would follow after the infantry. A detachment of two grenadier companies would escort the procession, formed left and right of the dais, marching in file. The soldiers would carry their muskets on the right arm.

[See also: 12. Chaplain; 138. Salutes; 154. The manual exercise.]

## 141. Funerary honours

One of the more sombre duties placed on infantry was providing funerary escorts. When a colonel died beneath the colours, the entire regiment marched. Majors warranted half a regiment and two flags; battalion commanders, their battalion and its flag; a captain, his company; a lieutenant or sub-lieutenant, his section.

A sergeant merited two squads led by a sergeant; a corporal, one squad with a corporal; soldiers merited four men, in other words, sufficient to carry his coffin. Sub-officers and soldiers carried their muskets under the left arm in the 'secure arms' position and drums were covered with black *serge*. The coffin was carried by four persons of the same rank, or four persons of the rank immediately inferior. The state would pay all expenses for a funeral of a soldier killed in action, or died within three months of being wounded. This included the price of gunpowder for a final salvo over the grave, announcing the deceased hero's departure for the afterlife. Napoleon also stipulated the protocol for his own demise. In the event of the emperor dying black crêpes would be put on the flags for a year. The same honours were awarded to colonels who died. In all other cases, the sign of mourning continued until the deceased officer was replaced. In addition, when a colonel died, all of the officer corps wore a black crêpe around their épées as a sign of mourning for their colonel for one month.

[**See also:** 126. Registering deaths; 127. Wills; 138. Salutes; 154. The manual exercise; 234. After the battle; 251. Interment of the dead.]

Soldiers of the 76th Line reclaim their colours from an arsenal in Innsbruck, Austria in 1805.

*Part V*

# Tactical Organisation & Drill

## 142. Introduction

The French tactical system was set down in the *Regulation concerning the exercise and manoeuvres of the infantry* of 1 August 1791, a document which remained in use throughout the Napoleonic period. Before exploring this document, it is perhaps useful to provide some background and context on why the French system developed as it did.

In medieval combat the principal means of fighting was shock, in other words, the collision of two bodies of troops in hand-to-hand combat. The most appropriate formation for infantry was to form a dense mass, and the most appropriate weapon was the pike, or other pole arms. In this respect, there was little to distinguish the medieval solider from the time of Alexander the Great. When firearms began to render shields and armour ineffective, the tactics employed on the battlefield naturally adapted. The Swedish King Gustavus Adolphus (1594–1632) is credited with the innovation of increasing the frontage of an infantry formation at the expense of its depth in order to maximise fire power. At the beginning of the 18th century a four rank system was common in Europe, but the infantry of Frederick the Great of Prussia fought in three ranks during the Seven Years War (1756–1763). The three rank solution allowed all ranks to fire simultaneously while the formation remained sufficiently solid for shock actions. The 1791 regulations were, in essence, the French interpretation and refinement of Frederick the Great's tactical system.

The principal difficulty of Frederick's system was manoeuvring a long, thin line of men over any significant distance. Firstly there were obstacles, features of the terrain, defiles, etc., which could break up a formation; but more important still was the difficulty of maintaining the exact alignment of a battalion, let alone a line of battalions, while moving at anything beyond a snail's pace. If alignments were not strictly maintained, there was a danger the line might fragment and become vulnerable to cavalry attack, or the battalions would converge and become confused.

Through the course of the 18th century there was a great debate in France about the best formation for infantry to adopt. After the Seven Years War one camp wanted to adopt the Prussian *ordre mince* ('thin order'), while others remained wedded to the idea of deep formations (*ordre profond*) because these were more favourable for rapid movement, taking an offensive approach and delivering shock attacks (until the slaughter of 1914 many French military theorists remained obsessed with the notion battles are ultimately won by élan and irresistible shock action rather than firepower). The leading exponent of the *ordre profond* was François-Jean de Mesnil-Durand. His concern with Frederick II's system was it being too 'German' to be acceptable to French soldiers. In order to act with the required level of precision, the men had to perform as automatons, utterly devoid of independent thought. This was not the best way to exploit the supposed French genius for intrepid action. In the other camp was the Count de Guibert. Having studied the Prussian army at close hand and debated tactical matters with Frederick II in person, Guibert was convinced (rightly, the battle of Waterloo ultimately proved), that deep formations ran the risk of being shot to pieces long before they could deliver their shock attack. Guibert's solution was based on a pragmatic mixed system employing deep formations when manoeuvring, and thin formations when delivering musketry. After many trials and tribulations, Guibert's philosophy won the day. A military committee was formed under the direction of Viscount de Noailles which led to the publishing of the 1791 infantry regulations. According to this document, a battalion would be subdivided into platoons (*peletons*), which could either be arranged in a linear formation for firing (a formation described as *en bataille*), or stacked into 'columns' of platoons for manoeuvre (*en colonne*). Columns had a frontage of just one or two platoons, rather than eight or nine platoons in the line; they were therefore much easier to manoeuvre over battlefield terrain. The regulations did contain one sop to the exponents of the *ordre profound* which was the attack column (*colonne d'attaque*). This formation was two platoons wide and four deep, and there were no instructions for manoeuvring the column except in a straight line.

The 1791 regulation was over four hundred pages long, subdivided into five parts, which included an organisational summary, three 'schools' (the soldier, the platoon and the battalion) and a final section entitled 'evolutions of the line'. These detailed every motion, from the stance of the soldier without arms, the methods of loading and firing, not to mention a plethora of instructions for manoeuvring columns of various descriptions through a variety of potential situations. Although very interesting, there is only space in this section to introduce the most general concepts and routines. English speaking readers who wish to delve more deeply into the minutiae of drill and manoeuvres, might profit from obtaining a copy of John MacDonald's contemporary translation of it.

Several additional caveats should conclude this introduction. The war broke out in 1792 – the first spring after the introduction of this regulation – at a time of great social upheaval when a great many experienced noble officers emigrated from France and when a large number of sub-officers or National Guard Volunteers had been newly promoted to the rank of officer without formal training. It is therefore perhaps true to say the finer details of the 1791 regulations were not properly realised until the period after the treaty of Luneville in 1801 and before the Ulm campaign of 1805. Although this regulation was the cornerstone of infantry tactics, it is equally important to understand it did not entirely keep up with the organisational changes which took place in the 1790s and under Napoleon's reign, such as the increase from two to three field battalions per regiment, nor the reduction of the number of companies per battalion in 1808. It also failed to address tactical innovations such as fighting in skirmish formation (*en tirailleur*), firing by rank, and the formation of 'Egyptian squares' to counter cavalry attacks. Bardin attempted to correct these shortcomings with his *Infantry Manual*, and even included a proposed revision of the schools of the soldier and the platoon in his 1813 edition. Many marshals and generals had their own opinions on tactics and would issue specific instructions prior to going on campaign. The grand tactics are therefore beyond the scope of this work – we instead focus on the lower level, 'mechanical' routines which underpinned the system.

A motley assortment of French grenadiers from the mid-1790s. The figure with the sashes and plumes is a 'representative on mission', a type of political commissar send by Paris to put down rebellions.

# Chapter 19

# Tactical Organisation

## 143. Tactical composition of a battalion

The battalion was the basic tactical building block of the French Army. A regiment or half-brigade in the field tended to be formed of two or three battalions. Two regiments typically made up a brigade, and two brigades made up a division. In the early 1790s, some divisions were labelled 'advanced guard' divisions, and had a more significant light cavalry presence; but in general, every infantry division contained a mix of line and light infantry (typically 2:1 in ratio). Under Napoleon, the Army Corps system became predominant, with several infantry divisions collected under the command of a senior general (typically a marshal of the empire) with the necessary supporting arms and services to enjoy a certain degree of operational independence. These were the essential structures applied to infantry in the field throughout the period.

In turn, each infantry battalion was composed of a number of sub-units. Administratively, each sub-unit was called a company (*compagnie*). However, when the battalion was assembled for manoeuvres, each sub-unit was referred to as a platoon (*peleton*). Although the two words are often used interchangeably, it is important to note there were differences; for example, a platoon was often temporarily composed of men from different companies.

Previous to the Napoleonic Wars, the term platoon had described a grouping formed of two companies. In the instruction of 1 May 1766 and 11 June 1774 it was established a platoon would be formed of a single company only. In 1770 the meaning changed so a platoon came to describe a half company. Then, in the regulation of 1 August 1791 the platoon settled on the single company solution, with a platoon being a subunit within a battalion composed of at least twelve files of men in three ranks (i.e. 36 muskets). Each platoon was divided into two equal sections.

The regulation of 1 August 1791 described the eight fusilier platoons as being paired to create four 'divisions' (not to be confused with the larger tactical term of the same name describing a formation composed of two brigades). The purpose of these divisions was primarily linked to manoeuvring the battalion, in column formation. The authors of this regulation added an additional layer of complexity, by deciding the right hand platoon of each division would be commanded by the most experienced captains. Thus in a two-battalion regiment, the captains of the fusilier companies would be distributed as shown in Table 14.

**Table 14:** Tactical composition of a battalion 1791.

| | | | |
|---|---|---|---|
| 2nd Battalion | 4th Division | 8th Platoon | 16th Company |
| | | 7th Platoon | 8th Company |
| | 3rd Division | 6th Platoon | 14th Company |
| | | 5th Platoon | 6th Company |
| | 2nd Division | 4th Platoon | 12th Company |
| | | 3rd Platoon | 4th Company |
| | 1st Division | 2nd Platoon | 10th Company |
| | | 1st Platoon | 2nd Company |
| 1st Battalion | 4th Division | 8th Platoon | 15th Company |
| | | 7th Platoon | 7th Company |
| | 3rd Division | 6th Platoon | 13th Company |
| | | 5th Platoon | 5th Company |
| | 2nd Division | 4th Platoon | 11th Company |
| | | 3rd Platoon | 3rd Company |
| | 1st Division | 2nd Platoon | 9th Company |
| | | 1st Platoon | 1st Company |

When in 1794 the implementation of the half-brigades took place, this principle was reapplied; partly to ensure an even spread of experienced captains across all three battalions, and partly for political reasons, because the government wished to eliminate all traces of the Royal Army battalions. When allocating companies to the new battalions, a system was adopted called *tiercement* (lit. dividing into thirds). The senior captain, regardless of his parent regiment or battalion, was allocated 1st Company, 1st Battalion; the second 1st Company, 2nd Battalion and so on. The result of this was the majority (but not all) new battalions were composed of a mixture of officers and men from across the original units. However, once allocated in the new formation, captains naturally became 'wedded' to their companies, and they did not reorganise every time there was a vacancy. Thus in practice, over time the allocation of the companies / platoons was no longer an accurate reflection of the seniority of the captains. Nor was there any attempt to place lieutenants and sub-lieutenants according to their seniority.

The regulation of 1 August 1791 described a two battalion regiment, with the first company of grenadiers occupying the right of the first battalion, and the second battalion occupying the left of the second battalion – the first and second places of honour in the line. However, when the regiment was being exercised, the grenadiers would unite and form two, equal-strength platoons on the right of the line. This avoided the problem of having to pair the grenadier platoons with centre companies. On active service the field service regulations of 1792 required all the grenadier platoons of a brigade or division to be united as a special battalion. Grenadiers were therefore often detached from their parent battalions, at least before 1808.

The voltigeur companies were created between 1804 and 1805, officially replacing the second company of fusiliers / chasseurs. In the instructions concerning their formation, there was no indication where the voltigeurs should stand in the line. Like the grenadiers, voltigeurs were often detached from their parent battalions, either being assigned to advance or rearguard functions, or they operated in advance of their parent battalion, scouting and skirmishing.

The imperial decree of 18 February 1808 reduced the number of platoons in a battalion from nine to six. It continued with the practice of pairing companies to form divisions, but only when all six companies were present (i.e. four fusilier, plus two elite). When one of the elite companies was not present, the remaining companies would manoeuvre and parade by platoon only. According to the decree, grenadiers were assigned to the right of the battalion, while voltigeurs were recognised as occupying the left of the battalion. In addition to being the most practical position for a platoon which would often be detached from the main body of the battalion, the left of the line was considered the second place of honour.

In the 1813 edition of the *Infantry Manual*, Bardin condemned the placement of the voltigeurs on the left of the battalion as being 'contrary to the natural system of *endivisionnement*'(as the process of forming divisions was called). Bardin counselled for the voltigeurs to be placed on the left of the grenadiers, so the elite platoons might form a division on their own. Without any more detailed guidance from the 1808 decree, the obvious interpretation followed by many was for the grenadiers and voltigeurs to be paired with the neighbouring fusilier company when forming a division. Mixing elite and centre companies in this way was anathema to Bardin. According to Bardin, some regiments only ever paired their four fusilier platoons. Grenadiers and voltigeurs were each said to be at the same time a platoon and a division. He supported this approach and documented it in his revision of the 1791 regulations which appeared as an annex to the 1813 infantry manual. According to Bardin each battalion ought to have adopted the structure given in Table 15.

Table 15: Tactical composition 1808 (Bardin formula).

| | Voltigeurs | | |
|---|---|---|---|
| Left half battalion | 2nd Division | 4th Platoon | 4th Company |
| | | 3rd Platoon | 3rd Company |
| Right half Battalion | 1st Division | 2nd platoon | 2nd Company |
| | | 1st Platoon | 1st Company |
| | Grenadiers | | |

Under the system Bardin described in 1813, the grenadiers were no longer automatically separated from their parent battalion, as described in the 1 August 1791 regulations. However, it appears Bardin's recommendation was not universally accepted, and he ultimately lost the argument. An anonymous 'major' (later identified by Bardin as Heffmeyer), published a work titled *Livret de commandemens, ou Tableaux synoptiques des manoeuvres d'infanterie* (the work was undated, but Bardin's dictionary gives the year of publication as 1815). This document described how the elite companies should form divisions with the centre companies, as per the 1808 decree. Heffmeyer's structure is given in Table 16.

Table 16: Tactical composition 1808 (Heffmeyer formula).

| Battalion | 3rd Division | 6th Platoon | Voltigeurs |
|---|---|---|---|
| | | 5th Platoon | 2nd Company |
| | 2nd Division | 4th Platoon | 4th Company |
| | | 3rd Platoon | 1st Company |
| | 1st Division | 2nd Platoon | 3rd Company |
| | | 1st Platoon | Grenadiers |

In this system the companies are assigned to platoons, very similar to the original system from 1 August 1791. The main difference here is the grenadiers are labelled as 1st Platoon. It is also interesting to note 1st Company, 1st Battalion would have the eagle guard assigned to its second section. Another small interesting detail is the impact on this structure to the appearance of the battalion. After 1811 the company pompoms worn on the shakos would not have followed the correct numerical sequence.

As with many details from the Napoleonic era, it is likely different regiments adopted different solutions. From later regulations, it appears the Heffmeyer model was the one which most regiments adopted and was the one the French army stuck with, much to Bardin's chagrin. Reflecting on the practice of forming divisions and the practical difficulties it raised, Bardin later described *endivisonnement* as 'a vice.'

[**See also:** 144. Assembling the platoon; 145. Assembling the battalion; 164. Battalion formations and manoeuvres.]

## 144. Assembling the platoon

Before a battalion could assemble, each platoon was first prepared by the sergeant major. As a point of principle, it is important to state the squads and ordinaries in which the men were administered and quartered had no tactical function at all. When the platoon was formed, all the men in a company would form up in a single rank in height order (regardless of squad, etc.), the tallest on the right, and the shortest on the left. The sergeant major would then count the men and divide them into three equal portions. The tallest men in the right hand third would be the front rank; the shortest men in the third on the left would become the middle rank; while the middle third would form the rear rank.

The sergeant major would order the men to form up in three ranks. This could be done with an alignment to the right, left, or centre of the line. When the ranks were formed, the corporals were placed in height order on the flanks of the front and rear ranks of each section. The sergeant major would then number the files making each man say his number. When he reached the section split he would tell the two men in the middle 'you are the left of the first' or 'right of the second' respectively. The men in the front rank were known by the denomination 'file leader' (*chef de file*).

Once the ranks were formed, the officers and sergeants would then take their positions. Ordinarily the captain would stand in the front rank on the right of the platoon. However, during some manoeuvres, or when the platoon was about to commence firing, the captain would move to a position two paces to the rear of the file closers' rank, at the centre of the platoon. Directly behind the captain, on the right of the third rank was the first sergeant, who was known as the replacement sub-officer (*sous-officier de remplacement*). This sergeant would be the guide to the right of the platoon and would maintain the interval with the platoon to the right. When the platoon was about to fire, the replacement sergeant would fall back into line with the file closers (thus allowing the captain to pass by him). The lieutenant would stand to the rear of the centre of the second section, two paces behind the third rank. The sub-lieutenant would stand two paces behind the rear of the centre of the first section. The sergeant major would stand in line of the file closers, behind the right of the second section. The second sergeant would stand to the left of the second section, in the same line, except in the leftmost platoon of the battalion, when he would stand to the left of the front rank and act as the left hand guide for the battalion. In 1791 each company only had two sergeants on a peace footing, with a third added when the regiment was put on a war footing. This third sergeant would stand behind the left of the first section. Later, a fourth sergeant was added, located behind the right of the first section. This line of officers and sub-officers was known as the rank of the file-closers (*serre-file*); in other words, the men who were at the rear of the files.

[**See also:** 24. Captain; 27. Sergeant major; 142. Tactical Organisation & Drill (introduction); 143. Tactical composition of a battalion.]

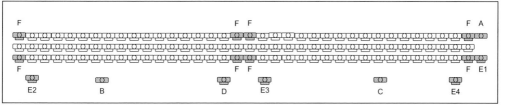

**Diagram A**: Fusilier platoon 1794.
Key: A captain; B lieutenant; C sub-lieutenant; D sergeant-major; E1 first (replacement) sergeant; E2 second sergeant (on leftmost platoon, the sergeant stood on the left of the front rank); E3 third sergeant; E4 fourth sergeant, F corporals.

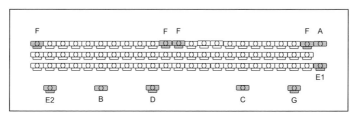

**Diagram B**: Grenadier platoon 1794.
Key: A captain; B lieutenant; C sub-lieutenant; D sergeant-major; E1 first (replacement) sergeant; E2 second sergeant (on leftmost platoon, the sergeant stood on the left of the front rank); F corporals; G quartermaster corporal.

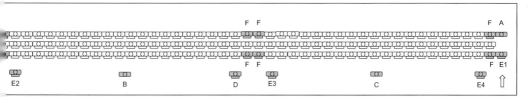

**Diagram C**: Infantry platoon 1808.
Key: A1 captain; B lieutenant; C sub-lieutenant; D sergeant-major; E1 first (replacement) sergeant; E2 second sergeant (on leftmost platoon, the sergeant stood on the left of the front rank); E3 third sergeant; E4 fourth sergeant, F corporals.

## 145. Assembling the battalion

The adjutant was responsible for ensuring the battalion was properly assembled under arms. Once the platoons were formed, the sergeant majors would go to the adjutant and inform him how many files their platoons were composed of. It was the adjutant's task to equalise the strength of the platoons. This was extremely important. For a battalion to perform manoeuvres in an orderly fashion, and to spread the number of muskets evenly along the line, each platoon had to contain an equal number of men. Over the course of a campaign, casualties were unlikely to be evenly spread, so the adjutant's first task every day on campaign was to borrow men from the stronger platoons to reinforce the weaker ones.

When the sergeant majors had reported the strength of their platoons, the adjutant would use a pencil to work out the average strength of them. He would then make the necessary adjustments, taking the surplus files or individuals from the left of the strongest platoons and marching them to the rear and centre of the battalion, and then directing them to the left of those platoons with a shortfall. It is not stated explicitly, but it appears logical the substitutes returned to their parent company (and their ordinaries) when the battalion was dismissed each day.

A skilful adjutant ought to be able to equalise a battalion of 800 men in less than five minutes. Once the task was completed, the adjutant would ensure the men in each platoon were assembled in height order and ensure the three ranks were correctly aligned. From memory he would make the roll call of the sub-officers, musicians, fifers, drummers and sappers, ensuring they were all correctly placed in the line. If sergeants were missing, the adjutant would decide which corporals would take their place.

As a final measure, two sub-officers would be selected from among the best marchers to perform the role of general guides (*guides généraux*), who were also known under the generic term *jalonneurs*. One would be placed behind the right hand platoon, the other behind the leftmost platoon, both taking position in the rank of file closers. These sub-officers, and the standard bearer in the middle, would be the three guides of the battalion.

A note should be added about equalising elite companies. Prior to 1808, when grenadier companies were with their battalion they were not equalised with the fusilier platoons. However, if the grenadier platoons were united, then they would equalise amongst themselves. After 1808, when elite and centre companies were the same strength, and in regiments where the elite companies formed divisions with centre companies, then they had to equalise with centre companies in order for the divisions to work correctly. There was a precedent for this from the 18th century, with so called false-grenadiers (*grenadiers postiches*). These were officers and men who would cover absences in the elite company.

[See also: 7. Lieutenant colonel; 8. Battalion commander; 9. Adjutant major; 16. Adjutant; 143. Tactical composition of a battalion; 146. Placement of the colour guard; 147. Placement of drummers and musicians; 148. Placement of sappers; 149. Tactical placement of senior officers and staff; 164. Battalion formations and manoeuvres; 231. Battle tactics.]

## 146. Placement of the colour guard

In 1791 the colour guard (*la garde du drapeau*) was composed of a sergeant major who carried the flag and the eight quartermaster corporals from the fusilier companies. The sergeant major stood in the front rank, flanked by two quartermaster corporals, with the other six formed behind in two ranks. The colour guard formed the left three files of the second section of the fourth platoon and was considered part of

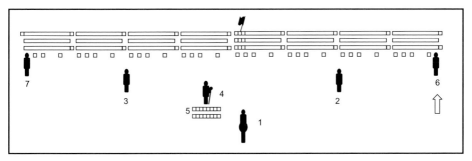

**Diagram D**: Battalion in line 1791 (grenadiers detached)
Key: 1 – Lieutenant-colonel (battalion commander); 2 – Adjutant-major; 3 – Adjutant; 4 –
Drum-major; 5 – Drummers (note: musicians would be behind); 6 – general guide (right);
7 – general guide (left).

this section. When the platoons were equalised, this meant the colour was actually very slightly off-centre.

When battalions were reduced to four fusilier companies in 1808, the colour guard formed the left of the second section of the second fusilier platoon. The colour guard was composed of an eagle bearer and two assistants in the front rank; a middle rank composed of one quartermaster corporal from the fusilier companies, and two corporals chosen for their precision under arms and in marching; with the remaining three fusilier quartermaster corporals in the rear rank. The quartermaster corporals from the elite companies never formed part of the colour guard because they were liable to be detached from the battalion at any instant. Instead the grenadier *fourrier* would stand between the sub-lieutenant and the fourth sergeant, while the voltigeur *fourrier* would stand behind the left of the second section (i.e. in the place normally reserved for the second sergeant, when this sub-officer was not required to act as the left hand guide of the battalion). The colour guards for ensigns were located in the same manner, but the front rank was formed by a sergeant major, and two sergeants.

[**See also:** 13. Eagle bearer; 17. Second and third eagle bearers; 45. Ensign bearer; 94. Flags and eagles; 164. Battalion formations and manoeuvres; 169. Volley firing; 233. Duties of sub-officers in battle.]

## 147. Placement of drummers and musicians

The drummers of each battalion were formed in two ranks, fifteen places behind the fifth platoon of their battalion. The drum major would be located with the drummers of the first battalion, the drum corporal at the head of the second battalion's drummers. The musicians were placed two paces behind the drummers of the first battalion.

[**See also:** 18. Drum major; 19. Drum corporal; 20. Chief musician; 37. Drummer; 38. Cornetist; 145. Assembling the battalion.]

Platoon of drummers being led by a drum major. Note the drummers all carry musketoons.

## 148. Placement of sappers

Every battalion had a number of infantry sappers, but their placement in the line was not discussed in the regulations. When a regiment was formed in line, the general solution was to place them in the intervals between battalions, level with the third rank, so they did not get in the line of sight between the guides responsible for maintaining alignment. When the regiment was on the march, or

Musician, drum major and sapper (circa 1813). Note the leather case for the axe underneath the haversack. (Beyer)

in the presence of the enemy, all the sappers in the regiment would unite on the right in two ranks, at a distance equalling the front of one platoon (approximately twenty metres). On parades they would march in front of the drum major, at a similar distance.

After 18 February 1808, each battalion was permitted four sappers and a corporal. An alternative location for the sappers was with the general guides on either side of the battalion. The corporal and two sappers would take position two paces behind the right hand guide, while the remaining two sappers stood behind the left guide.

[See also: 46. Sapper; 164. Battalion formations and manoeuvres; 165. Infantry squares.]

## 149. Tactical placement of senior officers and staff

The colonel was mounted and placed thirty paces behind the rank of the file closers, opposite the centre of the interval which separated the two battalions of his regiment. The battalion commanders were also mounted and were located twenty paces behind the file closers of their battalion, directly behind the file of standard bearer. When a regiment expanded to four battalions in 1808, the colonel would position himself between the second and third battalions, if all four were present. If there were less than four battalions present, he would position himself behind the eagle bearers (i.e. behind the centre of the first battalion).

The adjutant major and adjutant of each battalion would be located on foot, eight paces behind the file closers' rank, directly behind the centre of the left and right half battalions respectively. When a second adjutant was added to the battalion staff in 1808, the second would place himself eight paces behind the second file of the grenadier platoon so as to act as the right hand guide of the battalion.

[See also: 5. Colonel; 7. Lieutenant colonel; 8. Battalion commander; 9. Adjutant major; 16. Adjutant.]

## 150. Two rank formations

The French could adopt a two rank system in several circumstances, for example, during peacetime when the battalion was not on a war footing; if casualties reduced the size of the platoon significantly; or perhaps as a ruse to make a body of troops look larger than it actually was. In the latter case, the third rank would be used to extend the number of files in each platoon.

Perhaps the most notable example of this tactic can be found in a letter from Napoleon to Marshal Marmont on 13 October 1813, three days prior to the fateful battle of Leipzig: 'My intention is that you place your troops in two ranks instead of three. The third rank is of no use when firing; it is even less use with the bayonet. When one is in closed column, three divisions will form six ranks and three ranks of file closers. You will see the advantage this will have: your fire will be better; your strength will be thrice; the enemy, accustomed to seeing us in three ranks, will think our battalions are one third stronger.'

[**See also:** 143. Tactical composition of a battalion; 144. Assembling the platoon; 164. Battalion formations and manoeuvres; 167. Musketry (Introduction).]

## 151. Composition of detachments

When on active service, a regiment was often required to provide men for various detachments. The structure of a detachment was different to the normal tactical unit:

- A full detachment was composed of eight service squads, each composed of eight men. The detachment would be led by a captain, lieutenant or sub-lieutenant, two sergeants, four corporals and four chosen men (corporals after this grade fell out of use). The detachment would also have a drummer.
- A half detachment had four service squads with a drummer, a lieutenant or sub-lieutenant, one sergeant, two corporals and two chosen men.
- A quarter detachment was formed of two service squads, commanded by a sergeant, one corporal, and a chosen man.
- A petty detachment was formed of one service squad and a corporal.

Where there were several regiments in a place, each provided the full complement for a detachment – they never mixed officers and men from different regiments.

[**See also:** 181. Duties & routines (introduction).]

*Chapter 20*

# Arms Drill

## 152. Tone of command

Commands were given in an animated voice, the volume of which was in proportion to the number of men who were being addressed. Like so much else at this time, the manner of giving commands varied between corps, depending on the whim of the commander, and the tradition of the corps. Generally speaking, each command was broken into a cautionary word, followed by a word of execution. The motions were executed quickly, but precisely.

[**See also:** 7. Lieutenant colonel 9. Adjutant major.]

## 153. Position of the soldier without arms

Before a recruit could carry a musket, it was first necessary for him to learn to stand like a soldier. The position of the soldier at attention was described as follows: heels on the same line, close together but comfortable; toes angled out, approximately forty-five degrees from centre; knees straight but not locked; the body perpendicular to the hips, leaning slightly forward; shoulders back; arms hanging naturally; elbows touching the body; the palms facing outwards, with the little finger of each hand touching the rear of the trouser seam; head up without strain; the chin inclined, but without covering the neck; the eyes fixed on the ground about fifteen paces ahead. If the heels were not placed on the same line, the shoulders would not be square. The heels were not required to touch because bowlegged men with large leg muscles would not be able to do this. The purpose of the soldier leaning forward slightly was to achieve a degree of equilibrium, countering the weight of the pack and equipment. Once this martial pose was perfected, the recruit would be shown how to turn to the right and left on his heels, and how to make a half turn to the right.

[**See also:** 152. Tone of command; 154. The manual exercise; 155. Marching & manoeuvres (introduction).]

## 154. The manual exercise (*maniement des armes*)

Other than loading (which is dealt with separately), soldiers were trained in a variety of techniques for carrying their musket, placing it on the floor, presenting arms, fixing bayonets, and so on. The main commands are given below along with their nearest contemporary English equivalent.

- **Shoulder arms** (*portez vos armes*): the soldier at attention would carry the musket with the stock resting against the left shoulder and the butt supported in the left hand. The left arm was left very slightly crooked to enable the soldier to flex the joint very subtly. If the arm was fully extended, it would very quickly tire from supporting the weight of the musket.
- **Present arms** (*présentez vos armes*): the musket was held in front of the body, the barrel over the left eye, the ramrod channel facing outwards, the lock level with the last button on the jacket (*veste*). The right hand held the musket just below the trigger guard, the left hand gripping the stock with the little finger resting on the frizzen spring, and the thumb pointing upwards along the barrel.
- **Order arms** (*reposez sur vos armes*): from the shoulder arms position, the soldier would straighten the left arm, while reaching across the chest and grasping the musket at the second band above the lock. The weight of the musket was transferred into the right hand, and was then brought across the body and lowered to the right side of the body, with the ramrod facing outwards. The musket was then gently lowered the last remaining inches to the floor so it did not strike the ground hard. From this position the platoon commander could order *en place – repos* (stand at ease). This allowed men to relax, but did not allow them to break ranks. Typically they were required to keep one foot in the correct position.
- **Arms inspection** (*inspection des armes*): from the order arms (*reposez* …) position, the soldier would make a turn and a half on the left heel, carrying the right foot six inches behind the left foot in a perpendicular line. The barrel of the musket would be inclined, the ramrod turned inwards towards the body. The bayonet would be withdrawn from its scabbard and attached to the musket; then the ramrod would be withdrawn and inserted into the barrel. The inspecting officer or sub-officer would then walk along the ranks and successively inspect each man. As the inspector stood before the soldier, the latter would raise the musket in his right hand, bring it across the body and then grip the stock with his left hand between the band over the ramrod channel and the frizzen spring. The musket would be held so the left hand was level with the chin. The inspector would seize the weapon and then inspect it, checking the touch hole, the lock and so on. He then handed it back to the soldier who removed the ramrod and then returned to the order arms position.
- **Spring ramrod** (*baguette dans le canon*): This was a simpler method of inspecting the men's muskets, and could be used to check for fouled cartridges. The soldier would put the ramrod into the barrel as with the arms inspection

method, but would then return to the order arms position. The inspector would walk down the line checking the muskets visually. If he believed a musket might be loaded, he could stop and raise the ramrod up a little and let it drop. If he did not hear a metallic strike, this indicated the barrel was fouled. As the inspector passed, each man would repeat the first movement to remove the ramrod.

- **Ground arms** (*vos armes à terre*): from the order arms (*reposez ...*) position the soldier would turn the musket ninety degrees so the lock faced towards the body. The soldier would then seize the corner of his cartridge pouch with the left hand, then advance the left foot as if about to march off. Instead, the soldier would bend forward and place the musket on the ground, the lock facing upwards. The soldier would then recover his position and let go of the cartridge pouch. The reverse of this movement was *relevez vos armes* (Take up arms).
- **Support arms** (*l'arme au bras*): This was the habitual position of the soldier on guard duty, during movement, or in battle. From the shoulder arms (*portez ...*) position, the soldier would move his right hand across the body and take the weight of the musket off the left hand. The soldier would then bend his left arm, so the lock of the musket rested in the crook of the left arm. The right hand would then fall back to the right side of the body.
- **Slope arms** (*l'arme à volonté*): on route marches this command allowed the men to carry their musket over whichever shoulder they pleased, in one or both hands. The only requirement was for the extremity of the barrel to be pointing upwards (a precaution against accidents).
- **Remove bayonet** (*remettez la baïonnette*): from the shoulder arms (*portez ...*) position the soldier would seize the musket with the right hand as if going to the order arms (*reposez ...*) position. The left hand would seize the barrel higher up and then place the musket gently on the ground. The bayonet would be removed from the scabbard and fixed to the musket. The soldier would then reverse the movement and return to the shoulder arms position. This movement could also be performed from the order arms position, without shouldering the musket.
- **Secure arms** (*l'arme sous le bras gauche*): in wet weather this position allowed the soldier to invert his musket, lowering the barrel towards the floor and tucking the stock under the left armpit. This would prevent the barrel from filling with water and also gave some protection to the firing mechanism. It was also the position for carrying the musket in funeral processions. This position could not be adopted without first removing the bayonet.
- **Fix bayonet** (*baïonnette au canon*): this could be performed from either the shoulder or order arms positions. Once the bayonet was fixed, the men would return to the original position. The reverse movement was *remettez la baïonnette* after which the bayonet would be returned to its scabbard.
- **Charge bayonet** (*croisez la baïonnette*): from the shoulder arms (*portez ...*) position, the soldier would turn the musket inwards and grip the stock two inches below the lock. The soldier would turn his body to the right, forming his feet into a 'T'; right foot behind the left. At the same time the musket would be allowed to fall forwards. The left hand would catch the musket just forward

of the first *capucine*, the band located at the termination of the ramrod channel. The right hand would press the stock into the hip, and the left hand would hold the musket at an acute angle, the tip of the bayonet level with the eye.

- **Trail arms** (*descendez vos armes*): the midpoint of the musket would be taken in the right hand and carried towards the right of the body. The purpose of this command was to enable the men to pass through wooded terrain without snagging their bayonets, or to use the musket to help them climb steep banks or ditches.
- **Pile arms** (*armes au faisceau*): since the introduction of the bayonet, it was common for regiments to stack their arms in a *faisceau* (lit. a bundle of sticks) when resting on field exercises or when in the bivouac. When a battalion was in line formation, the commander could order *mettez vos armes en faisceaux*. At this command the platoon commander would order his men to form a pyramidal stack of three muskets for each file, so the stacks formed a line the same width and alignment as the battalion.
- **Advance arms** (*portez l'arme comme sergent*): this position saw the musket carried on the right of the body, the barrel towards the shoulder and the right hand gripping the lock, with the thumb and index finger round the trigger guard.

Plate showing the cross bayonets position. Soldiers would have to press together to ensure the third rank's bayonet extended beyond the front rank.

Officers also had their own version of arms drill for holding their épées. When in ranks, the épée was carried in the right hand, the hilt level with the right hip and the blade resting on the right shoulder. When out of ranks, the hilt was in the right hand, placed forward of the right hip, the blade in the left hand, the point exceeding the four fingers, with the thumb along the blade, the left elbow bent, the forearm a little in front, the left hand four inches lower than the left shoulder. To salute, the épée was raised so the blade was perpendicular, with the flat of the blade over the right eye, with the guard level with the right nipple. The blade was then lowered in a graceful motion, so the right hand ended up by the right thigh with the blade pointing downwards. When the dignitary passed, the officer would reverse the motion and return to the habitual position.

[**See also:** 86. Musket; 92. Officer's épée; 152. Tone of command; 210. Maintaining the musket; 212. Training (introduction); 213. Basic training.]

Fighting on the barricades towards the end of the imperial period. A wounded drummer passes cartridges to an officer decorate with the cross of the Legion of Honour.

*Chapter 21*

# Marching & Manoeuvres

## 155. Introduction

In order for great formations of troops to march in a cohesive manner, a near-mechanical form of marching was required. Such a system of movement had been perfected by the army of Frederick the Great and this had inspired the French in their great evaluation of the military sciences after the Seven Years War. Two types of march were recognised: the cadenced step and the non-cadenced step. The former was where soldiers all stepped off on the same foot and advanced by a set distance at the same pace; the latter was performed while in column of route and was made indifferently from one foot or the other. At the same time there were a number of different cadences which allowed the movement to be accelerated or slowed as required.

The style of march employed by the French was not a goosestep or a stomp, but a graceful and energy-efficient step. At the cautionary order 'forward' (*en avant*), the soldier would put his weight on the right leg, and at the second command 'march' (*marche*), would step off with his left foot, projecting it forward with the toes pointing downward and the knee turned somewhat outwards. The foot remained low towards the ground and travelled over the shortest possible line. The foot was placed flatly on the ground, without stamping, at a distance of two feet (French) measured from heel to heel, with the whole weight of the body coming to rest on the forward foot. The soldier did not move his arms from his side during the movement; his shoulders remained square and his head did not turn. In order to prevent the line breaking apart or from being compressed, each soldier maintained light elbow contact with the fellow on his right hand side (or left if the 'guide' was on the left flank).

The French also employed an oblique step which allowed platoons to advance diagonally while remaining parallel to the line of advance. When making the oblique to the right, the right foot would be placed two feet from the left foot at an angle approaching forty-five degrees. The left foot would then be placed 17 inches (French) in front of the right foot. When making the oblique step, soldiers would turn their right foot inwards slightly in order to prevent the left shoulder coming forwards and breaking the line. The left oblique followed exactly the same principles but was led by the left foot.

## 156. Ordinary pace (*pas ordinaire*)

This pace was used in everyday situations and particularly in training sessions for new recruits. At the end of the Seven Years War the 'ordinary pace' of French infantry was just 60 steps per minute, i.e. one step per second. Recruits were then taught to march by making them walk opposite a pendulum which determined the pace by its oscillations. In 1766 the ordinary pace changed to 70 steps per minute; however recruits were still trained at the 60 step pace. The regulation of 1 August 1791 increased the ordinary pace to 76 steps per minute, bringing it in line with the Prussian model. This pace remained unchanged throughout the period.

[**See also:** 155. Marching & manoeuvres (introduction); 37. Drummer; 162. Comparison chart of movement rates; 175. Older firing systems; 178. Deploying skirmishers; 231. Battle tactics.]

## 157. Accelerated pace (*pas accéléré*)

The 1 August 1791 regulation also introduced an accelerated pace of 100 steps per minute. Napoleon later ordered all manoeuvres should take place at this speed. It should not be confused with the old manoeuvring pace (*pas de manoeuvre*) which was measured at 120 steps per minute.

[**See also:** 144. Assembling the platoon; 155. Marching & manoeuvres (introduction); 162. Comparison chart of movement rates; 163. Platoon manoeuvres; 164. Battalion formations and manoeuvres; 175. Older firing systems.]

## 158. Charge pace (*pas de charge*)

The charge pace was measured at 120 steps per minute. This was the equivalent of the outmoded 'double pace' (*pas redoublez*) and the 'manoeuvring pace' (*pas de manoeuvre*). When the charge pace was ordered at the cross bayonets position, the ranks would press together and the men take smaller steps so as not to trip one another. The file closers would also press forward ensuring the platoon was as dense as possible at the moment of impact with the enemy (Lejeune's depiction of Chiclana shows the sergeants turning their muskets horizontally and using them to form a buttress across the haversacks of the rear rank).

[**See also:** 20. Chief musician; 37. Drummer; 162. Comparison chart of movement rates; 164. Battalion formations and manoeuvres; 166. Bayonet charges.]

## 159. Route pace (*pas de route*)

When marching from one place to the next, infantry regiments could adopt a more relaxed form of march known as the route pace. Before setting out, each battalion would form a column of sections (i.e. half a platoon frontage). As the column moved off, the ranks would open slightly and this allowed the men to carry their muskets over either shoulder at slope arms (l'*arme à volonté*). More importantly, the men were not required to keep step. In other words, the march became a walk which averaged 85–90 paces per minute. It is unlikely many European roads were wide enough to accommodate a full half platoon, so the files which extended beyond the edge of the road fell back and reformed behind the rest of the section. If the road widened, or the section halted, the men who dropped out would quickly scamper back to the correct place. To uneducated passers by the column of sections might have appeared somewhat shambolic. However, there would always be a halt before entering a town to allow the stragglers to catch up, and for the ranks to be dressed.

[See also: 53. Uniform – general description (introduction); 154. The manual exercise; 155. Marching & manoeuvres (introduction); 162. Comparison chart of movement rates; 164. Battalion formations and manoeuvres; 221. On the march; 222. Halts on the march.]

## 160. At the run (*pas de course*)

This pace was described by the great theoretician, Count de Guibert in his 1772 *Essai général de tactique* as being a triple pace, something in the region of 200–250 steps per minute. In theory one could order a regiment to move at *pas de course*, but it was generally accepted the unit's cohesion would quickly fall to pieces. Instead it was adopted in the wars of the Revolution as the pace used by skirmishers.

[See also: 162. Comparison chart of movement rates; 176. Skirmishing (introduction); 179. Skirmishers: movement and communication; 180. General remarks on skirmishing; 218. Gymnastic and fitness exercises; 233. Duties of sub-officers in battle.]

## 161. Miscellaneous paces

During the wars of the Revolution, General Custine instructed Adjutant General Meunier to introduce a new pace in the French Army of the North. This became known as the 'unique pace' (*pas unique*) and was 90 steps per minute, but with a 26 inch stride, rather than usual 24 inches. This pace does not appear to have been widely adopted. Separately, in the month of *Brumaire XII* the minister of war gave a new instruction on camping. Sub-officers pacing out a camp would take a metre long stride called the metric step (*pas mètrique*). An instruction to provide tents to the soldiers may have been more useful.

[See also: 226. Arrival at camp.]

## 162. Comparison chart of movement rates

Table 17.

| Pace | Cadence<br>(steps per minute) | Distance*<br>(metres per minute) | Km<br>(per hour) |
|---|---|---|---|
| Ordinary | 76 | 49.4 | 2.9 |
| Accelerated | 100 | 65 | 3.9 |
| Charge** | 120 | 78 | 4.6 |
| Run** | 240 | 156 | 9.3 |
| Route | 90 | 58.5 | 3.5 |

* The 2 foot pace is measured at 0.65 m.

** It was generally acknowledged these paces could only be maintained over short distances.

## 163. Platoon manoeuvres

When operating as part of a battalion, each platoon had to manoeuvre in a cohesive formation. To properly align the platoon, the first three files of each platoon would be designated as guides (*guides* – not to be confused with the general guides). The rest of the platoon would align on the guides, with their heads slightly inclined to the right, looking down the line for the guides. The captain would ensure the front rank was straight; the replacement sergeant would observe the centre and rear ranks. Each file would be numbered. If the captain or sergeant were not satisfied with the alignment they would call out the file number and direct the man to *rentrez* or *sortez* as required. At the command '*fixe*' all the soldiers would turn their heads to face directly forward. Soldiers would maintain light elbow contact to the man in the direction of the guide, but were cautioned not to press in that direction too heavily.

Perhaps the simplest platoon manoeuvre to describe is the *conversion*, whereby the platoon would wheel to the left, or (if the guide was on the left of the platoon), to the right. Wheels could be made from a fixed pivot or a moveable one, if the platoon was in motion and required a change of direction in march. On a fixed pivot wheel to the left, the soldiers marched while looking towards the wheeling flank. The soldier on the right of the line would take an ordinary two-foot pace, while the pivot man marked time, gradually turning in the direction of the wheeling flank. The soldier on the right would maintain elbow contact with the man to his left, without pushing or pressing inwards. When poorly executed, the middle of the platoon might buckle because of the pressure of the men on the right pushing inwards. Equally the platoon might split in two if the men on the right did not maintain sufficient contact with the left. If the *conversion* was made while on the march, the same principles applied, except the pivot maintained forward momentum by taking a six inch pace and tracing out an arc as the wheel was performed. If the pivot did not take this precaution, the distances between the platoons would not have been maintained.

If the guide was on the right of the platoon, and the commander wished to turn to the right, he could execute a turn (*tournez*) in that direction. At the command 'march', the platoon commander would turn at an angle up to ninety degrees and keep marching. The whole platoon would also make a turn, anticipating the likely direction of march, but unlike with a wheel, the platoon would be momentarily fragmented. The soldiers on the outer edge of the platoon would accelerate until they caught up and the alignment was restored. Turns could be made to the left, if the guide was on that side of the platoon.

[**See also:** 144. Assembling the platoon; 152. Tone of command; 164. Battalion level manoeuvres; 154. The manual exercise; 155. Marching & manoeuvres (introduction); 169. Volley firing; 178. Deploying skirmishers.]

## 164. Battalion formations and manoeuvres

When a battalion wished to advance in line, at the command 'forward' the front rank of the colour guard would advance six paces forwards. At the same time the second rank of the colour guard would advance to fill the gap in the front rank, thus maintaining the interval in the front rank. The alignments on the flanks were maintained by the two general guides (sub-officers on the extreme right and left of the battalion), who also advanced six paces ahead of the battalion so they could view the colour guard.

Of course, manoeuvres in line were notoriously difficult over anything but short distances, so the preferred formation was to form a column for manoeuvring. Columns could be formed on the right, left or centre of the battalion, and have a frontage of a section, platoon, or division (i.e. two platoons). The distance between each platoon or division could also vary. An open column (*colonne ouverte* or *colonne à distance entière*) maintained a sufficient interval between the platoons or divisions for the battalion to wheel perfectly into line. Columns could close up to half distance (either a section or platoon's distance, for a column of platoons, or divisions, respectively), or could form a mass (*colonne serrée en masse*). In this case the file closers would stand one pace behind their platoon, with a three pace gap between the third rank and the next platoon or division.

The 1791 regulations also allowed the formation of an attack column (*colonne d'attaque*). The attack column was first described in the ordinance of 17 February 1753, and was formed from two battalions joining together at the centre (the first division being formed of the eighth platoon of the right battalion, and the first platoon of the left battalion). This formation was used in the Seven Years War. By 1791 the attack column was formed by a single battalion only, two platoons wide, and each formed at 'section distance', in other words the distance between the divisions was the equivalent of a half a platoon. The column was formed on the centre, which is to say the fourth and fifth platoons were at the front. The troops marched at the accelerated pace when forming these columns.

Bardin describes how attack columns were used to assault enemy field works and defensive bridgeheads during the wars of the Revolution. The column would be formed five or six hundred metres from the works and would march at the accelerated pace, in a straight direction (there were no instructions for manoeuvring these columns other than forwards). The column would be preceded by skirmishers who would fire on the enemy positions, and sappers who would clear obstacles from the column's path. At seventy metres (one hundred paces) the column would accelerate to the charge pace. The attack column could either press home its charge, or redeploy into line from the centre. The advantage of the central deployment was the two lead platoons could open fire while the other platoons re-deployed back into line. The 1791 regulations recommended using the two rank firing system in this case. If the grenadiers were with their parent battalion they would typically form the tail of the column, standing at the midpoint between the two platoons forming the rear division. If they were to lead the attack, a superior officer would tell the grenadier captain to take position at the head of the column. However, once thus placed, they would prevent the lead division from opening fire. Drummers were always placed at the rear of the column.

Bardin also described a battalion column (*colonne par bataillons*), where a number of battalions were deployed into line, one behind the other, with thirty or forty paces between each. Bardin credited this innovation to Prince Eugene at the end of the 17th century, and cited examples of the tactic being used at Jemappes (1792) and perhaps erroneously at Austerlitz (1805).

The column of route (*colonne de route*) was formed by sections (i.e. half a platoon frontage). The ranks would open twice the usual distance, the men were free to

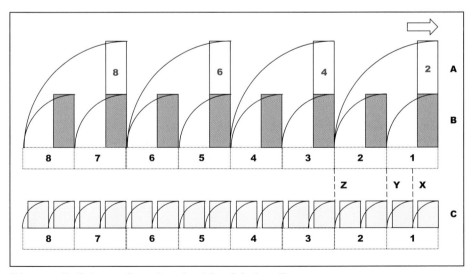

**Diagram E:** Columns, formed on the right of the battalion.
Key: A – Column of divisions; B – Column of platoons; C – Column of sections; X – section distance; Y – platoon or half distance; Z – division, or full distance.

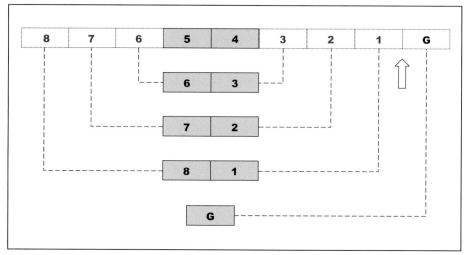

**Diagram F:** Attack column, formed on centre of battalion.

carry their muskets *à volonté*, and were not required to march in step. Unlike other formations, they were not required to be silent. If the rear of the column ever became separated, drummers at the rear would sound the *rappel*. This would cause the head of the column to halt. Bardin claimed this manner of marching was unpopular with officers because they had set positions and this prevented them from chatting to one another. When troops marched in file, the officers could congregate to the side of the platoon.

[**See also:** 143. Tactical composition of a battalion; 162. Comparison chart of movement rates; 163. Platoon manoeuvres; 165. Infantry squares; 166. Bayonet charges; 169. Volley firing; 231. Battle tactics.]

## 165. Infantry squares

The square was a four sided formation (often rectangular in appearance) used predominantly as a defensive formation against cavalry, or during a retreat. Bardin described the formation as a mobile citadel. Squares could be formed of a single battalion or larger formations such as brigades. They might be six ranks deep or three ranks deep. Larger formations might have their corners protected by grenadiers, or incorporate regimental artillery. Squares might also be protected by skirmish screens. The commanding officer was located in the centre of the square from where he could direct its fire.

The formation of squares as a defence against cavalry was described in the final part of the regulations of 1 August 1791, titled *Evolutions of the Line*. This instruction supposed the dispositions against cavalry attack would be made at brigade level. If four battalions marching in a column of divisions through open country were harassed by enemy cavalry, the battalion columns would first close up to a section's distance. The regimental artillery (as existed in 1791) would be placed level with the interval between the battalions, about eight or ten paces off either flank. If it was felt necessary, men from the rear rank of each battalion column could be deployed on the flanks to fire at any cavalry coming within range.

The march of the column would continue, unless the enemy cavalry appeared in strength and began forming for a charge. In this case the column would halt and the skirmishers would be called in. The second division from the head of the column would close up to within one pace of the file closers of the leading division. At the rear of the column, the last division would close up on the division in front of it. All the divisions in between would wheel by section (i.e. half platoon) left and right respectively to face towards the open flanks, one section behind the other. They would align on the front and rear divisions. The two divisions at the rear would turn about. Grenadier sections would be placed to cover the flanks of the two leading and rearmost divisions and use the gun limbers (*avant-trains*) as barricades to protect them. If grenadiers were unavailable, fusiliers would be drawn from the third rank of the interior sections. The intervals between the battalions would be protected by artillery, with the caissons forming a barricade behind them. The general and senior officers, drummers, and musicians remained in the interior of the square.

If the enemy cavalry charged, the outermost sections would commence a two rank firing, while the innermost sections remained passive at *l'arme au bras*. If the enemy cavalry pressed on, the senior commander would command 'interior sections, close on mass' (*sections intérieurs, serrez en masse*). At this caution, the file closers behind the front sections would quickly move out of the way, and take position behind the interior section. The commander would order 'march', at which the interior sections would advance to within one pace of the rear rank of the exterior section. The front section would continue to fire until the enemy was almost on them, and then present bayonets. The rear three ranks would make ready, and when they saw the faces of the enemy cavaliers, would fire point blank over the heads of the front three ranks, then cross bayonets. All six ranks would press together so as to better withstand the shock. If the charge had been repulsed (which was likely, unless artillery had significantly weakened a part of the formation), the battalions could reform their columns and continue on their way.

If the troops were in line formation when threatened, the 1791 regulations called on them to form column with a section distance before then deploying into the square described above. There was also a simplified means of forming a square type formation, one that was particularly recommended to isolated battalion columns menaced by cavalry. The column would quickly close up in a mass. The front two divisions would face forwards, the rear two turn about. In the two middle divisions, everyone would face left or right and the three files on either flank would commence two rank firing. The practicality of this tactic is obvious, but it made a terribly inviting target for enemy artillery.

Bardin expanded on the subject of squares in his infantry manual, describing so–called 'Egyptian squares' – a tactic dating from the French expedition of Egypt

(1798–1801). These squares were only three men deep and could be executed by battalions formed in platoons or divisions, and took the form of an oblong. They could be formed while already in a column, or while in line of battle. Essentially the process described was very similar to the 1791 square. The front division would halt and form the front of the square. The second division would close up to within platoon distance, and then break: the right platoon would wheel ninety degrees to the right, the left platoon, the same to the left. The third sub-division would do the same and thus the sides of the square would be formed. Finally the rear division would close up the gap then make a half turn to right, thus facing outwards from the square and forming the reverse face. All the file closers, drummers, musicians, sappers, and superior officers would enter into the square. In a variation of this, two battalions could combine to make a larger square.

[**See also:** 4. Regimental artillery; 7. Lieutenant colonel; 90. Bayonet;154. The manual exercise; 170. Two rank firing; 172. Firing by rank against cavalry; 176. Skirmishing (introduction); 233. Duties of sub-officers in battle.]

**I**

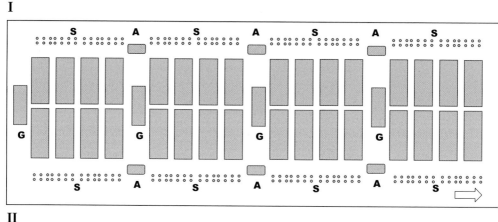

**II**

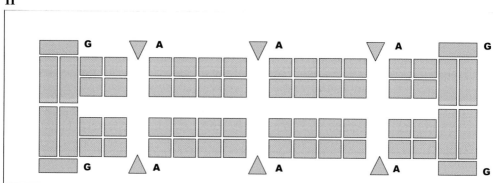

**Diagram G**: Anti-cavalry formations (1 August 1791).
I. Column of four battalions closed up with skirmishers deployed.
II. Square of four battalions with artillery deployed.
Key: A – artillery; G – grenadier platoons; S – skirmishers deployed.

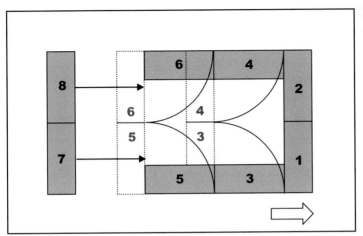

**Diagram H:**
Column of divisions formed in square.

## 166. Bayonet charges

French infantry considered themselves almost invincible when it came to the use of the bayonet in close quarters fighting. It was believed bayonet attacks suited the French temperament, but despite this, no official training regime for bayonet fighting was recommended. As with many aspects of the regiment, it was left to individual colonels to decide if a school should be established for practicing the handling of the bayonet (*maniement de la baïonnette*), much in the same way as the colonel might have his men instructed in fencing.

In a battle, if the commanding general wished to make his men advance with 'crossed bayonets', he would instruct them to adopt this position before commencing the march, ordering:

1. Regiment / battalion, forwards, charge pace (*régiment / bataillon, en avant, pas de charge*)
2. March (*marche*).

At this command the three ranks would press closely together, and move forward precipitously, taking shortened steps so as not to trip over one another. The file closers would also close up behind the third rank.

The moment of impact is rarely described simply because it rarely occurred. Either the advancing force was shot to pieces and lost its cohesion before the moment of impact, or the defending force did not stand to meet the charge. When two adversaries did meet, the result is unimaginable. The combat became one not of skill, but of momentum and push; at some point breaking up into a series of individual combats, with bayonets, side arms, inverted muskets and fists.

[See also: 90. Bayonet; 150. Two rank formations; 154. The manual exercise; 158. Charge pace; 173. Firing from the cross-bayonets position.]

*Chapter 22*

# Musketry

## 167. Introduction

Prior to the outbreak of war in 1792 the French Army had developed a series of complex firing systems in order to deliver volleys as effectively and efficiently as possible, using all three ranks in the process. These volleys could be delivered by platoon, half battalion or battalion. Latterly Napoleon attempted to introduce a system of firing by rank, something he considered more effective than other forms of volley fire. The French also employed a type of independent fire which consisted of a two rank 'rolling fire'; also the fire from individual skirmishers.

Although formulated with a high degree of precision, there were fundamental problems with three rank firing solutions. Experience in the field demonstrated the impracticality of making the front rank kneel in order for the middle and rear ranks to fire over their heads. Placing great emphasis on shock action, the French Army were generally unwilling to adopt a two rank formation or to employ the third rank as a reserve, or pool of skirmishers – solutions which were adopted by other nations. The result of these shortcomings was, according to Bardin, that in action, once the order to open fire had been issued, men would blaze away at will with very little control regardless of them being in ranks or detached as skirmishers. This sort of *feu de billebaude* (chaotic firing) was accepted as being the norm for the French infantry.

Bardin admitted the French never matched the British in musketry. In his opinion, the British trained more regularly, put greater resources into target practice and had more reliable munitions. French musketry on the other hand failed to produce any great effect despite their musket being, in Bardin's opinion 'without contradiction, far superior to those of other nations'. Bardin's believed the primary fault lay with poor instruction and training. Too many soldiers valued the volume and rapidity of fire against precise aiming. French military theoreticians agreed unanimously that rapid fire was the cause of poor aim. If soldiers were trained to place their faith in the speed of loading they would rush and probably become more nervous in the face of the enemy. Not only this, rapid firing caused the musket barrels to overheat and become fouled, and caused the men to expend their ammunition prematurely. Even if soldiers did take the time to aim, they often had the bad habit of aiming at the centre of the opponent's body regardless of the range. The result of this was musket balls all too often did nothing but plough up fields, or whistle harmlessly over their opponents' heads.

## 168. Loading procedure

The maximum rate of fire when firing at will, using ball cartridge was three or four shots a minute, properly rammed, with priming charge applied; although it was apparently possible for a highly trained soldier to load and fire up to six times per minute, even if using a ramrod. There were three methods of commanding men to load: in twelve motions, in quick time, or at will. There was no difference in the procedure of loading, only the number of commands given. Recruits were taught the slower, 'twelve motions of loading' (*charge en douze temps*) version first, and once they had mastered the various moves, they were allowed to progress with decreasing interruption.

The twelve motion loading procedure taught the soldier the most efficient way of loading the musket, with the fewest moves and without disturbing his neighbours. The procedure can be summarised by the following steps:

1. **Load arms** (*chargez vos armes*): In the first motion, the man would half face to the right, forming his feet into a 'T', and turn the musket into his body with the lock facing outwards and the right hand gripping the narrowest part of the stock. This motion threw the right shoulder backwards and created a channel for the muskets of the rear two ranks to fall into. On the second motion the musket was allowed to sink into a slanted position with the stock pressed against the body by the right forearm two inches below the breast. The left hand supported the barrel, which was held so the top of it was level with the eyes.
2. **Open pan** (*ouvrez – le bassinet*): The soldier would flick open the cover over the pan with his thumb and then the right hand would pass to the cartridge pouch, lifting the outer flap.
3. **Handle cartridge** (*prenez – la cartouche*): A cartridge would be seized between the two fore-fingers and thumb and brought to the mouth ready to be bitten open.
4. **Tear cartridge** (*déchirez – la cartouche*): The top of the cartridge was bitten off and the hand lowered bringing the cartridge to the pan.
5. **Prime** (*amorcez*): The soldier was allowed to glance downwards while a small amount of powder was poured into the priming pan. After priming, the third and little fingers would rest against the back of the pan preparing to close it.
6. **Shut pan** (*fermez – le bassinet*): The pan would be sprung closed and the narrow part of the stock would be seized between fingers and palm without letting go of the cartridge.
7. **Cast about** (*l'arme – a gauche*): In the first motion the right arm would stretch out, swinging the musket to the left, so the barrel was perpendicular and the stock resting against the left thigh. At the same time the foot position would change, so the weight of the body spun on the left heel with the right foot carried forward and coming to rest so the heel was against the ball of the left foot. In the second motion, the musket was gently lowered so the butt plate rested on the ground and the right hand was next to the barrel in order to insert the cartridge.

8. **Charge cartridge** (*cartouche – dans le canon*): The soldier would glance at the muzzle and pour the powder down the barrel, followed by the ball and wadding.
9. **Draw ramrod** (*tirez – la baguette*): The ramrod would be seized between thumb and forefinger and raised to the full extent of the arm. When the arm was fully extended, the soldier would quickly swap hand position, seizing the ramrod backhanded at the middle of its length. The ramrod would then be fully withdrawn from its pipe socket and inverted so the butt of the ramrod was over the muzzle. In the second motion the ramrod would be inserted into the barrel as far as where the hand gripped it.
10. **Ram down cartridge** (*bourrez*): Maintaining light pressure on the ramrod with the thumb, the right hand would run up to the top of the ramrod. The soldier would seize the tip of the ramrod and then drive it forcibly into the barrel ramming home twice, or until the charge was fully rammed home.
11. **Return ramrod** (*Remettez – la baguette*): The ramrod would be withdrawn from the barrel and seized in the middle of its length. The hand would then invert the ramrod so the tip could be inserted back into the pipe socket. The ramrod was then pushed down into the channel.
12. **Shoulder arms** (*Portez – vos armes*): The musket would be raised with the left hand as high as the shoulder. The right hand would seize the small of the stock. The left hand would fall to support the butt plate and the right hand fall to the right side of the body. The feet would be returned to their usual position.

Once this system was perfected, the soldier would move onto an abbreviated system known as loading in quick time (*charge précipitée*). The object of this exercise was to emphasise the key loading processes. At the command to load (*charge précipitée*), the soldier would complete all the motions of loading in four phases:

1. All the motions up to and including priming.
2. From closing the pan to inserting the cartridge into the barrel.
3. Withdrawing the ramrod and ramming the cartridge home.
4. Returning the ramrod and shouldering the musket.

After this, soldiers practised loading at will (*charge à volonté*). Other than the initial instruction to load, no other words of command were given until the men had reached the shoulder arms position. Instructors would point out the best and quickest soldiers were those who performed the process with coolness and without apparent hurry, because they did not interfere with the men either side of them, did not spill powder while priming, or drop their cartridges, and were able to insert the ramrod at the first attempt.

[**See also:** 67. Cocked hat; 86. Musket; 87. Carbine; 167. Musketry (introduction); 169. Volley firing; 170. Two rank firing; 173. Firing from the cross-bayonets position; 180. General remarks on skirmishing; 212. Training (introduction); 216. Target practice.]

## 169. Volley firing

Volleys were the simultaneous discharge of a group of muskets. Volleys could be fired by platoons, half battalions (sometimes referred to as 'wings') or full battalions.

Platoon firing was conducted so the firing 'rolled' along the front of the battalion in a predetermined sequence. At the command 'platoon firing' (*feu de peloton*) the captains would quickly fall out of the front rank and take position behind the centre of their companies, two paces behind the file closers. At the same time the replacement sub-officers would fall back on the same line as the file closers, opposite their usual place in the line, and the battalion's colour guard would also fall back slightly, so the front rank of the guard was in line with the third rank of the platoons either side of it.

When the command 'commence firing' (*commencez le feu*) was given by the battalion commander, the captain of the first platoon would order 'first platoon, make ready; aim; fire!' (*premier peloton; armes; joue; feu*). At the command 'make ready' the front rank would throw back their leg and kneel down on the right knee. The second and third rank men would turn their body to the right, forming their feet into a 'T'.

At the command 'aim', all three ranks lowered their muskets to the aiming position. In so doing, the third ranker took a half step to the right in order to find a channel for his musket, past the second rank man. There would then be a pause before the captain ordered the men to fire, or to return to the 'make ready' position. If the men had fired, the captain would command 'load' (*chargez*).

Immediately after the first company had fired, the captain of the third company would order his platoon to make ready, aim and fire. The fifth and then seventh companies would follow suit, each captain waiting in turn. After this, platoon fire was executed alternatively by the first and second platoons of each division. The commander of the second platoon would wait until he first saw one or two muskets shouldered before giving the command to make ready. The commander of the first platoon of the pair would likewise wait for the second to near completion before ordering a subsequent volley.

The battalion commander could also order his battalion to fire by wings or half battalions. At the command 'fire by half battalion; right half battalion, make ready ... etc. (*Feu de demi-bataillon; demi-bataillon de droite; armes ...*) the platoons of the right half of the battalion would fire first. The battalion commander would then wait until he saw muskets being shouldered after loading before ordering the left hand wing to make ready, aim and fire. Battalion fire and half battalion fire could be direct or oblique. In the latter case, the battalion commander would order 'oblique to the left / right' as required after the order 'make ready' and before 'aim'.

The battalion commander would order ceasefire by a very short roll on the drums. This was followed by a single beat on the drum (*coup de baguette*), which was the sign for the captains, replacement sub-officers and colour guard to retake their places in the line.

[**See also:** 86. Musket; 165. Infantry squares; 167. Musketry (introduction); 168. Loading procedure; 176. Skirmishing (introduction); 231. Battle tactics.]

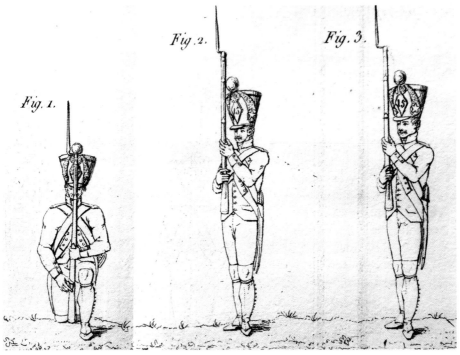

The 'make ready' position for each of the three ranks in platoon firing.

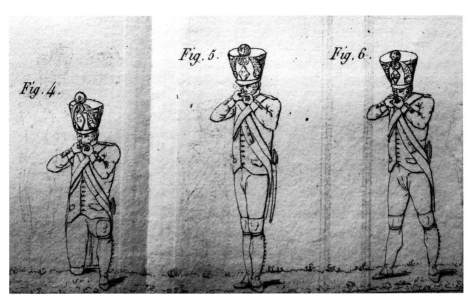

The 'aim' position. Notice how the third rank (fig.6) steps to the right to fire past the second rank (fig. 5).

### 170. Two rank firing (*Feu de deux rangs*)

The French sometimes employed a species of firing by file which was considered particularly useful against cavalry because there was no break in the firing for horsemen to exploit with a charge. The objective of this system was to allow all the muskets in a platoon to be used without the front rank having to kneel. There had been experiments with three rank firing while standing, but when soldiers wore packs and were further encumbered by their camping equipment, the men in the third rank could not always press forward far enough to avoid shooting the front ranker in the back of the head. The French had experimented with just the front two ranks firing by file (see regulation of 20 May 1788), with the third taking a pace backwards and remaining passive in reserve, but the loss of one third of the platoon's firepower was undesirable.

In this system, firing commenced from the right hand file of the platoon and without further orders rippled along the files to the left of the platoon. During this firing the front rank would remain standing, with the second rank men taking a half step to the right to fire through the channels between the files. The third rank man would remain passive in the first phase of firing, holding his musket as if about to make ready.

As soon as the front rank fired, they would load and continue firing in the same order, sending ripple after ripple along the line of the platoon. When the second ranker fired, he would turn, swap guns with the third ranker and take a second shot, causing a second ripple of fire to roll down the line. Meanwhile the third

The chaos of a fire fight 1813, in Saxony. These infantrymen appear to be using the two rank firing system. (After Raffet)

ranker would load his musket. The second ranker would then follow a sequence which went load, fire, exchange, fire, load, fire, exchange, fire, load, etc. In theory this system ensured a constant hail of balls from along the platoon.

However, there were numerous disadvantages with the system. Firstly it was very difficult to stop the men once the order to commence firing had been given. Unlike volley fire, there was no break in the firing for the men to hear the ceasefire drum roll over the sound of the gunfire. Equally, once the platoon began taking casualties, the synchronisation of fire would begin to break up. If a second rank man was hit the file was reduced to a single musket while the third ranker decided if he should break ranks (something he was not allowed to do) and move forward into the gap created in the second rank. Even if he took the initiative to do this, if the second ranker was killed or unconscious, he would first have to move the body out of the way before stepping forwards. Another problem was the third rank might strike the front rank with the bayonet while in the act of loading. Unlike platoon firing, where the motions of loading were synchronised across all three ranks, in two rank firing, the front and third ranks would almost certainly be at different stages of loading. A final consideration was the third rank man would have no idea if the gun he was loading had actually discharged or not. This could easily result in double loading and was the cause of accidents.

[**See also:** 164. Battalion formations and manoeuvres; 165. Infantry squares; 169. Volley firing; 171. Firing by rank; 172. Firing by rank against cavalry.]

## 171. Firing by rank (*feux de rang*)

Around the time of the Camp of Boulogne there was an attempt to revive an old practice of firing by rank. This system had fallen out of favour because it was impractical for the third rank to fire when the men were wearing haversacks. However, the Napoleonic version of this system was considered to have numerous advantages: the firing was as well fed as usual systems, but two thirds or five sixths of muskets were in reserve at any one point. It also allowed the front rank to 'cross bayonets' without interrupting the fire of the third rank, and it was deemed less chaotic than the two rank firing system.

The Napoleonic *feux de rang* could be executed by battalion, half battalion or platoon, but never 'at will'. In the case of battalion firing, the commanding general would command:

1.  Fire by rank by battalion (*feu de rang par bataillon*)
2. Commence firing (*commencez le feu*)

The battalion commanders would then repeat the first command, followed by the orders:

1. Battalion, make ready, third rank, – aim – fire (*bataillon, armes – troisième rang, – joue – feu*)
2. Second rank, – aim – fire (*deuxième rang, – joue – feu*)
3. First rank, – aim – fire (*premier rang, – joue – feu*)

The third rank was the first rank to fire, followed by the second, then the first. The third rank men would step six inches to the right in order to be able to aim through the gap in the files, thrusting the left leg forward and leaning into the man in front, so the barrel of the musket cleared the heads of the men in the front rank. After firing, the third rank would load automatically without any command, then go to the 'make ready' position waiting for new orders.

At the next command, the second rank would aim and fire in the normal method and load automatically, finishing in the make ready position. On the third command the first rank would follow suit. As soon as the front rank had arrived at the 'make ready' position, the battalion commander could begin the firing sequence again.

This system really came into its own with half battalion firing. Here the battalion commander could fire in succession the three ranks in one half, then, while waiting for the men to finish reloading, he could order the second half of the battalion to fire. A similar effect was produced by platoon firing, the primary difference being the command to fire was given by the individual captains.

[**See also:** 164. Battalion formations and manoeuvres; 165. Infantry squares; 172. Firing by rank against cavalry; 173. Firing from the cross-bayonets position.]

## 172. Firing by rank against cavalry

When faced with a cavalry charge it was widely recommended a proportion of the battalion's fire ought to be held back in reserve. This is because cavalry would often attack with a reserve, the first wave drawing the fire, with the second falling upon the unloaded infantry. Therefore the standard battalion fire was unsuitable as all three ranks discharged simultaneously. Commanders instead relied on the two rank firing system, or firing by ranks, the latter presenting the double advantage of allowing the men to remain in the 'crossed bayonets' position. In this case the commander would give the following commands:

1. *Feu de rang par battalion* (fire by rank by battalion)
2. *Croisez la baïonnette* (cross bayonets)

At the first command, the three ranks would 'make ready'; at the second they would 'cross bayonets', with the third rankers stepping forward on the left foot and pushing their bodies forward forcibly and ensuring their musket barrels extended past the front rank as much as possible. From this position the commanding general could execute a fire by rank; or fire all three ranks at once (a perilous feat).

He could also order his troops to advance, or even to return to the shoulder arms position.

[**See also:** 165. Infantry squares; 170. Two rank firing; 171. Firing by rank; 173. Firing from the cross-bayonets position.]

## 173. Firing from the cross-bayonets position

If enemy infantry had approached to within thirty paces, it was generally supposed there would be insufficient time to fire and reload before the *shock* occurred. Therefore it was advisable to fire on the enemy infantry at the last instant from the crossed-bayonet position. This species of firing could be accomplished by rank, or by all three ranks simultaneously, something which was considered extremely dangerous and often resulted in accidental injuries to the front rank.

In the first case, with the men already in the cross-bayonets position, the colonel could order the ranks to fire in turn by giving the commands:

1. *Feu de bataillon par rang* (battalion fire by rank)
2. *Commencez le feu* (commence firing)

After this the battalion commander would instruct his battalion to fire. At this command the three ranks fired in turn, firing from the hip, keeping a strong grip on the musket with the right hand, and turning the musket ninety degrees anticlockwise, so the firing mechanism faced upwards – a precaution to stop the priming charge from igniting the neighbouring man's cartridge pouch, or burning his clothes. The second and third ranks were urged to take care not to shoot their comrade in the front rank and to ensure they fired through the interval in the files, with the third ranker pressing forwards to ensure the barrel projected beyond the front rank. After firing, the men would not reload, but would remain in the crossed bayonet position, braced for impact.

In the second case, when the commander wanted everyone to fire simultaneously, he would order:

1. *Feu de bataillon* (battalion fire)
2. *Commencez le feu* (commence firing)

After this the battalion commander would instruct his battalion to fire.

[**See also:** 158. Charge pace; 172. Firing by rank against cavalry; 171. Firing by rank.]

## 174. Independent fire (*feu a volonté*)

During the wars of the Revolution this type of fire was extremely common. It could be performed in ranks, although in the chaos of combat the third rank could only fire with great risk of hitting their comrade in the front rank. This species of firing was the only one used by skirmishers and voltigeurs during the period.

[**See also:** 3. Light infantry regiments; 33. Chasseur; 36. Voltigeur; 86. Musket; 87. Carbine; 167. Musketry (introduction); 168. Loading procedure; 176. Skirmishing (introduction); 180. General remarks on skirmishing.]

## 175. Older firing systems

There were several types of firing which were known from previous regulations which survived into the Napoleonic wars but did not feature in the 1791 regulations. The first was called fire 'without movement' (*feu sans movement*) and was executed by a formation more than three ranks deep. Each rank knelt except the last rank, which fired first. After this each rank in turn would stand and fire. This system saw very little use in the Napoleonic wars, but Bardin thought it worth recording in the infantry manual all the same.

In addition to platoon fire, Bardin discussed a fire by section (*feu de section*) and also a *feu de division* (i.e. a pair of platoons) whereby the two odd platoons in the centre of the line fired first followed by the next two even numbered platoons, etc. This system could be made with an element of movement, the subdivision advancing out of the line before firing. This was based on the Prussian *Chargiren mit Pelotons im Avanciren und Retiriren* used by Frederick the Great. The step was six inches. However, the French found this system extremely impractical and ceased to perform it in 1776. This regulation also suppressed the *feu de file* – a form of voluntary fire by all three ranks while standing.

Interestingly Bardin did not include 'fire while advancing' (*feu en avançant*) described in the *Evolutions of the Line*. This was performed alternately by odd and even numbered battalions. The odd number battalions would advance at the accelerated pace. After thirty paces they halted and fired. Meanwhile the even numbered battalions marched at the ordinary pace. When they drew level with odd battalions they would accelerate for thirty paces and then fire. A similar technique could be used in retreats, the odd numbered battalions firing and reloading, then marching off, followed by the even numbered battalions.

[**See also:** 169. Volley firing; 170. Two rank firing.]

*Chapter 23*

# Skirmishing

## 176. Introduction

Although the use of skirmishers in battle was not entirely innovative, the French Army of the 1790s was noted for its tactic of throwing large numbers of troops forward in loose skirmish formations to engage and harry the enemy line. The word given to these skirmishers was *tirailleurs* ('shooters'). Bardin claims this word was unknown to the military before the 1790s. Despite the widespread use of skirmishers, there was very little in terms of instructions for skirmishing. Bardin did not comment on the practice in his infantry manuals. The regulations of 1 August 1791 only mentioned *tirailleurs* in the context of protecting the flanks of columns against enemy cavalry. The 1792 field service regulations are more helpful, but only give very brief advice on the employment of light infantry, calling for it to be employed in skirmish formations and to be sent forward to discover the enemy positions and, in particular, to fire on enemy gunners.

Skirmishing was not the exclusive preserve of light infantry. Line infantry were equally familiar with the practice. There are even examples of grenadiers being used as skirmishers (Coignet at Marengo, for example). There are stories of entire battalions being thrown forward as skirmishers; in some respects, in the 1790s one might consider the entire first line of infantry as being nothing more than a thick belt of skirmishers with a line of battalions behind in support, feeding more men forward as required. Some authorities claim this tactic was borne out of necessity, French troops in the Revolution not possessing the training or temperament to deliver volleys in the conventional fashion.

Initially the tactics employed by line infantry skirmishers were very rudimentary. An officer would call for volunteers to go forward and pepper the enemy line with musketry. There were no instructions as such, except to use one's intelligence, take shelter if it could be found, and run back on one's parent unit if threatened or called on to fall back. Such orders as were required were shouted by the officers and sergeants patrolling the rear. French soldiers proved to be exceptionally resourceful at this type of fighting, goading the enemy line into wasting precious volleys on an elusive target, and also distracting the enemy from the movement of infantry formations behind the skirmish screen.

In addition to skirmishers, use was made of flankers (*flanquers*). These were men who would protect the flank of a column on the march, or would cover any exposed flank when the battalion was in line formation. These troops could respond to any threat as it arose, without disturbing the alignment of the line. During the expedition to Egypt (1798–1801) the French found themselves faced with large attacks by light cavalry. Employing square formations for protection on the march, infantry found the rear of the squares were often exposed to attacks. Skirmishers were therefore used to protect the rear face of the square as it marched, running back to the square when the enemy cavalry pressed home an attack. They were also useful for driving away mounted skirmishers who came to fire on the square. When the voltigeurs companies were created in 1804 and 1805 the onus of skirmishing increasingly fell on them.

There are very few formal instructions for skirmishing. An instruction for the service and manoeuvres of light infantry written in 1804 by Colonel Guyard suggested skirmishers might be deployed by sending one or two files from each platoon ahead to scout the way ahead or protect the flanks. The commander would command '*éclaireurs, en avant – marche!*' and the required number of files would advance to between 50 and 100 fathoms ahead. Bardin made it clear he was not a supporter of formal systems for skirmishing and, in particular, the means of sending signals to skirmishers, which he believed were 'inexecutable' on the battlefield. 'In the presence of the enemy', Bardin wrote in his dictionary, 'every *tirailleur* acted on inspiration.'

## 177. Skirmishing – the Davout instructions of 1811

A set of instructions for skirmishing survives from October 1811 when Marshal Davout addressed the subject in an order to the generals of his Army Corps. By 1811, in Davout's Corps at least, the centre companies were far less practised in skirmishing than the voltigeur companies. Davout was concerned his voltigeurs might not always be available to perform the role for the parent battalion, so he ordered skirmish training to be undertaken by all of the infantry within his Army Corps. Davout recommended men from the centre companies were mixed with the voltigeurs during training so they would benefit from their experience. The following articles in this section elaborate on Davout's scheme and provide an overview of the general principles involved in skirmishing in the latter half of the Napoleonic period.

[**See also:** 3. Light infantry regiments; 33. Chasseur; 36. Voltigeur; 160. At the run; 164. Battalion formations and manoeuvres; 165. Infantry squares; 176. Skirmishing (introduction); 178. Deploying skirmishers; 179. Skirmishers: movement and communication; 180. General remarks on skirmishing; 231. Battle tactics.]

## 178. Deploying skirmishers

Although it was possible for skirmishers to be drawn from a number of different companies, experience had shown it was better to draw skirmishers from a single company. Under Davout's system, when a captain was instructed to scout ahead of a column or to cover a line, he would take his company 200 paces in front of the formation he was protecting and form a cordon of skirmishers. To do this he would divide his company into three sections (not the usual two). The captain would take command of the centre section and retain with him the sergeant major, two sergeants, two corporals and the drummers (or cornetists) plus a portion of the men. This body would act as a reserve section, from which the captain could send men to replace those out on the cordon, or to collect casualties.

The lieutenants would each take one of the flanking sections and would march them off one hundred paces to the left and right of the centre section. If the company had four drummers or cornetists (Davout's instruction implies this was sometimes the case), the lieutenants would each take one for their sections. The lieutenant commanding the section on the right would order his first and second ranks to face to the left and to march off, leaving a fifteen pace interval between each file. The third rank would remain static and act as a reserve. The sub-lieutenant would do the same in reverse with the left section, and the two wings of the cordon would meet in the middle ahead of the reserve. Once this occurred the men would face front. The ordinary pace would then be beaten on the drums and the line of skirmishers would advance one hundred paces ahead of the three section reserves. These section reserves were also referred to as the reserve platoons, or the officer escorts. Each reserve had to be at least six men strong to be considered effective.

When protecting the flank of a column, the same deployment procedure was followed, but instead of the skirmish cordon advancing in a line, it would march by the flank, keeping pace with the column. If attacked, the skirmishers would face outwards, away from the column, forming a cordon perpendicular to the column's direction of advance. If the captain had to protect both flanks of a column with a single company, he would send his two lieutenants to either flank, retaining a smaller escort comprising of the sergeant major, one sergeant, two corporals, one or two drummers (or cornetists) and ten fusiliers. The captain would take his escort to the flank which was most likely to be threatened.

[See also: 37. Drummer; 38. Cornetist; 164. Battalion formations and manoeuvres; 174. Independent fire; 176. Skirmishing (introduction).]

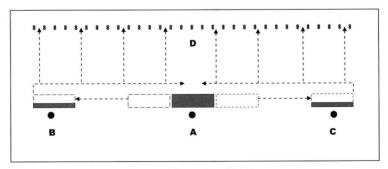

**Diagram I:** Platoon deployed in skirmish formation (1811).
Key: A – Captain and central section reserve; B – Lieutenant and left section reserve; C – Sub-lieutenant and right section reserve; D – chain of skirmishers deployed from right and left sections.

## 179. Skirmishers: movement and communication

Skirmishers moved at the same pace as the column or line they were protecting, always maintaining the interval between them. When covering the head of a column the skirmish line would form something of an arc ahead of it. If the main body changed its direction of march, the skirmishers would have to move at the run (*pas de course*) in order to keep up. They would often use the running pace when clearing woods or a village and in circumstances where there was no threat from cavalry. Skirmishers would also run when falling back on their reserve platoons.

Due to the extended distances involved, communications were by drum or voltigeur's cornet. No mention was made of using whistles, although Swiss regiments in French service were known to use them. In terms of drum calls, some of the standard *batteries* were employed, but with different meanings for skirmishers.

**Table 18:** Drum and cornet voltigeur signals.

| Movement | Cornet calls | Drum calls |
|---|---|---|
| Deployment | *Déployement* | *La breloque* |
| Rallying | *Ralliement* | *Aux drapeaux* |
| Retreat | *Retraite* | *Retraite* |
| March to the right | *Marche à droite* | *La grenadière* |
| March to the left | *Marche à gauche* | *Les trois coups de charge* |
| Charge | *La charge* | *La charge* |
| March slowly | *Pas ordinaire* | *Pas ordinaire* |
| March quickly | *Marche précipitée* | *La charge avec roulement* |
| Stop | *La messe* | *La messe* |

When skirmishers were deployed the parent body was advised not to beat drum signals needlessly, in particular those that would order the skirmishers to move to the left or right.

Sometimes communications had to be managed by sending sub-officers up and down the cordon to give vocal commands. When a sub-officer was sent to deliver instructions to the skirmish line, he was always to be accompanied by a soldier from the reserve.

If the parent body retired behind the skirmish cordon, the captain commanding the skirmishers always had to maintain some visual contact with the main body in order not to lose its direction of march. If his view of the main body was obscured, he was to detach several of his men to monitor its movements for him.

[**See also:** 176. Skirmishing (introduction); 37. Drummer; 38. Cornetist.]

## 180. General remarks on skirmishing

Once deployed, skirmishers were always to remain in pairs to provide mutual assistance. For protection they would take it in turns to fire, waiting for their comrade to reload before firing. If charged by enemy cavalry, skirmishers were advised to hide in holes, ditches and hedges from where they could continue to fire on the horsemen safely. If this was not possible they were to run back to the nearest reserve. As soon as there was a threat of cavalry attack, the officers would order their escorting reserves to form a circle or mass and to face outwards ready to act as a rallying point.

When marching, deployed in open country, the skirmishers would have to remain calm, alert and silent, to listen for instructions. The officers and sub-officers would have to pay attention to the ground, looking for areas of natural advantage they could fall back on if suddenly attacked. If they were covering the flank of a column they would have to clear the thickets and climb the hillocks and gullies to ensure the enemy was not lying in wait.

When marching through woods where the ground was broken with ditches, hedgerows and ruins they would advance carefully and, if they encountered the enemy, use the best possible cover to set up ambushes. If the enemy had laid an ambush, the proven tactic was to have a few brave men attempt to turn their

Line infantry skirmishing. Note one of the soldiers is ramming a charge while walking. Loading while moving was considered an essential skill for skirmishers.

position, climbing up onto a rock or ruin and to get behind their position. In almost all cases, the enemy would break off contact for fear of being encircled and would sustain considerable loss in doing so.

If a building was encountered on the march, the captain would send an escort to check it. If the enemy was believed to occupy the building, word would be sent back to the column commander to prepare for action. When a village was encountered, the captain would remain outside it with his escort and take up the most advantageous position possible. The lieutenants would go into the village and take up positions with their escorts on the principal routes and act as rallying points for the skirmishers who would quickly clear the buildings, outhouses and gardens.

When faced with a village or entrenchment occupied by the enemy, the best advice was for the skirmishers to rush the flanks and rear of the position, drawing the enemy reserves to the extremities. The captain would then attack the centre with his reserve. The same principle applied if the initial attack was made on the centre and the reserve struck a flank. The key to the operation was the speed and impetuosity of the attack. When skirmishers encountered a fixed position they were to roll along it, probing for the flanks.

[**See also:** 160. At the run; 174. Independent fire; 176. Skirmishing (introduction); 231. Battle tactics.]

*Part VI*

# Garrison Service

# Chapter 24

# Duties & Routines

## 181. Introduction

For every day of battle a soldier experienced, there might be weeks, months or even years spent in garrison. When not tearing across Europe on campaign, soldiers would often be found in purpose built barracks (*casernes*). These were located in important cities, or garrison towns, which were classified as being 'open' (i.e. a town or city), part of a citadel or fortress (*place fort*), or in a castle (*château*). In these places the soldiers submitted themselves to highly regimented routines, which were considered necessary for building the soldier and maintaining public order. These routines were described in the *Ordinance to regulate the service in the fortifications and in the quarters* (1 March 1768); and the *Regulation concerning the interior service, police and discipline of the infantry* (24 June 1792), a document Bardin refers to as the 'police regulations'.

Other than the business of training, cleaning, eating and maintaining uniforms and equipment, in terms of the duties performed in garrison, each regiment was required to provide manpower for five types of duty:

1. For detachments, escorts and the guarding of exterior posts which might not be relieved for a number of days.
2. Men for general guard duty, who would be relieved daily.
3. Guards of honour for general officers and dignitaries.
4. For fatigues, such as receiving distributions of food, straw or fuel for heating; for carrying vegetables, cooking, and making cartridges for the next campaign.
5. Making the rounds and patrols.

Regiments might also be required to provide detachments for service on ships, because the French did not have a dedicated 'marine' infantry. They might also be required to provide detachments for works in besieged places.

## 182. Lodgings and the arrangements of the bedchamber

When a battalion lodged in barracks it did so by company, following the same order as if forming a line of battle. Corporals lodged with their squads; the two drummers were attached to the first and third squads. The sergeant major, sergeants and quartermaster corporal lodged together in a separate room, if possible in the centre of the company. The drum major, drum corporal and musicians shared a room, as did the adjutants. The musicians were provided with a second room for practising in. If officers could not be housed in the military buildings they would receive a monthly sum to board with an inhabitant, or at an inn.

Each bedchamber door was labelled with the number of the squad and provided with a list of the men contained within it. The bedchamber was furnished with a number of wooden beds, each with a wooden frame 30 to 40 cm high, 190 cm long and 110 cm wide. Upon this frame sat a mattress (*paillasse*) filled with 15 kg of straw and a second mattress filled with 13 kg of wool, or a mixture three quarters wool and one quarter hair. For a pillow, the bed was provided with a tubular bolster 100 cm wide, 80 cm in circumference filled with 2 kg of wool. Upon each bed sat a woollen blanket, 280 cm long, 220 cm wide and weighing 10 to 12 pounds. There was also a sheet of semi-whitened linen 280 cm long and 190 cm wide. This sheet was changed once every twenty days in summer and once a month in winter. The bed also had the names of the men who slept there (there were typically two men per bunk).

At one end of the bedchamber would be a fireplace and a succession of shelves and pegs. Light came from candles in the hours of darkness. Haversacks were to be securely buckled and placed on the bolster at the bedhead. Dirty linen was placed inside the haversacks, not stuffed under the mattresses. Shoes were to be neatly arranged; coats and jackets turned inside out and folded in two. Headgear was placed next to the coat; muskets placed in the racks, each labelled with the soldier's name. Cartridge pouches and sabres were suspended by their belts; cooking utensils stacked neatly, fuel for the fire stacked in the corner next to the chimney if it was peat; beneath the bed if it was wood.

The master craftsmen would be accommodated as near to the regiment as possible. The master tailor was provided with one room for his lodgings and two for his tailors. The cobbler was provided with the same arrangement. The armourer was provided one chamber for his lodgings, one for a workshop and one for his forge and workers.

[**See also:** 14. Surgeon major; 48. Orderly; 83. Utensils and tools; 112. Deductions and funds; 133. Regimental prisons; 183. The daily routine; 243. Sanitation of bedding.]

## 183. The daily routine

In garrison the military day typically commenced with the duty drummer beating the reveille at six o'clock in the morning. This would occur an hour later between 1 October and 1 April, or differently if directed thus by the colonel. At the sound of the drum call, the corporals would wake their men, have them dress, form in a single line, and would then conduct a roll call (*appel*). If men had fallen sick or were otherwise indisposed, the corporal would inform the duty sergeant, who would in turn make a note of their name along with the number of their bedchamber.

After roll call, the corporal would have his men wash their hands and face. The beds would be left to air for half an hour and then be made. Meanwhile the bedchamber would be swept, the windows opened and everything put in the appropriate place. If the bedchamber was affected by foul odours, the corporal was advised to burn a few juniper berries which might be purchased by the ordinary fund. On the first day of each month, the corporal would also have the windows washed, inside and out. While these chores were being completed, the corporal or the appointed 'ordinary chief' would go out shopping, taking a man with him to carry the groceries.

At eight o'clock the regimental surgeon major would arrive in the guardhouse to review the names of any soldiers who had been reported sick. The surgeon major would then pay a visit to these men and decide if they could be treated in their bedchambers, or if they had to go to hospital. No one was excused duty without a certificate signed by the surgeon major and approved by the colonel.

At half past eight the drum major would assemble the drummers and inspect them. At nine o'clock the drummers would beat the signal for the guard. On hearing this, the corporals would inspect the men destined for guard duty. If a man was found improperly attired for guard duty he could be punished with four hours of fatigue duty in the barrack room.

After this the corporal would daily complete a report form (*billet de rapport*) detailing all movements and significant events in the last 24 hours. The quartermaster corporals would collect these reports and pass them to the quartermaster treasurer for verification, then to the sergeant majors who would pass them to the captains. If the captain wished to make a request on behalf of one of his men, for example, for leave, or permission to take work with the master craftsmen, this would be added to the report. When the captain had signed off the report, the sergeant major would take it to the duty adjutant.

At half past nine there were two drum rolls. The duty sergeant would begin by inspecting the men assigned to guard duty. If anyone failed this inspection, the corporal would be put in the guard chamber for eight days as punishment for presenting an ill prepared man. When the sergeant was satisfied with their attire he would issue each soldier with three ball cartridges.

Also at this time, the adjutant major and the duty adjutant would gather with the sergeant majors at the quarters of the duty battalion commander. The adjutant major would hand over the general report and answer any queries raised by the battalion commander. After this exchange of information took place the sergeant majors would go and check on the records of the rounds made over the previous day. Meanwhile the adjutant major and the duty adjutant would go to the colonel's quarters and make a report.

Prior to their arrival, the colonel would have received any necessary orders from the local garrison commander, or any general officer present. These orders were to reach the colonel by nine o'clock so he might digest them before the arrival of the daily report. After receiving the daily report from the adjutants, the colonel would announce the orders for the coming day. These orders would be recorded by the adjutant major in the regiment's register of orders (*livre d'ordres*). These would be transmitted to the sergeant majors by the adjutant.

At ten o'clock the drummer would beat a signal for morning soup, the first meal of the day. As the men ate, the duty lieutenant would make a tour of the bedchambers to ensure the men were eating and the bedchambers were clean. They would also check if the advances of pay (*prêt*) had been distributed fairly. At the same time the duty captain would make an inspection of the hospital, police chambers, prisons and cells.

At ten thirty there were three drum rolls, after which the duty sergeant would take the men chosen for guard duty to be inspected by the company's duty officer. If the officer was not satisfied with what he found, the sergeant ran the risk of being put in the guardhouse.

The battalion commander or adjutant major would arrive at the parade ground at eleven thirty. Soon afterwards the incoming guard would begin arriving and be formed into a single rank. Everyone would be in place by midday when the general parade would commence. The men would line up, sergeants included, with the officers four paces in front. The colonel or the next available senior officer would make a general parade. If a man was incorrectly dressed, the relevant duty officer would be reprimanded. To the left of the guard all the quartermaster corporals, plus one corporal and sergeant per company would form in three ranks and be inspected. The drum corps would also be present. The adjutant major would begin dividing the men into the required number of platoons, each one being assigned to a particular post. While this was occurring, the duty adjutant would begin assembling all the outgoing guards ready for handover.

After the incoming guard marched off, a drummer would beat the order. At this signal all the quartermaster corporals and duty sergeants formed a circle, starting with the most senior regiment. Inside this grand circle a smaller interior circle was formed by the adjutant majors, colour bearers (in fact, probably the adjutants), with the major of the garrison (a staff officer working for the governor) standing at the centre. This officer gave the orders for the following day, the number of detachments required, etc. After this the major broke the circle (*rompez le cercle!*) and each regiment formed a smaller circle where the details of the order were discussed and allocated. When these circles were broken, the quartermaster corporals went to their company officers (all officers were required to be present at the parade) and advised them of the orders.

Once relieved, the outgoing guard would return to the parade ground and reassemble. When the guard was changed, the outgoing guard was stood down. The duty sergeants would lead the men back to their quarters. On returning to their quarters the outgoing guard would discharge their muskets using a ball extractor, passing the cartridges to one of the duty sub-officers. They would then return to their quarters and set about putting their arms and equipment into order. The muskets would be put in their racks and the cartridge pouches hung on their pegs.

For those not assigned to guard duty, the afternoon was the time when the officers and men could receive instruction and training. This might take place in the open air or in sheds or larger halls called hangars. There was no training on Saturdays, and the afternoon would be spent repairing equipment and cleaning the barrack room furniture.

At five o'clock (four in the off-season) the duty drummer would beat another roll on the drums. This was the signal for 'evening soup'. Any soldiers found 'taken with drink' at this hour were confined to their quarters until the following morning and closely monitored throughout the remainder of the week. After the evening meal was consumed and the utensils tidied away there came a period of leisure. Soldiers who were not on guard duty or confined to barracks were allowed to visit the regiment's canteens and nearby taverns to drink, smoke, sing, tell tall stories and vie (or pay) for female companionship, until the beating of the retreat.

The hour of the beating of the retreat was set in the 1 March 1768 regulations as at sunset. However, with mealtimes in winter set at four o'clock, and sunset in winter occurring at approximately the same time, this would have prevented men from leaving barracks altogether. With unauthorised women banned from entering the barracks, enforcing this rule would have meant the French Army taking a vow of celibacy for the winter months, which is very unlikely. As a contemporary of the period, the solution to this conundrum was probably so obvious to Bardin he did not feel the urge to record it. An ordinance of 1691 set the retreat at eight o'clock from All Saints Day (1 November) until Easter, and at nine o'clock from Easter to All Saints Day. A revision of the *Services des places* from 1822 stated the retreat was beaten half an hour after sunset, except in the 'short days of winter' when it would not be beaten before six o'clock. Ultimately then, the commandant of the town could advance or delay the hour of the retreat as circumstances suited, provided he obtained the authorisation of the general commanding the military division.

At the appointed time all the drummers from the various regiments in the garrison would march behind their drum majors to the centre of the parade ground (*place d'armes*) and beat the retreat. The drummers would then separate and continue to beat the retreat as they marched towards their separate quarters. As the sound of massed drums echoed around the streets, soldiers had thirty minutes to finish their drinks and return to barracks.

Half an hour after the return of the drummers, the duty drummer would make three drum rolls and the gates to the barracks would be closed. The sergeants would make a roll call of their sections in the bedchambers under lantern light, in the presence of the sergeant major and duty lieutenant. Once this was completed, the corporal would put out the lights having made sure everyone was in bed. At this point the corporal was free to rest. However, if during the night he heard anyone get up, enter or go out of the bedchamber or speak in a low voice, he would pay attention to what took place, particularly those whose conduct appeared suspicious. Once everything was settled the duty adjutant would make a tour of the corridors to ensure everything was quiet.

[**See also:** 37. Drummer; 51. Worker; 110. Pay; 184. Police; 185. The police guard; 190. Passwords; 191. Rations & supplies (Introduction); 199. Food preparation (Introduction); 200. Preparing soup; 205. Cleaning & maintenance (introduction); 212. Training (introduction).]

## 184. Police

While in garrison, there was a rolling duty roster whereby a number of officers and sub-officers were assigned various service and 'police' duties for the period of one week. The word *police* came from the Greek word *polis* (city) and the Latin *politia* (civil administration). Essentially it referred to the administration of public order and the keeping of the peace. In the military sense *police* applied to the keeping of good order and subordination of the troops. It was, in effect, a rule of conduct and surveillance. Chief among the duty officers was the duty battalion commander who would daily receive reports on police and discipline and the duty adjutant. Below the duty battalion commander was a duty captain in charge of police, discipline and 'interior service'. The post of *capitaine de police* also rotated weekly, but all captains would still bear ultimate responsibility for their own companies. Each company would have a duty 'officer of the week', a post alternated by the lieutenant and sub-lieutenant. The duty officer would have under him a duty sergeant and corporal responsible for service and discipline (again drawn from a rolling weekly rota). If one of the lieutenants was absent, the sergeant major would cover for them. The period of duty ran from after parade on Sunday, until the following Sunday's parade.

[**See also:** 8. Battalion commander; 53. Uniform – general description (introduction); 131. The hierarchy of command; 185. The police guard; 190. Passwords.]

## 185. The police guard

Order was maintained by a police guard (*garde de police*), the size of which was determined by the commander depending on circumstances. The police guard was under the orders of the captain of police and was generally responsible for maintaining order and tranquillity, ensuring soldiers were not out of their quarters, improperly dressed or otherwise running amok. The adjutant was specially charged with overseeing the activities of the police guard. The police guard was commanded by an officer (usually termed captain of the guard) who held the keys to the guard rooms, and was responsible for the utensils and furniture found there. The guard was also assigned a duty drummer (*tambour de service*) to beat the required signals at various hours. Although the duty drummer was authorised to sleep in his usual bedchamber, in practice he would sleep in the guardhouse (*corps de garde de police*) so as to be on hand as necessary. Those men assigned to the police guard were excused general fatigue duties, and only did the chores necessary for their own service, the most junior men being chosen for these tasks first. They did not need to cook, as their share of the rations would be brought over by their ordinaries.

The rota for guard duty was made at the beginning of each month. Guard duty commenced at noon and lasted for twenty hours. In the warmer, southern departments of France, guard duty would commence at 10 o'clock in the morning to avoid having to stand on parade under the noon sun. When on duty, each man would serve just six hours on post, with the remainder of the duty spent in reserve in the guardhouse. This meant four shift changes were required for every post identified. In summer (May to the end of September) they might serve eight hours thus reducing the number of guards required for each position. This would give the men more nights off duty. The 1768 regulations stated soldiers should have six or at least five nights off between each stint of guard duty, but this was rarely observed. Where numbers were short because too many men had been granted leave to take work, or the guard was doubled due to wartime contingencies, soldiers might end up on post every other night. This was considered prejudicial to their development as it left very little time for training or exercises.

The incoming guard would begin preparing at nine o'clock. The detachment which provided the guard would assemble at midday at what was known as the general parade. Prior to the parade, a bill would be drawn up for each post detailing its size, and which officers and sub-officers would command it. The battalion commander or adjutant major would arrive at the parade ground half an hour before the parade commenced. The names of each post were written in large letters on one of the walls facing the parade square. The guard would arrive and form a line with their backs to this wall. The adjutant major would then divide the assembled guard into the number of platoons required to man the posts. The ranks would be opened and an inspection of the men took place. The guard would then march off and each

Two soldiers brawling in their barrack room. Note the row of muskets and the candle lantern.

detachment would be assigned. On the way, the outgoing guards would be picked up and would end up back at the parade ground to be relieved.

[**See also:** 37. Drummer; 9. Adjutant major; 133. Regimental prisons; 184. Police; 186. Making the rounds; 187. The sergeant of police; 188. Duties of the corporal of the guard; 189. Duties of sentries at the gates; 190. Passwords; 221. On the march; 225. Arrival at a *gîte*; 246. Guard duty.]

## 186. Making the rounds

A round was a type of patrol which toured the ramparts checking on the sentries and posts, ensuring they were correctly placed and each post knew the password. This was particularly important at night, ensuring the sentries were alert. The timing of the patrols was set by the ordinance of 1 March 1678.

To ensure the rounds were completed in the appropriate fashion, the corporal of the guard would be issued with a number of service tokens, which were known as *marrons* (lit. chestnuts). These tokens could be round or square and are variously described as being made of cardboard, wood, leather or lead. Each token had a time written on it, indicating the hour at which a round was to be made. In a practice which dated back to Roman times, the token would be issued to a patrol which would find at the end of their route a wooden box with a metal slot in it. They would drop the service token in the box and sign a register. The wooden box would be locked with a key, and at nine o'clock in the morning the corporal would go and check the boxes, unlock them and retrieve the tokens. At the daily parade the tokens would be handed over to the incoming guard. (There was another type of token which was used for distributions. These were allocated to the guard by a staff officer of the garrison and were used to claim the guard's share of fuel for fires and lighting at distribution times).

If the rounds discovered something of interest, they would alert the nearby posts and inform the commander of the place. If the sentries were found to be at fault, the round would inform the commander of the post. When two rounds encountered one another the first would cry 'who goes?' and the other would reply 'round' and say what sort. The soldiers of the least senior regiment would give the password. If of equal rank, the round which discovered the other had the right to demand the password from the other.

In garrison towns, rounds would also be made of civilian areas. At the beating of the retreat the corporal of the police guard would make a patrol of known *establishments* and begin encouraging the men to leave. At the sound of the drums tavern owners knew they were forbidden from selling drinks to servicemen. A helpful visit from the regiment's adjutants would have reinforced this message, along with the warning not to give credit to the soldiers, no matter how hard they pleaded or what threats they made. If civilian tavern keepers (*cabaretiers*) ignored this polite advice they would find an armed guard posted at their door with orders to refuse entry to all soldiers, thus spelling an end to a lucrative source of income. The rounds would also take in the regimental canteens, and repeat offenders for serving late drinks would be stripped of their livelihood. The retreat (known as the general retreat in some texts) did not affect the civilian population. However, at ten o'clock the town bells would toll signalling the start of a sort of curfew. At the sounding of this 'bourgeois retreat' all public houses had to cease business. Typically an hour was given to allow everyone to return home, after which no one was allowed on the streets without a lantern or firebrand. Anyone found lurking in the shadows after this time would be deemed suspicious by the patrol and taken in for questioning.

[**See also:** 34. Grenadier; 181. Duties & routines (introduction); 183. The daily routine; 187. The sergeant of police; 188. Duties of the corporal of the guard.]

## 187. The sergeant of police

The sergeant of police had onerous and manifold duties, the principal one of which was to ensure men leaving and returning to the barracks were correctly attired; sub-officers, drummers, grenadiers and sappers were armed with their sabres; coats were brushed, shakos worn, the plumes or pompoms correctly placed and the gaiters diligently buttoned. Woes betide anyone the sergeant of police saw returning to barracks obviously drunk or worse, improperly dressed.

The sergeant of police would examine carefully the 'strangers' desiring entry to the quarters. He would only allow those to pass who were spoken for by an officer or sub-officer, or if they had been granted written permission. Similarly, as a precaution against espionage, the sergeant would never allow a serviceman of a foreign power into the quarters without written orders. He would also make sure the sentry on the gate did not allow any women to enter, except those whose names were posted on a list in the guardhouse. If the sergeant found any women in the quarters he suspected were unauthorised, he would have them arrested and handed over to the civil authorities without delay. Nor would he allow any brokers of dubious goods or merchants of clothing to enter the barracks, or even to dwell within the vicinity of its gates.

Each morning the sergeant of police would have the police chamber and guardhouse, etc. swept by those in detention, confined to barracks or otherwise assigned to general fatigue duties. Later in the morning, half an hour after the drum for the morning soup, he would reassemble those same unhappy subjects and, with the blessing and guidance of the duty adjutant, zealously assign them to unpleasant chores such as cleaning the cesspits, the kitchens, and fire buckets.

At eight o'clock each morning the sergeant of police would hand the commander of the guard and the surgeon major the names of the sick. The sergeant would visit the discipline room and the cells each morning and evening. The sergeant would inspect the sentries, ensuring the corporal did his rounds punctually and diligently. He was responsible for ensuring the drum signals were executed promptly at the times indicated by the adjutant. Thus, whatever the drum major thought to the contrary, the duty drummer was under the sergeant of police's command.

If a distinguished person such as the colonel, or a general officer should honour the barracks with a snap inspection, the sergeant of police was required to accompany the dignitary throughout their tour, but not before sending the corporal of police scurrying off to inform the adjutant what was occurring.

At the beating of the retreat, he would assure himself the sentries were properly dressed for the rigours of the night, in their fatigue caps, smock frocks or greatcoats and, if the regiment used them, cartridge pouch covers. The sergeant of police would lock the barrack gates and, while evening roll call was taking place in the bedchambers, he would put the guard under arms, then pass through the canteens and eject anyone he found there, taking their names for his report.

At the drum roll for lights out, half an hour after roll call, the sergeant of police would ensure all lights did go out, the exception being those bedchambers still waiting for the return of men with permission to return late. When latecomers did arrive at the gates, they were not allowed to enter without the sergeant first being informed. The sergeant of police would check their names diligently against the adjutant's list of all men granted permission to miss evening roll call, for example those who were given leave to take work in town.

At six in the morning in summer, and at seven in the winter, the guard would change back into full uniform and the sergeant would inspect them. After the changing of the guard, the outgoing men would be sent back to their quarters. The sergeant of police ensured this was done in good order, that the bayonets were in their scabbards and no one had left their musket or haversack in the guardhouse.

There was one final piece of record keeping at the end of the shift. In the guardhouse there would be a register listing the men confined to barracks, the names of all those who came and went from the cells, those who arrived after roll call, the number of the barrack rooms found with lights on, and the name of senior

Off duty soldiers drinking and frolicking.

officers or distinguished persons who came to visit. The register would also contain the names of those listed sick or wounded; the time the medical officer visited; the hour men employed in pickets, or public spectacles returned; the names of recruits arriving in town; and everything of note and importance which occurred during the twenty-four hours of guard duty, such as men found to be drunk, quarrels, guards coming back in disorder, packages thrown from windows, or confined men who had sneakily exited the barracks. Every morning this register was handed over to the adjutant who diligently examined it and signed it off.

[**See also:** 16. Adjutant; 28. Sergeant; 37. Drummer; 59. Greatcoat; 70. Forage cap; 133. Regimental prisons; 183. The daily routine; 244. Sexual health.]

## 188. Duties of the corporal of the guard

Under the direct orders of the sergeant of the guard, were a number of sentries (the exact number determined by the commander) and a corporal of the guard. The corporal's first duty was to check the 'hall of discipline' and verify the number of men detained. Meanwhile the men would check all the utensils and equipment in the guardhouse and report missing items or breakages they discovered.

After the drum roll for 'lights out', if any of the bedchambers or canteens remained illuminated, the corporal of the guard would mount an investigation. Likewise, if any of the external lanterns were extinguished or fading, the corporal of the guard would relight them. During the night the corporal of the guard was required to make several rounds of the barracks, ensuring no one was out roaming the courtyards, the kitchens or staircases, or trying to climb the walls or trees. The corporal of the guard would also check rubbish had not been thrown out of the windows and no damage was being done. Another duty was to chase off any dogs lest their barking disturb those asleep. If anyone was found acting suspiciously the corporal of the guard had the power to arrest them. The corporal could lock anyone up, but he could not release anyone from prison without the adjutant's permission. The corporal would ensure the prisoners did not have their pipes with them in the discipline hall, or weapons, even under the pretext of cleaning them. He would watch the prisoners while they ate, and ensure they did not have alcoholic drinks. He had to search anyone coming to visit the cells to ensure they were not trying to hand over weapons or knives. If the corporal allowed women to visit he would receive a serious punishment.

Every morning after reveille, the corporal would return to the police hall and the cells, looking for damage, ensuring the inmates had not fallen sick. The inmates would tidy up, and the water in the jugs would be refilled. The corporal would also open the gates of the barracks. They would stay open all day, except in the case when all the occupants were confined to barracks. In such a case the only men authorised to leave were officers, the adjutant, the ordinary chiefs and the men they conducted to fetch supplies.

The corporal would also oversee guard change. When the guard changed the incoming guard would stand to the left of the outgoing sentry. Both men would present arms and the outgoing man would pass on any instructions given to him (these instructions were known as the *consigne*).

[**See also:** 16. Adjutant; 30. Corporal; 133. Regimental prisons; 189. Duties of sentries at the gates; 187. The sergeant of police.]


## 189. Duties of sentries at the gates

Sentries would remain in the vicinity of the gates through the course of the day. They would be relieved at meal times, eating in the guardhouse, and not returning back to their ordinary. When the barrack gates were closed after evening roll call, the sentries would withdraw to the inner courtyard, but remain outdoors. If a benevolent corporal allowed the sentry to shelter inside the guardhouse, the corporal would be severely punished. Each company would reserve eight old coats for use by the guards in the winter months and on days of bad weather. They would also wear their fatigue caps at night, rather than their formal headgear.

The sentry had two means of raising the alarm: by firing his musket, or by calling for help. There were a number of protocols attached to verbal challenges. For example, if the corporal was out doing his rounds or a patrol marched before the gates were shut in the evening, the sentry would cry out the challenge 'who lives?' (*qui vive?*), and stand to attention in the shoulder arms position.

When a general officer approached, he would be honoured with a cry of 'to arms!' (*aux armes!*); colonels or the commanding officer would be greeted with the shout 'call out the guard!' (*hors la garde!*). The sentry was also required to present arms when a general or superior officer passed, or 'shoulder arms' and stand to attention when officers or holders of the Legion of Honour passed. Sentries would habitually stand in the support arms (*l'arme au bras*) position.

On a more mundane level the sentry would pay particular attention to the comings and goings through the barracks. In what was presumably an attempt to interdict hidden contraband, persons bringing vegetables into the barracks were to be challenged unless accompanied by a corporal in uniform and carrying a sabre (i.e. on duty). To prevent the pilfering of military equipment and supplies, any soldier or 'stranger' leaving barracks with packets or haversacks was also to be challenged unless the corporal waved them past. Soldiers with a musket were not allowed to pass without the corporal confirming he was on actual service of some kind. Sentries were also required to prevent men confined to barracks from leaving. The names of these miscreants were held on a list in the guardhouse and were in any case easily recognised: men confined to barracks were required to remove the gaiter from their right leg.

If an officer made the cardinal error of arriving at the gatehouse in civilian clothes, the sentry was to inform his corporal who would tell the sergeant, who would report to the captain, who would in turn inform the commander.

On the subject of ladies, as a precaution against those of dubious status or intention, only authorised women (e.g. the cantineers and laundresses) were permitted to enter the barracks, unless the sergeant of police allowed it. In order for mistakes to be avoided, all women and other 'strangers' were required to speak with the corporal or commander of the guard on entry to the barracks.

Sentries were also required to keep good order in the vicinity of the gatehouse. They were not to suffer someone dumping rubbish (or worse) in the vicinity of their post, and certainly not in the interior of the barracks. Sentries were not to permit children 'foreign' to the regiment to gather in the courtyards where they would almost certainly play games which were prejudicial to the service, such as throwing stones. If children did misbehave they would be taken to the guardhouse until their parents came to collect them.

As a precaution against explosions, sentries assigned to guard duty at powder magazines were armed with halberds or other pole arms. The garrison commander was therefore required to provide two such weapons for every powder store.

[See also: 187. The sergeant of police; 188. Duties of the corporal of the guard; 246. Guard duty.]

## 190. Passwords

Passwords were a precaution against surprises and the means by which soldiers of the same army might recognise one another. Since time immemorial it had been the prerogative of distinguished persons to choose and issue the password; typically a marshal of France, the monarch, or army generals. Equally, it was considered a sign of distinction to be given knowledge of the password. There were three types of password used by French troops: the parole (*mot d'ordre*); its countersign; then a rallying cry (*mot de ralliement*) which could be used in combat to rally a body of men. Traditionally the parole would be the name of some noted deceased person or the saint of a town, with the countersign being the name of a town or country. The rallying password was a sort of cry consisting of a word or phrase, often the name of a general which could be used if troops became dispersed. It could also be used by patrols as they returned at night.

According to the 1792 police regulations the password would be issued each evening after the gates were closed. One hour before the closure of the gates the password would be issued by the commander of the town or the senior general to the officer responsible for closing the gates. Once the gates were closed, all the duty sub-officers would assemble on the parade ground and form a circle. The officer of the guard would place a corporal and six fusiliers four paces outside the circle, facing outwards, presenting arms. The officer entrusted with the password would remove his hat and tell the senior sub-officer of the senior regiment what the passwords were. These would then be whispered around the circle, man to man, clockwise. The circle was broken and the sub-officers went to tell their officers, removing their hat and whispering it into the officer's ear.

[See also: 139. Honouring dignitaries; 186. Making the rounds; 227. Duties in camp; 229. Outpost duty.]

*Chapter 25*

# Rations & Supplies

## 191. Introduction

Napoleon is often quoted thus: 'An army marches on its stomach' (the actual quote in French translates something closer to 'soup makes a soldier'). By comparison with the diet endured by the average peasant, French soldiers were generously catered for, in garrison at least. The official daily ration for each man consisted of half a loaf (750 grams) of bread, 250 grams of fresh meat, 30 grams of rice or 60 grams of dried vegetables, one sixtieth a kilo of salt, 250 ml of wine (or an equivalent portion of beer or cider). They were occasionally issued one sixteenth of a litre of brandy, and 50 cl of vinegar.

In garrison, most food was purchased daily by the ordinaries, but bread and other consumables were provided at formal distributions. The quartermaster treasurer was in charge of all distributions, or in his absence, the adjutant major, or adjutant. At the hour indicated for distributions, the duty drummer would beat the *breloque*. At this signal the duty sergeant and quartermaster corporal of each company would assemble. If it was for a distribution of bread, one man per ordinary would accompany them, dressed in a forage cap and wearing his smock-

The central figure (a light infantryman) has a water can (*grand bidon*) strapped to his haversack. Note the bread ration is tucked under the strap. Note the mess pan (*gamelle*) carried by the figure on the left. (Bcyer)

frock, or with his jacket turned inside out. The quartermaster treasurer would form the party into three ranks and march them to the distribution point, often accompanied by an armed detachment to maintain order and ensure fair play. The quartermaster treasurer would inspect the quality of the bread and verify the weight of it, then distribute it through the sergeants. The same process applied for distributions of sheets (*draps*), straw, and firewood.

## 192. Bread and biscuit

Bread was the principle sustenance of French soldiers and distributions were made every four days, the evening before the ration was due. When bread was distributed the quartermaster corporal would be present, usually with an officer. The quartermaster corporal would tell the officer how much had been received and then the officer would verify the weight and dimensions of the bread. 'Supply bread' (*pain de munition*) was made from three quarters wheat flour and one quarter rye, or good quality barley flour. The uncooked dough weighed three and half pounds before baking; after cooking each loaf was 27 centimetres in diameter (10 inches), 8 cm high (approx. 3 inches) and weighed 1.5 kg (3 pounds). Great importance was placed on examining the quality of the bread given to soldiers. In order to be judged 'good', the crust ought not to be burnt, but it had to be well cooked and golden in colour. On breaking the bread there should be a sweet balsamic odour and the loaf should leave an agreeable taste of hazelnut in the mouth.

When soldiers were stationed within the boundaries of the empire they were also provided with 125 grams of 'soup bread' (*pain de soupe*). This was a stale, white bread made entirely from wheat four which could be crumbled and added to thicken soup. This ration was not provided to soldiers on the march.

If bread was unavailable, a daily ration of 550 grams (18 ounces) of dry biscuit might be issued, (each biscuit weighed 275 grams). These biscuits were most commonly used in sieges or onboard warships rather than with field armies. They were made from wheat flour, rolled thin and cut into *galettes* which were usually about 5 French inches square. They were then cooked in a hot oven until golden brown (various recipes give the cooking time at anything from 35 to 60 minutes). The biscuits were then placed on a shelf in a dry sealed chamber and allowed to cool for up to a fortnight before being packed tightly into barrels and crates. When well made, a biscuit could last up to six years.

[**See also:** 56. Weight of arms and equipment; 82. Packing the haversack; 85. Wagons and horses; 110. Pay; 112. Deductions and funds; 132. General disciplinary measures; 133. Regimental prisons; 191. Rations & supplies (introduction); 221. On the march; 228. Provisions; 240. Rations; 252. Sieges; 254. Military hospitals.]

## 193. Meat

Fresh meat was issued at the rate of 250 grams (8 ounces) per ration, distributed as two thirds beef, and one third the meat of dairy cattle or mutton. The distribution of meat usually took place on alternate days, but in hot weather could take place daily. Where possible the animals were butchered the day before to allow the carcasses to cool. Each beef was calculated at 500 pounds (244 kg); in other words, one cow could feed a thousand men. The raw meat (including head, liver and offal) was issued in company sized lumps and then divided for each of the eight squads into pieces weighing two or three pounds each. On campaign, soldiers were cautioned not to let their meat spoil. It could be preserved by dry curing it over smoke, or, more practically, cooked and retained for the next meal break. Cooked or cured meats were issued when fresh meat was unavailable. Salt beef was distributed at the rate of 250 grams (8 ounces) per ration, while bacon was distributed at the rate of 200 grams (6 ounces).

[See also: 191. Rations & supplies (introduction); 200. Preparing soup; 201. Dry smoking meat; 203. Stock cubes; 204. Canned food; 228. Provisions; 240. Rations; 254. Military hospitals.]

## 194. Vegetables

The daily ration included 30 grams of rice or 60 grams of dried vegetables. The rice was sourced in Piedmont, India or the Carolinas, while the dried vegetables consisted of broad beans, peas, haricot beans or lentils, whichever was easiest to source locally. Ideally the distribution would be made so soldiers alternated between them daily, with the soldiers receiving four rice rations every seven days, and three vegetable rations. In barracks, the soldiers would purchase fresh seasonal vegetables to add to their meals, particularly potatoes, and at large, semi-permanent camps such as those around Boulogne in 1804–1805, they might also grow their own vegetables.

Dried vegetables could be very difficult to cook. Firstly they had to be sieved in order to rid them of small stones, dust and insects. The soldiers then had to find a suitable water source because dried vegetables cannot be cooked in hard water containing calcium sulphate. Soldiers were therefore instructed to use free flowing water, which was crystal clear, odourless and able to dissolve soap. River and rain water was preferred to water from springs and ponds, and they were taught never to use water from wells, or water which had come into contact with limestone.

## 195. Brandy (*eau de vie*)

Brandy was only distributed on the special order of a general, for example, after a forced march, strenuous field works, or on the day of battle. It was issued at the rate of one sixteenth of a litre per man (62.5 ml), a right not extended to officers.

The French Army insisted on this drink being made from distilled wine, rather than grain (i.e. vodka). The latter was considered extremely harmful to health.

[**See also:** 191. Rations & supplies (introduction); 200. Preparing soup; 202. Preparing broth from bones; 227. Duties in camp; 228. Provisions; 240. Rations.]

## 196. Vinegar

Vinegar was distributed by order of a general in hot weather, at the rate of 50ml (two spoonfuls) per man. The practice of mixing vinegar with drinking water dated back to Roman times. When vinegar was mixed with water the acidity killed harmful bacteria and the flavour helped to overcome the unpleasant taste of stale water. The sergeants were issued with a separate canteen (*petit bidon*) for carrying vinegar for their sub-division.

[**See also:** 28. Sergeant; 56. Weight of arms and equipment; 80. Petty equipment; 191. Rations & supplies (introduction); 210. Maintaining the musket; 227. Duties in camp; 228. Provisions; 241. Water and alcohol; 252. Sieges; 254. Military hospitals.]

## 197. Forage for horses

Senior infantry officers rode horses and at various times even company officers would have horses. Like men, horses need to eat, so this had to be factored into the supply chain. The principal staples were hay (grasses and other herbaceous plants cut and dried for feed), straw (the dry stalks of cereal plants, but with a lower nutrition content than hay), and oats. Forage for horses of infantry officers was issued at the following rates:

- On campaign: 5 kg of hay; or 5 kg straw; or 6.5 litres of oats.
- Travelling in the interior: 7.5 kg of hay; or 8.5 litres of oats.
- In garrison or depot 5 kg of hay; or 5 kg straw, and 6.5 litres of oats.

[**See also:** 85. Wagons and horses; 112. Deductions and funds; 227. Duties in camp.]

## 198. Fuel for heating and cooking

The fuel for heating and cook fires in garrison came in the guise of wood, coal, bituminous coal (*houille*), or peat, depending on the locality. Fuel was issued every five days. Troops in Paris and the interior of France received the full heating allowance from 1 November to 31 March. Those in the northern departments or the coastal regions received the winter allowance from 16 October to 16 April inclusively. Those in the south of France, from 16 November until 15 March inclusively. The remainder of the year only half a ration was issued. Adjutants, drum majors, sergeant majors, master craftsmen, sergeants and quartermaster corporals received a double ration throughout the year.

Firewood was commonly measured in steres, one stere equalling a cubic metre of piled timber or logs. In winter the ration would be 1/150th of a stere per man; in summer they would receive one 1/300th of a stere. In some departments wood was sold by weight and if so, it was issued at a rate of two kilos per man in winter or one in summer. Coal was issued at a rate of one kilo in winter or half in summer. If it was converted into briquettes of bitumous coal it would be issued at a rate of two briquettes in winter and one in summer. The briquettes were each 13.5 cm long, 5.5 cm high and 4 cm thick. They were delivered in packets of six or nine briquettes. Peat came in slabs (*tourbes*) typically measuring 10x5x5 cm. The ration was ten slabs per man in the winter and five in summer.

[**See also:** 112. Deductions and funds; 182. Lodgings and the arrangements of the bedchamber; 186. Making the rounds.]

A young soldier tends the a cauldron of soup. According to Elzéar Blaze, soldiers who were good cooks were kept well away from battles.

*Chapter 26*

# Food Preparation

## 199. Introduction

First thing in the morning, the chief of each ordinary would put on his sabre and go into town to shop for the two meals of the day. When out shopping, the chief would take with him one or more soldiers to carry back the supplies. The assistant(s) would be dressed in a smock-frock (*sarrau*), or jacket, or greatcoat, and a fatigue cap, but no weapons. The assistant would also bear witness to the probity of the financial transactions between the chief and his suppliers.

To deter the chief and his assistant from embezzling from their comrades, it was recommended the shopping fatigue was entrusted to a different fellow each day. Of course, one imagines this did not prevent irregularities occurring (after all, who would complain if the fellows who fetched one's dinner partook in a small refreshment on the way?). The chief was required to shop at a 'published market'; in other words he was not to cut corners by arranging a local merchant to bring supplies up to the barrack gates. The chief was to ensure the quality of the food and ensure there was sufficient quantity for everyone.

Kitchens came in many guises. Some bedroom chambers might be sufficiently large for cooking to take place locally. Other barracks had purpose built kitchens (the caserns at Versailles had the kitchens in cellars). In some the ovens (*fourneaux*) were linked, in other barracks they were separate. With no individual plates or bowls, the soup would be transferred from the pot to a communal mess pan. The soldiers would then eat '*à la gamelle*', which is to say like matelots in the navy, communally from the mess pan, each man taking a spoonful of soup at a time in strict rotation.

Under the watchful eye of the chief, every man in the ordinary (corporals excepted) would take turns preparing the soup (although men who had useful skills and who had permission to take work with the regimental tailor and other master craftsmen might exclude themselves from this chore for the fee of sixpence per day). The cooks would wear their forage caps and guard against food stains by turning their jackets inside out, or wearing a smock-frock.

The senior sub-officers never ate with the men while in barracks, but instead formed ordinaries with their colleagues in other companies of the same battalion. Quartermaster corporals could join the sergeants' ordinaries if they preferred. Another boon to their rank was the sub-officers could chose to hire a person 'foreign to the regiment' to manage their ordinary on their behalf. Of course, on campaign when beggars could not be choosers, the sub-officers were permitted to eat with the men under their command.

## 200. Preparing soup

The regulation of 1 July 1788 allowed French regiments two meals of soup per day. Although the manner of cooking might vary in practice, the official recipe for soup was given by Bardin as follows: Measure one litre of water for every quarter kilo (half pound) of meat; bring to the boil in a pot (*marmite*) over a large fire, then reduce the heat and add 8 grams of salt per litre of water. Add seasonal vegetables one or two hours before removing the meat (the meat was withdrawn and cut into portions). When the soup has boiled for five or six hours, and the broth is reduced to one fifth its original volume, the bread is added, leaving the pot on the fire until the last mess pan is filled, so the broth does not lose its warmth.

The meat ration was insufficient to prepare this meal twice a day. It appears one meal consisted of the meat broth described above, while the other was principally a vegetable dish. In French such a dish would be described today as *soupe à la graisse* – soup cooked with lard. The principal component of this dish would be potatoes to which would be added onion, and whatever seasonal vegetables were available.

[**See also:** 83. Utensils and tools; 108. The Ordinary; 112. Deductions and funds; 183. The daily routine; 191. Rations & supplies (introduction); 192. Bread and biscuit; 193. Meat; 194. Vegetables; 199. Food preparation (introduction); 254. Military hospitals.]

Soldiers preparing a meal in a *marmite* cooking pot. Note mess pan strapped to the haversack of the soldier smoking a pipe. (Beyer)

A soldier cooks meat on his sabre by holding it in the smoke of a bivouac fire.

## 201. Dry smoking meat

In the field, if the order to depart was issued before the soup had finished cooking, the soldiers were instructed to half cook it so as not to waste the meat and to prevent it from going bad. If there was not time for this, the soldiers were instructed to dry smoke it (*boucaner*), that is, cook it by exposing it to hot, thick smoke. Incidentally, this manner of cooking meats gave rise to the word buccaneer (*boucanier*) in the 17th century.

[See also: 193. Meat.]

## 202. Preparing broth from bones

During sieges and on long journeys there was a procedure for making soup from bones. One would collect the bones from the meat cooked the day before, or even better, uncooked bones, and crush them in a mortar and pestle. When they were reduced to a paste, they were spread over a diaphragm, which was a sort of white metal casserole dish, pierced with holes like a straining spoon. The diaphragm was plunged into a cooking pot (*marmite*) full of water and the bones allowed to simmer for six hours on an equal heat. This would produce 3.2 litres (three and a half pints) of broth, and half a pound of nourishing juices. The broth was covered and allowed to cool. As a by-product, this process would produce 60 grams of fat which could be used in the preparation of vegetables.

[See also: 83. Utensils and tools; 199. Food preparation (introduction); 203. Stock cubes.]

## 203. Stock cubes (*tablettes de bouillon*)

In order to reduce the weight of rations carried on long marches and provide a nutritious meal to soldiers, Dr Martin's 1801 *Manuel de l'officier de santé* contained an interesting recipe for preparing stock tablets. To prepare stock cubes, one took a whole calf or the third of an ox, washed and cleaned the flesh and put it in a cauldron mixed well with twenty pounds of broken deer antler and four buckets of water. This was cooked until the meat came away from the bone. The meat was then chopped and pressed between two iron trays. The juices of the meat were degreased and seasoned with salt and pepper, then added back into the stock. The mixture was then allowed to reduce over a lively flame until it coagulated into a firm jelly (the deer antler formed a gelatinous substance). The jelly was removed from the heat and then poured onto plates to cool. Once the jelly had cooled it was dried in a moderate heat until it hardened. It was then cut into tablets, each an ounce or two in weight. If prepared correctly, two ounces of this mixture was enough to provide one meal for a healthy man.

Bardin also discussed stock cubes in his dictionary. He recorded the English had already introduced them and stores of them were recovered after the battle of Hondschoote in 1793. They were a precious resource for seafarers, and during sieges, Bardin admitted, and by the late 1820s and 1830s they were being produced

Soldiers cooking with a *marmite*. Note the lid for the *marmite* resting on the haversack in the foreground. (Beyer)

by the million. However, although the process of using gelatine as a coagulating agent was known at the beginning of the 19th century it appears the process of creating stock cubes was not widely adopted by the French in the Napoleonic wars. One of the principal exponents of gelatine based rations was the pharmacist and all-round champion of salubrious living, Antoine-Alexis Cadet de Vaux. Noticing the number of bones left over from the butchering process, Cadet de Vaux proposed using these bones to create stock cubes. There were two main problems with the process. Firstly, the long cooking time meant the process was expensive in fuel. Secondly (and this is perhaps typical of French soldiers), rather than seeing the utility of having small, easy to carry, rations, stock cubes made from bone broth were perceived as being the food of the destitute, and therefore beneath the dignity of soldiers. Cadet de Vaux was even rebuked by a group of regiment children (hardly boys used to the finer things in life) who turned their noses up at the food and 'obstinately repulsed' the innovation.

[**See also:** 39. Regimental children; 202. Preparing broth from bones; 204. Canned food; 236. The medical officer's manual.]

## 204. Canned food

It is a popular yet erroneous belief Napoleon's soldiers were issued with canned food. The confectioner Nicolas Appert invented a system for preserving meats and vegetables by placing them in sealed glass jars and heating the contents to expel the air. Appert's technique was not properly recognised until 1810 when he was awarded a prize of 12,000 *francs* for the discovery. Experiments were undertaken by the French navy, but the glass jars were found to be heavy, fragile and liable to burst from pressure. The can was invented by the British who realised the practical benefits of using a lighter, stronger, tin container. In 1813 Bryan Donkin was able to supply the Royal Navy with food in tin cans. The Duke of Wellington was also a supporter of the process, tasting canned beef around the time of Vitoria in 1813. Although the French recognised the usefulness of the canning process, the invention came too late in the First Empire to be properly exploited.

[**See also:** 203. Stock cubes.]

*Chapter 27*

# Cleaning & Maintenance

## 205. Introduction

In any period of history, much of a soldier's time is spent cleaning and maintaining his uniform, arms and equipment, and the French Napoleonic infantryman was no exception to this rule. According to the 1792 police regulations no exercises or manoeuvres were planned on Saturdays so this day could be set aside for making repairs, cleaning equipment and the furniture in the bedchamber. On Sundays there would be a general inspection of the regiment by the colonel at 10.30. Every three months the colonel was advised to inspect the men's effects, a process apparently known as the booty review (*revue de butin*). In this inspection all the soldier's uniform, equipment, and weapons, would be inspected. During this the soldier would hold his account book in hand and new effects could be ordered. Extraordinary reviews usually took place prior to going on campaign with the more proactive generals ensuring their men were properly equipped. Each article issued to a soldier had an expected lifespan, and if the soldier did not want to spend his meagre wages exclusively on repair and replacing them, then it was essential he knew the following processes and procedures.

Corporals were to take particular care showing recruits how to treat their effects properly and to disassemble, then reassemble their equipment in order to clean and maintain it. Men were expected to make minor repairs of their own equipment. If the repair was too complex, the damaged article was presented to the captain who could authorise the regimental craftsmen to repair it. Damage caused while on leave would be repaired at the man's expense.

## 206. Cleaning the uniform

The uniform regulation of 1 October 1786 and the 'police' regulations of 24 June 1792 both required soldiers to keep their uniform clean. While laundresses would wash the soldier's linens, the men were responsible for cleaning the other uniform garments. This was a complex art in itself, as it was expressly forbidden to wash the uniform because woollen cloth loses its natural elasticity when washed and the lifespan of the article is shortened. Instead of washing, soldiers were expected to beat and brush their uniforms to maintain the highest standards of cleanliness.

If a garment was dirtied by spots of mud, grease or wine, a morsel of pipe clay moistened with some saliva would be applied. The pipe clay was allowed to dry out and then was removed by lightly scratching the cloth with the fingernail.

This would be followed with a beating of the garment with a clothes strap called a *martinet* (incidentally, this name is believed to derive from an infantry inspector under Louis XV called Colonel Martinet, who introduced the whipping as a military punishment. The whip was based on the British cat-o'-nine-tails. This correctional instrument proved more valuable for beating dust out of clothes than flogging the skin off men's backs.) If this method failed a little soap and water would be applied to the spot and this would be washed clean and allowed to dry naturally. The cloth was given a final clean by gently rubbing the material together.

Instead of soap, soldiers could apply some *pierre à detacher* (a removing stone). The best example was a bluish clay known more properly as fuller's earth (*terre à foulon*), an elastic clay used in the textile industry for removing grease and oily impurities from cloth.

If the stain still persisted one might take a pound of fuller's earth and a pound of *white of Troyes* (carbonate of lime – sometimes called *petit blanc* in French). These were crushed together and washed several times to remove their natural causticity. Into this mixture was added two large measures of 'salts of tartar' (potassium carbonate) and one ounce of turpentine. This mixture was worked into a dough which was allowed to half dry before being divided into portions each the size of an egg. When it was required for use, the stain would be moistened with a little hot water, and a light coat of the preparation added. The cloth was allowed to dry naturally and the spot would most likely have vanished.

If the coat had spots of tar on it, these could be dissolved with butter, which was in turn removed by washing with soap and water. Stains on scarlet cloth could be removed by applying some lemon juice.

In 1806 Napoleon experimented with reintroducing white coats for infantrymen. White wool posed particular problems in terms of keeping it clean. The tried and tested method of cleaning the coat used by soldiers before the Revolution was to spread it out on a table, and sprinkle it with some dry bran mixed with a little fine powder called Spanish whitener (*blanc d'Espagne*). This was rubbed into the coat with a piece of material. The coat was then beaten lightly so the whitener impregnated all parts of it. The coat was then beaten with a clothes strap until no more dust came from it. The coat was lightly brushed to remove any excess powder.

Although this process was known to be effective, it did wear out the material quite quickly. For this reason it was recommended only miller's bran (*son*) be used on white woollen cloth and they avoided any earth or chalk substances known to have caustic and corrosive properties.

Buttons and buckles were cleaned up with diluted whitener which was formed into a liquid dough and then rubbed against them. In order not to spoil clothes and jackets with this process, the buttons were inserted into a wooden button stick known as a *patience* (in reference to the care and time needed for this task).

[**See also:** 54. Materials; 55. Lifespan of uniforms; 80. Petty equipment; 205. Cleaning & maintenance (introduction).]

## 207. Whitening leather belts

The police regulations of 24 June 1792 required all white leather equipment to be whitened regularly. The most common and least expensive method of doing this was to produce a whitener by boiling several handfuls of miller's bran (*son*) in some water until the water went clear. A portion of pipe clay was diluted into this water and then allowed to cool.

Another method was to make a whitener from glue. To provide enough whitener for a company of men required 10 litres of water, 1.5 to 2 kg of pipe clay, 92 grams of Flanders glue (a light, transparent glue used in the textile industry), 120 grams of starch and 1.9 decigrams of indigo. This mixture was more solid than the previous method, but it was subject to flaking and if the belts became soaked with rain, the uniform could be stained blue. Some soldiers mixed pipe clay with milk. When this method was employed it was vital the belts were not held while they were still wet. They had to be hung freely so no folds would appear in the whitening and then left to dry in the air, not in front of a fire or in direct sunlight. Even when applied correctly this practice often left spots of fat on the belt.

Another solution could be made from powdered white lead – a traditional ingredient in paint. The powder was diluted in very clean water and left for twenty-four hours to remove all the caustic properties. The ratio of powder to liquid was described as being not too liquid or too dry. Prior to application the belts would be washed in clear water which was applied by a brush. Once cleaned the belts would be allowed to dry naturally without being heated or without the help of sunlight. When they were dry the solution would be applied with a brush in successive coats. After the first coat had dried, the belts would be lightly brushed. This would create a slightly coarse texture for subsequent coats to adhere to.

New leather belts might be difficult to whiten. Lime was used in the tanning process for removing hair and impurities from the hide. If the lime missed a part of the hide there might be grease spots on the leather which repelled the application of whitener. If this occurred the soldiers were told to scratch the affected area and to apply a solution of pipe clay and Spanish whitener without any glue. This process would be repeated until the grease spot was reduced and the belt would take the application of whitener evenly. In all cases the use of the varnish on belts to produce a gleaming effect was forbidden.

[See also: 76. Cartridge pouch; 80. Petty equipment; 91. Infantry sabre; 205. Cleaning & maintenance (introduction).]

## 208. Polishing the cartridge pouch

The 1792 police regulations required the cartridge pouch to be polished, even on its sides, using a wooden polisher. The infantry manual gave precise details for achieving a satisfactory finish, beginning with the process for making the polishing wax. For this, a pound of white wax was melted and mixed with a little gum arabic (acacia gum) and an ounce of ivory black (a pigment produced by charring animal bones). The mixture was brought to the boil, then removed, sieved and ground. If there was no white wax, yellow wax could also be used. In this case it was necessary to add two ounces of gum arabic, and to skim the mixture to give it brilliance. The mixture would then be coloured using vine black, a pigment made from burning the cut branches of grape vines, or the remains of crushed grapes.

If the cartridge pouch was new, the leather surfaces were rubbed with pumice. This removed the hardened blackening which covered the pouch, and which prevented the wax from penetrating into the leather. Without this precaution, the wax would soon flake. The polish was applied vigorously, and the wax was singed by holding the cartridge pouch over a small fire made from very dry straw. This warmed the wax, but not the leather. If too much heat was applied the cartridge pouch would become covered with pustules and would become brittle and crack.

This process was repeated until the coats of wax were blended together, and the finish was of an equal thickness. Any small holes or defects in the leather were to be smoothed over. The pouch was then polished with an *astic* (a polishing stick made of a hard wood) or a pebble, or a fork-toothed tool (*dent emmanchée*). The leather was then polished using cork of Liége, and then wiped with a linen buffer or a piece of fine cloth. The wax was not polished while warm, because it would tarnish. Once wiped clean without any spots, the cartridge pouch was rubbed lightly with the palm of the hand until gleaming (*miroitée*).

If the cartridge pouch had already been used, and was greasy, or the wax did not retain its gleaming finish, it was necessary to comb the leather with a knife, having heated the cartridge pouch over a fire. It was then polished and singed as with a new cartridge pouch, and finished in the same way. In summer, it was better to polish a cartridge pouch in the shade rather than in the sun, because the more the wax was softened the greater the difficulty of making it gleam.

If the corners of the outer flap had become creased, when the leather was warmed the crease could be removed by striking it with an *astic*, and then straightening it between the hands, until it cooled and preserved the correct shape. If the sides of the cartridge pouch were deformed, it was necessary to remove the wax by scraping the side with a knife. The internal wooden box was removed and the cartridge pouch was dipped in water. The wooden box was then reinserted with the box of another cartridge pouch placed on top of it. The pouch was then allowed to dry, with the sides of the leather pouch pressed against the wood. When the cartridge pouch dried, it would have resumed its original shape. In some regiments they reinforced the sides of the cartridge pouch with small boards because the leather at the sides of the pouch was not thick enough to retain its shape.

[**See also:** 76. Cartridge pouch; 80. Petty equipment; 205. Cleaning & maintenance (introduction); 209. Varnishing cartridge pouches.]

## 209. Varnishing cartridge pouches

Some regiments varnished their cartridge pouches, which dispensed with the need to use wax polishing techniques. The Imperial Guard and the Guard of Paris were particular exponents of varnishing, and found some economy in the method, because companies did not have to pay nine or ten *francs* per month for wax, and because many cartridge pouches deteriorated by the way of them singeing, or by the use of the hot pebbles with which the soldiers stretched and polished the wax.

Varnish was applied in a number of coats at a cost of 75 *centimes* per pouch. This preparation lasted for at least two years, without any other care than moistening the outer flap and the base with a little oil from time to time. The leather could remain in gleaming condition for a longer time, if the soldier was careful and was provided with a cartridge pouch cover.

[**See also:** 76. Cartridge pouch; 80. Petty equipment; 217. Polishing the cartridge pouch.]

## 210. Maintaining the musket

All infantrymen were taught the process of dismounting their muskets for the purpose of cleaning, maintenance and repair. First the ramrod would be removed from its channel underneath the stock; then the bayonet and the leather sling. The two screws holding the counter plate (*contre platine*) would be removed from the left side of the musket, allowing the lock (*platine*) to be removed. Next to be removed would be the breech screw (*vis de culasse*), which connected the end of the barrel to the wooden stock. There were three bands securing the barrel to the stock. The one closest to the muzzle was called the *embouchoir*. This was held in place by a spring on the 1777 models, and by a screw on the Year IX model musket. The next band was the *grenadière*, so called because it had a metal swivel loop underneath which held one end of the leather sling originally fitted to allow grenadiers to wear the musket over the shoulder while throwing grenades. This band was removed by releasing a spring, as was the final band, the *demi-capucine*, which terminated the ramrod channel. At this point the barrel could be detached from the stock. The pin for the lower sling swivel (*battant*) was removed, followed by the trigger guard (*pontet*), and the pin holding the trigger (*détente*). The last piece removed was the screw holding the *écusson*, the trigger guard plate through which the trigger passed.

Dismounting the lock was more complicated because of the strong springs which gave the firing mechanism the necessary tension. The lock was composed of twenty separate pieces. On the lock plate (*corps de platine*) was a movable hammer piece which held the flint. In French this piece was called the *chien* (lit. dog), but is better known in English as the 'cock'. The *chien* had a lower and upper jaw which were held in place with a locking screw. The next piece was the brass priming pan (*bassinet*), which was adjacent to the barrel's touchhole (*lumière*) and was covered by a piece called the *batterie* (better known as the frizzen in English). This piece included the striking surface, pan cover, cam and a pivot hole. Beneath this was a frizzen spring (*ressort de la batterie*) which acted on the cam of the frizzen and held it in an open or closed position. On the inner side of the lock plate were the main spring and those pieces comprising of the trigger mechanism. In order to unscrew the various pieces a spring dismounting tool (*démonte ressort* – also called a *monte-ressort*) was required. This tool was usually carried by the sub-officers, and allowed the user to pinch the spring, thus removing the tension from the fixing screws and allowing them to be removed. Bardin reckoned a good soldier could completely disassemble and reassemble a musket in twelve minutes.

Once a musket was broken down into its various components it could be cleaned. The metalwork on a musket was cleaned using emery powder mixed with olive oil (or sieved steel wool) applied with soft wood or rough brushes. The angles and curves of the weapon were cleaned using scrapers and spatulas. The barrel had to be laid on a bench or table before it was rubbed down lest the pressure caused it to bend. When emery or steel wool was not available, one could use pulverised sandstone (*grès*), sieved and moistened by olive oil. This material could also be used to remove heavier stains. For smaller stains, one could use burnt brick which had been properly crushed and then moistened by oil. These last two ingredients were also recommended for cleaning metal which had not been tempered.

Once all the pieces had been cleaned, they were wiped with a piece of cloth, so no emery, steel wool, sandstone, or brick remained. This ensured the surfaces would remain smooth. Once cleaned the weapons could be given a brilliant finish using *Tripoli* or cinnabar (mercury sulphide). Provided the soldier took great care of his weapon, this method of cleaning would be least prejudicial to the durability of the musket. Brass pieces were to be cleaned with *Tripoli* or crushed brick and vinegar. Fatty substances could not be used on brass as it would cause the metal to oxidise.

It was necessary for musket barrels to be washed on the inside to prevent rusting after firing. The barrel was washed until the water no longer came out black. The barrel was then rubbed by a dry piece of linen, followed by a piece of oiled linen. If this procedure was not carried out, there was a risk of rust which might block the touch hole or cause cracks at the end of the barrel which might cause it to burst. The linen was usually attached to the ball-extractor which was screwed into the end of the ramrod. Some men would simply wrap the linen around the large end of the ramrod, but this was frowned upon because pieces of material could be left in the barrel. It was recommended each squad had a wooden ramrod with a split at one end into which a piece of linen was inserted and fixed in place with thread.

It was forbidden to use the ramrod or the blade of the bayonet in the place of the turn-screw when tightening or releasing the jaws of the lock. Nor were men supposed to heat their ramrods under the pretext of enlarging the channel. Soldiers did this so the ramrod would rattle during arms drill and make a crunching sound which was pleasing to the ear – for soldiers at least. When the main spring was too hard, soldiers were not allowed to heat it to attempt to reduce the tension. Soldiers were also warned against rounding or altering the wooden stock in any

Grenadiers in fatigue caps
prepare soup and clean their
weapons in the bivouac.

manner, or oiling or applying tallow to the screws which went into the wood. Soldiers were forbidden from de-breeching their muskets, this procedure was only to be performed by an armourer. They were not allowed to remove the butt plates (*plaque de couche*) from their muskets, but had to clean them in situ.

If they lost the leads which held the flint in the jaws of the lock, soldiers would often take a lead ball from one of their cartridges and hammer the ball flat and create two lead sheets. They sometimes used the butt of their musket to do this, resting the ball against a hard flat surface and striking it with the metal plate at the end of the stock. This was all well and good, but they sometimes snapped the stock of the musket in the process and left the musket unusable.

[**See also:** 22. Master craftsmen; 77. Gun tools; 86. Musket; 211. Storage of weapons; 216. Target practice.]

## 211. Storage of weapons

The magazine or arms hall (*salle d'armes*) was a place chosen for being free from damp and sheltered from the sun. The weapons were to be well cleaned before being placed into storage and wiped down with an oily cloth. The barrels were plugged with a cork or wooden mannequin. Sabres and bayonets were also rubbed down with oil before being placed in their scabbards. If weapons had been in storage for any great length of time, they needed to be stripped down, cleaned, and re-oiled before being issued.

[**See also:** 86. Musket; 210. Maintaining the musket.]

*Chapter 28*

# Training

## 212. Introduction

There were several types of training for infantry soldiers while in garrison. In order to be classed as a qualified soldier, recruits had to pass through a succession of schools in which they learned marching, arms drill, and loading and firing. During the year there would be various exercises such as target shooting and practice manoeuvres, although the regulations of 1768 required colonels to ask the town governor for permission first before assembling his battalions and clogging up the streets, thoroughfares and gates. Gymnastic training as understood in the modern sense does not appear to have been given much consideration; however, there were several activities which provided physical exercise. Each regiment could also have a school for arms training which was managed by the master-at-arms. A provision for scholastic education was also introduced after the Revolution.

## 213. Basic training

The syllabus for marching and arms drill training was set out very briefly in the regulation of 1 August 1791. The colonel was responsible for general instruction of the officers, sub-officers and soldiers of the regiment. Military training was grouped into three distinct sections, known as schools (that of the soldier, the platoon, and the battalion). Soldiers would be assigned to an instructor (usually a sub-officer) who was deemed qualified for the task by his captain. This instructor would record the progress of the recruits, noting the dates at which they achieved competency in the various schools.

[See also: 5. Colonel; 24. Captain; 27. Sergeant major; 28. Sergeant; 47. Master-at-arms; 142. Tactical Organisation & Drill (introduction); 154. The manual exercise; 156. Ordinary pace; 166. Bayonet charges; 177. Skirmishing – the Davout instructions of 1811; 183. The daily routine; 212. Training (introduction); 216. Target practice; 217. Practising field works; 218. Gymnastic and fitness exercises; 245. Physical exercise.]

## 214. Instruction of officers

The instruction of officers followed the same school system taught to the men. If officers were to exercise command, it was believed they ought to be competent in the various drills and manoeuvres themselves. The colonel was required to assemble the officers at his quarters as often as necessary and explain to them, or at least have explained, the various principles set out in the regulations. Nothing in the regulation of 1 August 1791 was said about developing leadership skills, only that the officers should be frequently exercised in marching by the superior officers, teaching them the exact length and cadence of the step, and the accurate position under arms. Regiments may well have kept a library of military books to read, and they may have held debates to discuss tactics and strategy, but if so, these establishments were unofficial and instigated, or tolerated, by the colonel, not the minister of war.

[**See also:** 5. Colonel; 47. Master-at-arms; 118. Promotion to the officer corps; 154. The manual exercise.]

## 215. Instruction of sub-officers

Sub-officers were instructed by the adjutant, and to a lesser extent, the adjutant major and the field officers. They were required to understand the School of the Soldier and the School of the Platoon intimately; possessing an accurate knowledge of the manual exercise of the soldier, of the types of firing and marching. When a new sub-officer was created, it was the duty of the first sergeant to ensure he was properly instructed, with the adjutant overseeing the training. Colonels were also required to ensure the colour platoon and guides were properly exercised in marching, paying particularly attention to maintaining a straight line of march and a precise length and cadence of the step.

[**See also:** 16. Adjutant; 24. Captain; 27. Sergeant major.]

## 216. Target practice

There was an annual allowance of 250 kg of powder and 125 kg of lead per battalion for exercises and to provide ammunition to guards. After 26 May 1807 this allowance was set at 1 kg of lead and 2 kg powder for every four men. All corporals, grenadiers and fusiliers were required to perform this school once a year and a note was taken of the best marksmen. Recruits were to be given particular instruction and at the end of the exercise, attempts were to be made to recover the spent musket balls so they might be remoulded.

According to the regulation of 1 August 1791 targets were made from a rectangular board five and a half French feet high, and 21 inches wide (i.e. the same size as the body of the average soldier). The middle was marked by a band of colour three inches wide traced horizontally. The highest extremity was marked by a similar band. Soldiers would be exercised at firing from 50 fathoms, then 100 fathoms and finally 150 fathoms. At 50 and 100 fathoms the soldiers would aim at the lower band and at 150 the higher band. The soldiers would fire individually, at first without command, and then by command.

In order to compensate for the kick of a musket at shorter ranges, and the fall of shot over distance, the following aiming advice was given to always hit the target in the chest:

| Distance | Aiming point |
|---|---|
| 800–900 paces | 3 ft above the target |
| 600 paces | 1 ft above the target |
| 450 paces | Hat |
| 300 paces | Belt |
| 150 paces | Knee |

On the command 'fire', the soldier was to press the index finger forcibly against the trigger without moving the head, nor disturbing the alignment of the weapon. After firing the soldier was to remain in the aiming position until given the instruction to load.

The instructor was to recommend them to properly support the butt against the right shoulder in the aiming position; to support the weapon with the left hand, and to quickly align the breech and end of the barrel on the target band they were aiming at. They would practise adopting this position numerous times so they became proficient at quickly adopting the correct position and aim.

[**See also:** 86. Musket; 89. Ammunition; 167. Musketry (introduction); 212. Training (introduction).]


## 217. Practising field works

One of the most common peacetime exercises was the annual mock siege, simulating an attack and defence of a fortified place. These exercises would take place in the summer after the grasses on the glacis had been carefully cut for forage (the glacis was the sloped earthworks on the exterior of a fortress over which an enemy would have to pass. The angle of the glacis was such it afforded no cover to enemy troops from the defenders' fire). Gardens and fruit trees were not allowed on the exterior works and animals were not allowed to graze anywhere on the ramparts, ditches, etc. and if they were found the soldiers could confiscate them 'for their profit'. These mock sieges would be directed by the local engineer officers who would teach soldiers how to construct siege works such as breast works and covered ways. The engineers would also teach the soldiers how to best defend the fortifications, and how to achieve the best direct or flanking fires and show where crossfires might be possible. At first, exercises would take place without powder, but then this would be added for an additional element of realism.

Where possible, troops would also attend an eight day school on constructing field works such as ditches and redoubts. This involved the building of *fascines*, *gabions* and *claies*. Fascines are fagots or bundles of wood made with branches.

They were used by besiegers to protect workers while opening a trench. They were ten to twelve feet long and a metre in diameter. They could also be used to protect batteries, breast works, entrenchments, trenches and dikes. They were fixed in the ground with three or more pegs. One man could make one fascine in an hour. The most efficient system was to have six men for each metre required; two cutting branches, two for placing them, and two for holding them. Gabions were a sort of cylindrical basket without a bottom which could be filled with earth and stones. They came in various sizes. To make one of a metre in diameter, you traced a circle in the ground one metre across and then planted uprights. Smaller branches were then woven around the uprights to form a wickerwork effect. The *claie* was a trellis work which could be loaded with earth. They could be used as the foundation of batteries on soft ground, or to put over the top of ditches and then covered with earth to provide a covered, protected route. They could also be used as formers when rebuilding stone walls. *Claies* were usually five by six feet in size.

[**See also:** 195. Brandy; 229. Outpost duty.]

## 218. Gymnastic and fitness exercises

Generally speaking, Napoleon's army had no official form of gymnastic exercise. The reason for this was rooted in the system of warfare practiced in the 18th century, which was between large formations of troops, as opposed to single combat. Gymnastics was a form of self-expression incompatible with the 18th century mindset that 'immobility' was the highest form of military exercise. In common with this, the uniform of an infantryman was designed to restrict the movement of limbs and the head.

The only forms of exercise which were widely recognised and encouraged were dancing and fencing, both of which were viewed as being favourable to developing physical qualities, and to give the soldier suppleness and dexterity. However in both these examples, one imagines the driver for these activities was as much to provide a useful recreation as to enhance the men's physiques. Knowledge of fencing was of course useful for personal defence. Its purpose was partly a form of physical education, building strength, suppleness and improving nimbleness. It also taught the men to be confident in their bearing and to be 'imperturbable' in the face of danger.

The provisional regulation of 5 April 1792 did at least recommend conditioning soldiers about to embark on campaign by exercising the troops with route marches with arms and full equipment. These 'military promenades' were to be limited to several leagues at first, and then, as men began to become fitter (to be 'in breath') the marches would take place at midday in order to accustom the men to withstand the hot weather.

During the First Empire voltigeurs were trained to swim and run; and be able to keep up with cavalry moving at the trot; although nothing explicit was published in how this was achieved. Velites of the Imperial Guard also received gymnastic

Light infantry voltigeurs racing into action. Bardin believed voltigeurs corporals ought to be able to swim, run and leap ditches.

training. Although not a specific instruction itself, Bardin's original 1807 *infantry manual* recommended that corporals of light infantry and voltigeurs ought to be able to run, swim, leap ditches, and climb.

[**See also:** 39. Regimental children; 105. Velites; 212. Training (introduction); 245. Physical exercise.]

## 219. General education

The 1792 police regulations required each regiment to form a school between 1 October to 1 May to teach reading, writing and elementary arithmetic. The school was set up in a room in the barracks chosen for this purpose, and furnished with tables and benches taken from the surplus of those provided to the regiment. The colonel would choose two school masters from among the sub-officers in the regiment to manage the school. Their lessons were open to all men in the regiment and the council of administration was allowed to apply to the minister of war for a bonus for the school masters proportional to the work and progress made.

[**See also:** 212. Training (introduction); 117. Promotion.]

*Part VII*

# Service in the Field

# Chapter 29

# Opening the Campaign

## 220. Introduction

The provisional regulation of 5 April 1792 on the service of infantry on campaign set out how a regiment would prepare and act when required to go into the field. The regulation assumed an army would be formed in a camp before hostilities commenced; that all the various regiments would arrive there, and be assigned to a particular brigade. The regiment with the lowest number would be considered the senior in the brigade and take position on the right of the brigade (not that a low number imparted anything special on the regiment), and they would thereafter camp, march and fight in this order. A small note, but a crucial one: when the brigade was formed, the grenadiers would be formed into a battalion and placed under the command of a superior officer of the general's choice. The grenadiers would camp with their parent battalion, but would 'serve outside of the line'. If a regiment or battalion was detached from a brigade, its grenadiers would be returned.

Through the entire period, although military camps might not have always taken place at the outset of a campaign, there would still be a rendezvous point where the brigade was assembled. This might be a town, or fortress, but the important point was the process of brigading the regiments. It was also recommended that before the campaign commenced, the regiments would be reviewed by general officers. The 1792 field service regulations required those judged sick or unfit, or too young for active service to be removed from the line at this point and assigned to guarding the communications. The carriages belonging to officers and sutlers would also be examined to ensure they were properly registered.

## 221. On the march

On average the Napoleonic French infantryman would be expected to march eight leagues a day (approximately 32 km), at a rate of one league per hour. On occasions, the march might be extended, or 'forced', and on occasions, the march might even be accelerated, although this could not be sustained for long without leaving a great number of stragglers unable to maintain the pace.

For marches in peacetime, or in the interior, when a regiment set out a great deal of organisation was required so the troops would be provided with accommodation and sustenance along the route. The length and timing of the march was also vitally important in order for the men to arrive at their destination with enough time to cook and eat, preferably before nightfall.

The regiment's marching orders were written on a travel itinerary called a *feuille de route*. This set out an itinerary from the point of departure until the final destination, with all the various legs or stages (*étapes*) and evening lodgings (*gîtes*) on the way. Three days before the march commenced, the quartermaster treasurer would set out with a copy of the marching orders to arrange for quarters and provisions with the various local authorities along the route. On the day of departure an advanced party consisting of an officer, two sergeant majors and the quartermaster corporals would set out before the regiment to prepare the lodgings and bread at the destination so it was ready when the troops arrived. On arrival at that evening's *gîte*, this advanced party would present itself to the civilian mayor, or if a fortress garrison, the local commandant, or inspector. Forewarned by the quartermaster, these authorities would have taken the necessary steps to arrange for the soldiers to be quartered among the civilian population and for the correct weight of bread to be produced. Any troops who were classed as walking wounded, or excused duties would be sent ahead with this advanced party.

When preparing to march, the battalion would form in line and then each section would wheel to the right in order to form a column of sections. There was an advanced guard which was usually formed from half an elite company (particularly voltigeurs later on); but which could also be provided by an officer, sergeant, two corporals and two men per company. This body would remain in view of the head of the column and within the audible range of a drum. Behind the regiment there would be an escort for the regiment's baggage and a rearguard. The rearguard would be composed of half an elite company with one sub-officer per company and under the orders of a lieutenant or captain. The rearguard was not to lose sight of the regiment and to make halts at the same time. Its principal purpose was to ensure no one was left behind. The purpose of having one sub-officer per company was to identify which men had fallen out of the column.

The officer of the regiment's police guard would not leave until one hour after the troop's departure, looking for deserters. This final rearguard would hang back a league behind the main body, collecting stragglers and putting them into a wagon if they were unable to continue. Once the rearguard had passed, anyone found without written permission to be absent from their corps was at the mercy of the gendarmes, a party of whom would be following. These gendarmes would also check the side roads and villages as they went.

Soldiers detained in the guardhouse, or serving a prison sentence, were escorted by the police guard, located in the interval of the first and second battalions, or, in the case of only a single battalion being present, between the first and second companies. The regulations also spoke of a police *piquet* on the march. This was formed from two men per company, one sergeant, two corporals, and one drummer, under an officer. It is unclear if this was the same body as the police guard, or if it was sent ahead with the quartermaster corporals to help establish the next billet.

[See also: 10. Quartermaster treasurer; 29. Quartermaster corporal; 85. Wagons and horses; 159. Route pace; 185. The police guard.]

Cantineer rides at the head of a platoon of infantry. Cantineers are often shown riding side saddle, on a horse or mule laden with barrels and other stock.

## 222. Halts on the march

The age old practice was for regiments to stop midway on the route for an hour or two in order to rest and replenish their drinking water. For this reason the preference was to stop at inhabited places to secure potable water. The ordinance of 12 August 1788 recommended stopping for three or four minutes every hour to allow troops to catch up. Soldiers were not to remove their packs or sit down during this break, which became known colloquially as 'the halt of the pipes' (i.e. smokers could recharge their pipes and light them). Once this practice became established, the old 'grand halt' was reduced to an hour at most.

An additional halt was observed forty-five minutes into the march, presumably to ensure everyone was on the road and to adjust belts and equipment. Another halt was made fifteen minutes before arriving at the destination, a useful precaution to allow stragglers to catch up, and for the ranks to be dressed so the regiment arrived in a military fashion, not as a mob of refugees. Of course the commander could make additional, fewer, longer or shorter halts taking into account the urgency, the state of the road, the gradient of the road and the weather. If at any point in between a man needed to break ranks on the march, say to answer a call of nature, he had to ask an officer for permission, and leave his musket behind with a comrade while absent.

[**See also:** 159. Route pace; 241. Water and alcohol; 247. Marching.]

## 223. Night marches

A regiment might march at night for operational reasons, or to avoid the worst of the summer heat. In any case, there were strict control measures which had to be followed. Firstly the advanced and rear guards would close up on the main column so they were within calling distance of a voice. The strictest silence had to be maintained and sub-officers were charged with ensuring no one became lost. If part of the column became separated, the drummer at the tail of the column would beat the *rappel* as an order to halt. Once the missing column had re-joined, the same drummer would beat *aux champs* in order to proceed. There were to be no verbal commands.

[**See also:** 37. Drummer; 247. Marching.]

## 224. Duties of the baggage master

When ordered to march, the baggage master's (*vaguemestre*) first duty was to inspect the regiment's wagons and carts. He would take a piece of wood and hit the spokes of the vehicles wheels to ensure they had not split. He would then examine the rest of the vehicle in detail to ensure it was sound and in good working order. The day before departure, the baggage master would gather all the regiment's baggage. He would only accept packages which were properly sealed and sufficiently solid and which contained a 'legible and ineffaceable' inscription of what the package contained and who it belonged to. The officers' portmantles were not to exceed 12 kg each and were only to contain effects which would be in daily use. The baggage would be inscribed on a register, which listed the baggage belonging to the staff and then to each of the companies in order.

The baggage master would ensure the wagons were not overloaded carrying female sutlers or children. One man per company would be assigned to the baggage master for loading and unloading the wagons and they would do no other fatigues for the whole journey. When the regiment set out, the wagons would follow one hundred paces to the rear of the regiment. The lead wagon would contain the regiment's pay chest and papers. The baggage master might allow one wagon to stay behind with the rearguard in order to transport men who fell out on the march.

On the road the baggage master would ensure the wagons remained together and they only halted when the regiment stopped, unless there was an accident. He also ensured they did not become too strung out on the road. The wagon drivers (*charretiers*) were not to leave their horses, and no one was to climb up onto the wagons without a written order. When he encountered columns of troops, the baggage master would cede good road to the infantry. If a wagon did break, its baggage would be redistributed and the wagon thrown from the road. Everything which could not be reloaded or carried would be burned.

[**See also:** 23. Baggage master; 85. Wagons and horses; 116. Military postal service; 225. Arrival at a *gîte*.]

## 225. Arrival at a *gîte*

By the time the regiment arrived at its *gîte*, the quartermaster corporals should have made arrangements for billeting the soldiers of their companies on the local population. Each soldier or group of soldiers would be issued with a bill (*billet* – hence 'billeting') with the address of their hosts. The officer in command of the advanced party (known as the *capitaine de logement*) would have arranged inns for the officers and negotiated dinner at the price set by the colonel. This officer would also select a guardhouse for any prisoners the regiment might be escorting.

When the regiment arrived the first priority was to establish a police *piquet* to ensure order was maintained. The baggage master would conduct the wagons to this place, unless another had been indicated as the depot. He would have the baggage unloaded and examined. If the baggage was covered with snow, he would have it swept off. If the baggage was soaked by rain, he would do his best not to pile it together. There would also be a nominated distribution point where the bread ration would be issued.

The soldiers would then go to meet their hosts. When they reached their billets there were strict laws to protect the hosts. The hosts were not to be displaced from the bedroom they normally occupied. Soldiers were entitled to nothing more than a bed, such as could be provided, a place at the fire for warmth, and candlelight to see by. They were not to go visiting other homes in the night, nor wander about gardens and vineyards, pilfering fruits, vegetables or anything else belonging to the inhabitants. Before the companies dispersed, these rules would be given to the soldiers in the form of a *ban* – or proclamation. Once everyone had settled down an officer would inspect the billets to ensure everyone was present and there was no disorder. An hour after retreat, the sergeants would make the same rounds, ensuring no one had strayed since the officer's visit.

The commander of the police guard would hear the complaints of civilians, maintain good order among the soldiers, send men to where there was trouble, make patrols immediately after the retreat and then from hour to hour through the night. Any inhabitants who caused disorder were to be escorted to the civil authorities to be punished. The guard commander would also distribute billets to men who arrived late, unless he had received orders to arrest them and put them in prison.

[**See also:** 23. Baggage master; 185. The police guard; 221. On the march.]

## 226. Arrival at camp

When going into camp, a portion of the sub-officers and soldiers would be sent ahead to mark it out, under the order of the quartermaster and a battalion commander. The 1792 field service regulations spoke of the need to cut the grasses in some seasons. This task would be performed by four of the officer orderlies (*domestiques*) per battalion, equipped with scythes.

At the approach to a camp the drummers would beat and the soldiers come to the shoulder arms position. Each battalion would place itself in line at the head of the camp. The space in front of this line was known as the *bandière* a word we might translate as the line of the colours. In other words, it was the line on which the soldiers made their piles of arms, and where the colours were planted. When the battalions were lined up in front of the *bandière*, the wagon master would discharge the camping equipment, giving three pennants (*fanions*) per battalion to the general guides on the wings and centre of the line. He also discharged three ropes per battalion. These ropes were marked with alternate red and black bands, indicating the correct spacing between each tent. If these ropes were unavailable, the camp would be paced out using a 'metric step'. A bayonet would be planted in the ground and a cord attached to it. Using the centre of the *bandière* as the pivot point, the extent of the camp was marked by tracing a circle.

A battalion would generally camp on ground equal to its frontage. The tents were usually arranged by half-companies, so each half company had a 'range' of five tents lined up one behind the other. There were therefore two ranges per company. This could be transformed into more of a square by having one range per company, ten tents deep. The lines of tents were parallel to the *bandière*. The ranges were perpendicular to the *bandière*. They were alternatively spaced by lanes which were referred to as grand streets and little streets, respectively (a grand street was twice the width of a small street). When camps were established for a long period of time, soldiers had a habit of naming these lanes after great battles and generals.

When the measuring was completed, each corporal would take six men to collect and erect the tents. They would leave their packs and muskets under the guard of their comrades and then pick up the necessary canvases, poles, pegs and mallets. These items were deposited in the nearest grand street. The first range of tents would be composed of the squads and sections under the orders of the lieutenant; the second range, the sub-lieutenant. The first tent of the first range would be assigned to the sergeant major and the quartermaster corporal. The second and third tents would be occupied by the first and fifth corporals; the fourth and fifth tents were occupied by the second and sixth corporals. The second range would be composed of (from front to rear) the tents of the four sergeants, the eighth corporal, the fourth corporal, the seventh corporal, and the third corporal. When all the tents were in place, there was a roll of drums, at which all the tents were raised – a very Prussian touch. The soldiers with the mallets would quickly hammer the pegs in to secure the tents.

As the tents were going up, the officers would mark out where the arms would be piled. In a camp, there were small bell tents which would keep the muskets out of the rain. The regiment's sappers would form their own stack of arms with their axes. Once the soldiers' tents were erected, the officers' tents would be lined up behind them; also the laundresses and cantineers. Behind the battalion would be the battalion commander, with the colonel's tent at the centre of the regiment. The cook fires would be located between the soldiers' tents and those of the laundresses.

The soldier's camp latrines would be located on the other side of the *bandière*, shielded by an improvised screen if time and resources permitted. Officers had their latrines behind the line of the senior officer's tents.

As a footnote, we must remember tents fell out of use around the time of the great levies of men in 1793. Although canvas tents were not used, camps were formed on numerous occasions. At these, the tents were replaced with wooden huts. On campaign, the French Army usually bivouacked, forming a line and piling its arms in the usual way, but then made the best use of whatever rudimentary shelter could be found or made. Often this was nothing but a large fire around which everyone sat.

[See also: 83. Utensils and tools; 84. Tents; 85. Wagons and horses; 220. Opening the campaign (introduction); 227. Duties in camp.]

## 227. Duties in camp

As much as possible, usual military routine was followed while in camp. Service might be armed (i.e. detachments, exterior guards, guards of honour, police or piquet duty), or fatigues such as gathering distributions or forage. Service generally lasted twenty-four hours, and grenadiers were usually exempt. Other than providing guards, the principal duties were assisting the baggage master, carrying cooking pots, mess pans, water cans, and tools; attending distributions of raw meat, bread, vinegar, etc. In camp soldiers would reap the crops and grasses, forage, look for vegetables, water, firewood and straw. Fatigues might also include the manufacture of light fortified works, or, in siege, the manufacture of gabions and other defensive structures. The battalion commanders would each provide sufficient men for these duties. Service would begin with the senior regiment controlled by the senior adjutant major. Sergeant majors would hold a register listing the order of seniority in the company and the drum major would have a list of the drummers in order of seniority.

In camp orders and passwords were transmitted at midday. Having been set by the general in chief and then cascaded down through the generals of division and brigade, not to mention their staff officers, the daily orders would be transmitted to the battalion commanders. All the officers on picket duty, each quartermaster, adjutant major, adjutant sub-officer, sergeant major, the duty sub-officers and baggage masters assembled at the centre of the corps, twenty paces in front of the piles of arms. The sergeant majors and sergeants formed a circle, carrying their muskets in their right arm. The corporals formed a second circle, presenting arms and facing outwards to ensure no one approached. Between the sergeants and the corporals stood the others named above, and the drum major. Only the battalion commander entered the circle. He would then issue the orders, explain who had been assigned to guard duty, or what services were required overnight or the following day. The battalion commander would issue the password to the officers and adjutants. The first sergeant major in the circle would then advance

Soldiers gathering forage. The standing grenadier appears to be asking for some vegetables. Note he has a bayonet tucked into the front of his greatcoat. The figure in the background has a scythe for collecting forage. (Beyer)

into the circle and be told it. He would retire, then tell the sergeant to his left and so on. As the sergeants were told the password they would present arms until everyone in the circle had been told. The circle would be broken and the sergeant majors would go and tell their officers what was planned for the coming day. The quartermaster would pass on any instructions to the sutlers, baggage masters and the officers' domestics.

At sunset a gun would be fired or the drummers would beat the retreat. At the sound of the retreat, all fires would be extinguished and the regimental canteens closed. Soldiers had to return to their tents within an hour. All the companies would line up in a single rank in the main roads of the camp for roll call.

In camps which lasted more than two days, the troops would be exercised as often as possible. Infantry would be manoeuvred by battalion, regiment, brigade, and, if necessary, by division. The exercises would include firing. The soldiers would never use the cartridges in their pouches, only powder specially given for the training session.

[See also: 185. The police guard; 190. Passwords; 191. Rations & supplies (Introduction); 199. Food preparation (introduction); 200. Preparing soup; 229. Outpost duty; 242. Air quality.]

## 228. Provisions

When on campaign the distribution of rations was often sporadic at best, with the supply chain very often falling victim to the rapidity of marches, poor road conditions and inadequate vehicle provision, not to mention corruption and general incompetence. This forced soldiers to 'live off the land' (in other words to forage or steal) or face starvation. In equal measure, soldiers forced to undergo sieges were also likely to see a fairly drastic deterioration in the quality and quantity of foodstuffs distributed. Unlike in garrison, where the ordinary chiefs would go shopping each morning, on campaign all provisions were issued. The campaign rations consisted of bread or biscuit, rice, dried vegetables, fresh meat, or salt beef or bacon, brandy, wine, vinegar, and salt. Where possible, distributions were made every four days at the head of the camp. An officer or sub-officer was always present to maintain order. Officers were only provided with rations on campaign, receiving one and a half rations each, but no brandy or vinegar.

[**See also:** 191. Rations & supplies (introduction); 197. Forage for horses; 198. Fuel for heating and cooking.]

## 229. Outpost duty

One of the most important duties was to protect the camp with a system of outposts and sentries. This type of role was traditionally assigned to light infantry, but could be performed by line infantry. The instructions for performing this service were given in the 1792 field service regulations and other works, notably Frederick II's *instructions to light troops and to officers serving in the forward posts*, a work which Bardin listed as essential military reading in 1813.

Around every camp or bivouac would be a series of forward posts or pickets (*piquets*) which were designed to provide early warning of attack, and act as a deterrent against deserters. In summary, each picket would be formed of a grand guard where the officer and a reserve was stationed. Ahead of this would be a number of 'little posts' commanded by corporals, and beyond them a chain of sentries. There would also be patrols thrown out ahead of the chain, probing the suspected route of enemy advance. If the enemy did come into contact with a patrol, or sentries, the soldiers would progressively fall back on their supports, buying time for the men in camp to take up arms and prepare a defence.

Battalion commanders had a special responsibility for inspecting the grand guards around a camp. They were to be placed so they could be seen from a distance, but also provided with shelter from fire by earth banks or a parapet made from branches or trees. The battalion commander would observe the roads or tracks by which the enemy might debouch. The battalion commander would also identify the tracks which should be patrolled at night. The battalion commander would explain how he wanted the post defended and how many sentries were to be thrown ahead.

An officer placed in command of a post would employ all means possible for its defence. He would create an entrenchment, the back of which was left open in order to receive reinforcements. If the post was in a village or farm, he would place the grand guard behind a stone wall, such as might be found around a cemetery.

He would also barricade roads leading to the post. He would indicate an assembly point in case of an alarm. He would recognise the fords, defiles and tracks which the enemy might use. He would also identify a means of retreat if attacked by superior numbers (unless of course they had been instructed to hold out until the last extremity), and take measures for defence such as making an abatis, barricades, ditches, and entrenchments, using villagers to help if necessary.

Sentinels were posted within calling distance of the post they were covering. If they were not in direct view of the post, a corporal and four men would form a 'little post' at a location from where communication could be maintained. Before going out, corporals would check they had primed their muskets and their flints were well placed. The sentries had to fix bayonets and while on post they were not to put down their weapons, sit, read, sing, nor speak unless absolutely necessary. Sentries placed near artillery or stores of gunpowder in the camp were to be armed with a sabre or a bayonet 'in hand' (presumably a precaution against accidental explosions). Sentinels were relieved every two hours, or every hour in severe cold weather. If a grand post was approached, a sergeant and four fusiliers would call out 'halt there – who goes?' After the response 'France' the sergeant would ask, 'which regiment' or 'what rank'. When he recognised the party or individual, one of the four fusiliers would be sent to the commander of the post to report who had passed. Any strangers who merited the attention of the guard were to be taken to the chief of staff or the duty general officer. Enemy drummers or trumpeters were not allowed to approach the camp. If they were seen they were told to halt while the commander of the grand guard was summoned. If a lieutenant or sergeant received a written message from the enemy signallers then they would take it to the camp and have it passed to the chief of staff or commanding general. If a reply to the message was required, the enemy signallers were told to wait within musket range of the forward posts and not to approach it. The reply would be taken out to them at the appropriate time. If enemy deserters were found by the sentries, they were to be disarmed and taken to the chief of staff for questioning. If there were large numbers of deserters they were to be disarmed and guarded outside the camp until a solution was found for dealing with them. Anyone who was caught trying to leave the camp without permission was to be arrested and handed over to the gendarmes.

As night fell, the password and rallying cry could be issued to the officers of the guard. Soldiers were told to cover the locks of their muskets to keep them dry against rain and dew. If the musket did become fouled with rainwater the preferred way to clear the barrel was by firing a charge. Firing would occur between nine and ten o'clock in the morning in the presence of an officer of the picket who would ensure there were no accidents. If the charge had become too damp to fire, a sergeant major would order the men to clear their barrels using a ball extractor.

At night the little posts were to withdraw on the grand guards. Sentries were told to roam around their area of control, because fixed sentries could be avoided in the darkness. If in close proximity of the enemy, officers were not to undress at night, and they were to forbid anyone from leaving their post. They were advised to patrol the lines of sentries from time to time to ensure they remained vigilant. The timings of these rounds were not to be regulated. If the officer decided to go on patrol himself, he would take two men with him, always leaving orders before he departed. When he returned he would stop when the sentries cried 'halt there' and wait for a corporal and two men to advance and recognise them.

At daybreak the officers and men would border the parapet and remain there in readiness. When it was fully light, a sergeant and four men would be sent out to discover any enemy movements. This sergeant was given specific instructions on which places to search and where the enemy might position ambushes. When observing the enemy at a distance the direction of march could be gauged by observing the reflection of sunlight on their musket barrels and bayonets. If the reflection was towards the observer, the formation was advancing directly at them. If very few reflections were seen, it indicated the corps was retreating, and reflections to the left and right meant they were marching to the flank.

[**See also:** 59. Greatcoat; 80. Petty equipment; 134. Military justice; 210. Maintaining the musket; 227. Duties in camp; 246. Guard duty.]

*Chapter 30*

# The Day of Battle

## 230. Introduction

Once two armies had come into contact, there would often be numerous skirmishes and clashes between the outposts as the two adversaries probed one another's strength and intentions. Much of this fighting would be accomplished by light cavalry, but occasionally infantry divisions or even whole army corps might find themselves unexpectedly engaged. Most campaigns of the Napoleonic period were decided by one or two cataclysmic pitched battles where the rival armies lined up and contested their strength and resolve over a day, or sometimes two. At the end of this contest, one side would usually cede ground to its adversary, or sue for an armistice, temporary or otherwise.

## 231. Battle tactics

The preparations for a pitched battle during the Napoleonic Wars had changed very little since the 17th century. Gustav Adolphus is credited with employing two lines of battle with a reserve force behind. This system of deployment would have remained familiar to Napoleon's generals and sure enough, the Field Service regulations of 1792 describe the standard battle formation as being two lines of troops, three hundred paces distant. The reserves were to be placed three hundred paces behind the second line in the places allocated by the commanding general. (The second line might be formed in column or in line. In the former case it allowed the battalion to advance more quickly to reinforce the first line; in the latter the thin depth meant the column would suffer less from artillery fire. There is evidence from memoirs that men in the second line might be able to open ranks to permit the passage of cannonballs rolling along the ground). The artillery was to be placed in the most advantageous positions available from where it could fire on enemy troop formations.

As the infantry brigades deployed, light infantry would be sent ahead to screen the deployment and to discover the enemy's dispositions. Infantry regiments would form in order of seniority from the right. This prerogative was considered a non-negotiable point of honour (Bardin considered this practice a potentially disastrous piece of vanity). Depending on the situation, generals might form their brigades in a variety of formations. The simplest to describe is a line of battalions, either deployed into line, or remaining in columns with sufficient deployment space either side of them. Another popular tactic was the *ordre en echelon* where a line of battalions formed something of a diagonal line in order to refuse a flank. The front of each battalion remained parallel to the enemy line, but each successive battalion was placed to the left and behind of the first battalion. The interval between each echelon was normally one hundred paces, but could be more or less depending on the views of the commander. (The echelon could also be formed with the left battalion leading). The *ordre mixte* was composed of a mixture of lines and columns. Although this system has been popularised in modern histories, Bardin did not stress any particular importance to it, and was fairly light in his description of the system, writing it had been used occasionally in Spain and also in an attack on the Russian redoubts at Borodino in 1812. Battalions might be placed *en potence*: at right angles to the main line to protect a flank. Other battalions might be set at an angle to the enemy line in order to make concealed marches against the enemy flank; a tactic favoured by Frederick II, and apparently copied by Napoleon.

The advice given in the regulations was that care should be taken when locating the reserve, and the commanders of the reserve instructed on which corps they were to support and replace in an action. Commanders of the reserve were instructed to vigorously charge any enemy troops which broke through the line of battle, or to fall on the flanks of an obstinate enemy. Divisions should be placed so they were mutually supporting and could come to one another's aid.

Troops who had been issued clear instructions were best able to execute the orders of the commanding general. The instructions were to be said clearly with as few words as possible; lengthy oratory was frowned upon. At the same time commanders were not to underestimate the enemy or show excessive fear of the foe. If a commander had assured his troops the enemy would flee after receiving a single volley, the confidence of his men would likely falter if the enemy continued to press on after the first discharge. If a commander had told his men the enemy would abandon their positions, but they met heavy resistance, they would assume the enemy had been reinforced, or the general was incompetent. Even the bravest troops would hesitate or be intimidated in these circumstances. Success depended on the troops remaining silent and maintaining good order. The men had to obey their officers exactly and demonstrate sufficient 'firmness and courage' with increasing proportion to that shown by the enemy.

The engagement would usually commence with artillery fire. Battery commanders were instructed to direct their fire on enemy troop formations and not waste their ammunition on counter battery fire. The primary role of light infantry was to attack the enemy batteries, advancing in a lose skirmish formation which was less vulnerable to artillery fire, and making use of natural cover. Once within range of the enemy guns, the light infantry would open fire and kill the gunners as they served their pieces.

Attacks were to be made simultaneously at different points of the enemy line to divide their opponent's attention. The line infantry would advance until one hundred paces from the enemy, and then redouble their speed to press home the attack. If the enemy line broke, the line infantry would slow to the ordinary pace, or would halt and reform. The light infantry and grenadiers would be hurled in pursuit of the enemy, although they were cautioned not to get too far ahead of their supporting battalions. (The more astute will notice the doctrine of 1792 describes a shock action as being the principal tactic – it does not describe halting the columns in order to deploy into line for musketry.)

If an attack was repulsed, and the troops had become disordered, there was no point trying to rally them under intense enemy fire. This often proved impossible and only resulted in heavy losses. It was better to allow the men to fall back out of range before trying to rally them and attempting to renew the attack. The regulations of 1 August 1791 stated the commander should order the beating of the *breloque*, at which the battalion would break and run. When the battalion commander wanted to reform, he would plant the colours and beat *au drapeau*. Each captain would rally his platoon six paces behind the new line of battle.

Sensible advice was given on the subject of retreats, because the fate of battles was considered as always uncertain, no matter how good the dispositions made beforehand. Before giving the order to retreat the commander was to indicate to his divisional commanders, the wings and the reserve, the points on which they were to retire. If two lines wished to pass through one another (for example, the first line retiring behind the second), intervals in the line could be opened by doubling the sections; in other words the second section of each platoon could stand behind the first. When the passage of lines had been completed, the line would be restored.

[**See also:** 143. Tactical composition of a battalion; 155. Marching & manoeuvres (introduction); 164. Battalion formations and manoeuvres; 165. Infantry squares; 166. Bayonet charges; 167. Musketry (introduction); 176. Skirmishing (introduction); 250. Battles.]


## 232. Role of officers in battle

According to the 1792 field service regulations, nothing would assure the confidence of French soldiers more than being led by men who inspired them: 'For it is a very different thing to order men to march into danger, than to lead them there.' Prior to giving battle the following advice was given to officers to help prepare their men for combat. While on campaign troops ought to be ready for action at all times, with their weapons in good order. However, when about to give battle, officers should give the greatest attention to inspecting the soldiers' weapons, ensuring they were provided with fresh flints and these were well placed and secured. Prior to combat, the movements of infantry regiments were to be arranged carefully so the men went into battle fresh. The soldiers ought to eat before going into action so they were best able to support the fatigues of the day. Soldiers were not to remove their haversacks before fighting. When worn correctly they were not considered a particular hindrance to the movements of the body. The only possible exception to this rule was in mountainous or difficult terrain, if a general officer gave permission. Officers were to point out the advantages of favourable ground, and the routes to be taken if a retreat was necessary. During an advance the officers and other file closers were to maintain the alignment and order of the ranks. If they gave the order to open fire, they would hold back a portion of their fire if there was a threat of cavalry attack.

When given a post in range of an enemy attack, the officer was instructed to entrench himself by creating a redoubt. In a village it would be unlikely the detachment could hold the perimeter, so a walled place like a cemetery would be nominated as a defensive point. If the enemy arrived in force, the sentries would be called in and a message sent to the general. If static defence was impossible, the officer would fall back on the main body. If the officer decided to sit in a position and wait for support, he would take his own council, speak to the troops in a firm tone and not listen to any summons on the part of the enemy. Above all he was not to fall for enemy ruses and waste ammunition against feints. He would put a few fusiliers on a parapet to keep watch on the enemy, but keep the bulk of his men together.

[See also: 144. Assembling the platoon; 152. Tone of command; 214. Instruction of officers; 231. Battle tactics; 234. After the battle; 235. Prisoners of war; 252. Sieges.]

## 233. Duties of sub-officers in battle

When given notice of a battle, corporals would speak to the men of their squad, reminding them not to open fire until the command was given and to remain immobile when the drum call for ceasefire was made. The corporal would remind them not to drop their cartridges on the floor; not to spill any of the gunpowder; to ram the ball home properly, and not to leave the ramrod in the barrel. After firing, the men were reminded to look at their touchholes and if they did not see smoke coming out this was an indication of a misfire. In this case they were told to use their vent picks and to re-prime. As a final measure the corporal was to inspect the arms, ensuring flints were placed correctly, the men had vent picks at the ready, and sufficient cartridges.

During the battle, corporals were to keep watch on the file closers, guides, and colour guards. If they fell in combat, the corporal was to replace them urgently. They were to stop the men from breaking ranks to steal from the dead, and to remind soldiers this carried the death penalty. The same applied to those who went to mutilate or finish off wounded enemy soldiers. The corporal would stop men from leaving the ranks to go in search of cartridges. When a man was out of cartridges, it was the responsibility of the file closers to issue fresh cartridges. If the ranks were thinned by musketry or artillery fire, the corporals were to encourage the men to close up in the direction of the flag. The file closers were responsible for pulling the wounded out of the ranks and directing them, as soon as it was possible, to the field hospitals. Missing files in the line would be restored by transferring men from one rank to another.

If enemy cavalry attempted to charge, the battalion columns would close up to form dense masses. The file closers would step forward and press close to the third rank. Corporals were to remind the soldiers their best hope was to remain steady and to open fire at point-blank range, and then cross bayonets at the point of impact. If the line broke before impact, the cavalry would charge through the gaps and cut them down. If the soldiers' courage appeared to be waning, corporals were reminded the regulations did not forbid the hitting of men in flight.

During the battle, the drum major would send a party of drummers to go and look for cartridges in the caissons of the divisional artillery. These would be given to the file closers who would distribute them to the men. Meanwhile the remainder of the drummers would remain to perform rolls and signals, or to beat the charge.

If called upon to make an assault on a walled position or a town, the sub-officers were to remind the men not to quit their posts in order to commit pillage. A penalty of five years in irons was on the statue books, but more severe penalties could be announced by the general officer commanding the assault. There were two types of assault infantry might be called to make, one by escalade (in other words using ladders to cross a rampart or wall), and the other by advancing in force against a breach. In the first case the troops would approach the defences at the run, with as little noise as possible, and without becoming disordered. The ladder would be planted and everyone would scurry up and over the defences as swiftly as possible.

In the second case, it was assumed artillery had battered a breach in the defences, the rubble from which had fallen down and formed a sort of ramp by which the breach could be approached (i.e. made practicable). The troops would set out in attack columns and once the rampart had been gained, the sub-officers were to rally their troops on the crest of the breach rather than allow them to shelter in the rubble. It had to be assumed the enemy would have prepared an additional line of defences inside the breach, so sub-officers were to get their troops into order and commence firing in the regular manner as swiftly as possible.

While stuck in the breach, there was always the danger of the enemy igniting a mine which they had hidden in the rubble. The sub-officers were specially charged with examining the breach for any signs of a mine and, if they found one, to locate the match which might ignite it. All this was to be done in such a way as to not let the soldiers realise what was going on because they would certainly flee if they suspected they were about to be blown up.

[See also: 144. Assembling the platoon; 146. Placement of the colour guard; 215. Instruction of sub-officers; 232. Role of officers in battle.]

## 234. After the battle

After the battle the infantry brigades would form in line and post sentries around them. Any baggage would be brought up from the rear and the tents pitched, if they existed. If the troops bivouacked in the open, the brigadier general was required to stay with his men and to guard against disorder. The first priority was to recover the wounded of both armies and to transport them to the field hospitals in the rear. The officers and men detailed for this work were to be assisted in this unhappy task by enlisting the peasants and wagons from nearby villages.

Peasants assist with collecting two young, wounded soldiers.

Soldiers were under pain of death if they quit the ranks in battle to loot the dead. However, after the battle, squads were sent with an officer to search the enemy dead. Booty was taken back to the regiment and shared out among the companies. Soldiers sometimes received bounties for collecting weapons off the battlefield and rounding up horses. The dead were quickly stripped of their equipment and clothing, then buried anonymously in mass graves. Occasionally they were cremated on pyres if insufficient tools or time were available for interments.

The day after a battle, colonels would present to the general of division any men who had been distinguished in action. In turn the general commanding the division would take these men and present them to the commander in chief, and give an account of their deeds. Their names would be forwarded to the government. After a battle, the sergeant majors would draw up lists of all missing persons. If three witnesses could attest to what happened to the missing person (i.e. killed, wounded, captured), this was recorded.

[See also: 118. Promotion to the officer corps; 119. Awards and national recognition; 126. Registering deaths; 141. Funerary honours; 235. Prisoners of war; 241. Water and alcohol; 242. Air quality; 250. Battles; 251. Interment of the dead; 254. Military hospitals.]

## 235. Prisoners of war

There was no formal international treaty on the treatment of prisoners of war, but there were recognised conventions and bilateral treaties which would often be drawn up between the belligerents on the subject. With the exception of the guerrilla war in Spain, most belligerents treated enemy prisoners reasonably fairly.

Captured officers in particular could expect to be looked after by enemy officers as if one of their own. It was common for exchanges to take place, with an agreed 'tariff' on the worth of an officer or common soldier. At the end of hostilities, arrangements would be made to release and repatriate all prisoners.

Perhaps a more interesting aspect is the French policy toward its soldiers being taken prisoner. There does not appear to be any stigma attached to soldiers who were captured while on outpost duty, or while carrying messages, or who had been wounded. However, officers who had been charged with the defence of a post were only authorised to surrender after mounting a long defence, if all hope of relief was gone, and one of the following criteria applied: they had run out of ammunition; they had run out of food having reduced soldiers' rations and were at the end of starvation or thirst; to have lost the majority of his men. Being concerned about the welfare of his men or civilians, or the protection of a town was not considered an acceptable excuse. Nor were French officers to give their parole and offer not to serve in the war again. They were expected to remain in captivity until exchanged. If an officer fell into enemy hands having satisfied the above criteria he would continue to receive half pay for the duration of his captivity. If his conduct was not considered satisfactory, then he might face the full weight of the law for any number of charges from treason to deserting his post, depending on the consequences of his action.

[**See also:** 81. Non-regulation equipment; 110. Pay; 74. Tattoos and jewellery.]

*Part VIII*

# Health & Medical Provision

*Chapter 31*

# Health & Hygiene

## 236. The medical officer's manual

Surgery and the science of preventing sickness and disease were still very much in their infancy at the turn of the 19th century. By modern standards, there was no real concept of hygiene. Although soldiers appear to have washed their hands and face every day, they rarely bathed. Soldiers were routinely infested with their own 'garrisons' of lice and fleas, but beyond the nuisance value, this was considered a normal part of everyday life during the Napoleonic era. To address many of the common plights of soldiers, in 1801 the professor of the military training hospital in Strasbourg, Dr Jean-Jacques Martin, published a multivolume instruction manual for medical officers serving in the army titled *Manuel de l'officier de santé*. In addition to details on medical procedures, symptoms, and recipes for a variety of potions and concoctions, Dr Martin outlined the most common ailments, injuries and diseases which afflicted the army, particularly the infantry, a component of the army he expressed a great deal of sympathy for. His observations and recommendations were based on the injuries and diseases he witnessed through the wars of the French Revolution. The entries in the remainder of this section form a précis of his observations, notes and recommendations.

[**See also:** 14. Surgeon major; 237. Health of recruits; 238. The effect of clothing; 239. Hairstyles and headgear; 240. Rations; 241. Water and alcohol; 242. Air quality; 243. Sanitation of bedding; 244. Sexual health; 245. Physical exercise; 246. Guard duty; 247. Marching; 248. Forced marches; 249. Bivouacs; 250. Battles; 251. Interment of the dead.]

## 237. Health of recruits

Service in the infantry was considered the unhealthiest in the army. The clothes provided for infantrymen were lighter than those provided to horsemen, and so the former were more exposed to the influences of bad weather. They were also worse paid and in general, relatively little care was made in the recruitment of infantrymen compared to cavalry troopers. The men chosen for service in the heavy cavalry were the biggest, most robust men; almost all of them drawn from the agricultural classes who were for the most part hardened to fatigue and inclement weather. When infantry recruits were selected the medical was usually confined to the 'exterior constitution' of the body, its size, strength and structure. An examination of the eyes and the other organs of sense was considered to give a good indication of the internal constitution. However, recruits subject to dizziness, epilepsy, convulsions, asthma, habitual palpitations of the heart, 'maladies of spirit' (i.e. depression or other mental health issues), ringworm or other incurable and deep rooted skin infections, or men predisposed to bleeding, pulmonary disease, dropsy, gallstones, and the obstructions of the abdominal viscera, all ought to be rejected. These pre-existing conditions were likely to be exacerbated by military service and prevent the men from adequately performing their duties, or worse, they might communicate their diseases 'by contagion' to infect those who were in good health.

[**See also:** 100. Military conscription; 101. Recruitment council.]

## 238. The effect of clothing

In a bid to scrimp on cloth, uniforms were generally poorly proportioned. Garments which were too narrow and constrained the body's natural movements were the cause of disease, bleeding, strokes, swellings, inflammations of the lower extremities and corns in the feet. The buckles and ties which fastened breeches and the jacket hampered circulation in the organs of the groin and vessels of the lower extremities. Specific recommendations to improve clothing included:

- replacing buckles and ties with buttons (the adoption of pantaloons and short gaiters eventually helped this);
- providing enough linen for soldiers to change twice every ten days;
- to reinforce the knees of soldiers' breeches with leather to prevent them suffering damage to the joint while kneeling (pads had been sewn into gaiters for a time, but this was not re-adopted);
- providing all soldiers with a woollen greatcoat with sleeves and a hood which could be worn over their uniform in very cold weather (greatcoats were not widely issued until 1806 onwards).

[**See also:** 41. Laundress; 54. Materials; 59. Greatcoat; 61. Breeches and pantaloons; 62. Gaiters; 63. Footwear; 108. The Ordinary; 112. Deductions and funds; 218. Gymnastic and fitness exercises.]

## 239. Hairstyles and headgear

The fashion of wearing pomade, grease and powder in the hair or moustaches prevented perspiration, caused skin rashes and nourished vermin. The manual recommended the fashion ought to be suppressed. Leather headgear was considered healthier than felt because it better protected the wearer from humidity and heat, and did not need to be covered with oilcloth in the rain. It was also useful for headgear to have a visor to protect the eyes from rain and sunlight (at the time of writing, the shako had yet to be universally adopted).

[**See also:** 50. Barber; 66. Infantry helmet; 67. Cocked hat; 68. Shako; 69. Bearskin cap; 70. Forage cap; 71. Plumes; 72. Hairstyles ; 73. Beards and moustaches; 80. Petty equipment; 81. Non-regulation equipment; 110. Pay; 112. Deductions and funds.]

## 240. Rations

If well made, supply bread was considered very healthy for soldiers, although recruits from towns took time to adjust to the level of bran in the mix, which was greater than they were used to. That said, the bread was sometimes adulterated by unscrupulous bakers who could mix the dough with ash, sand, lime, plaster and so on. When criminal deceit was suspected, a thin slice of the bread was to be mixed with water and heated on a stove. As the bread disintegrated any foreign objects would sink to the bottom of the vessel. If one suspected the flour had been mixed with alum (used as a whitener by some bakers), it could be tested with a solution made with salt tartar (sodium tartrate). When inserted the adulterated bread would turn the water cloudy and a white powder would be deposited. Bakers might also add the root of jalap to bread which caused a dirty foam to form when the bread was digested. If bread was eaten too warm or too cold, it was known to cause 'dangerous constipations' among soldiers. Meat needed to be fresh and to come from healthy animals. Rather than distributing corrupted meat, to avoid 'putrid diseases' it was better to limit the diet to vegetables and especially potatoes. If soldiers ate too much salty and smoked meat they put themselves at greater risk of scurvy.

[**See also:** 191. Rations & supplies (introduction); 192. Bread and biscuit; 193. Meat; 194. Vegetables; 228. Provisions.]

## 241. Water and alcohol

Although essential for the health of soldiers, pure and uncorrupted drinking water was often very difficult to procure. 'Dangerous mixtures' in water could be cleared by boiling it, although having cooked the water it was necessary to leave it exposed to the air for a time in order for its natural taste to return. Water could also be purified by filtering it through a layer of sand. However when the lack of a fire, sand or time made filtering impossible, in order to avoid sickness, soldiers were recommended to mix the water with a twentieth part of brandy or a tenth part of vinegar. It was also observed eating pickled foods such as sauerkraut also prevented 'the disastrous effects of fetid and corrupt waters'. Brandy was accepted as an indispensable necessity for soldiers, but it was considered necessary to prevent the worst excesses of its consumption. Although drunkenness caused disorder, it was also believed to have a detrimental impact on health, causing inflammatory fevers, strokes, dropsy and malignant fevers.

[**See also:** 40. Cantineer; 80. Petty equipment; 81. Non-regulation equipment; 83. Utensils and tools; 133. Regimental prisons; 191. Rations & supplies (introduction); 194. Vegetables; 195. Brandy; 196. Vinegar; 222. Halts on the march; 228. Provisions; 247. Marching.]

## 242. Air quality

Air quality was considered as important as the quality of water for its impact on health. There was an inevitable degradation in air quality when a large multitude of people gathered, caused by their breath, perspiration and excrement, as well as the fumes from the cooking of food, fires, gunpowder smoke, and the detonation of artillery fire.

Camps ought never to be located on former battlefields where the corpses were only buried in shallow graves. If the ground was wet, drainage ditches were required. Butcher's shops, field hospitals, kitchens and latrines were to be sited as far away from the centre of the camp as possible. Every three or four days, new 'ditches of easement' ought to be dug and the former ditches covered over with earth to contain the 'putrid emanations'.

In barracks the soldiers ought not to sleep with burning coals in their bedchambers, not just because of the fear of fire, but also because of the potentially 'dangerous vapours' (by which they meant carbon monoxide poisoning).

[See also: 83. Utensils and tools; 226. Arrival at camp; 246. Guard duty; 252. Sieges.]

## 243. Sanitation of bedding

In camps, soldiers slept on straw which needed to be renewed as often as possible. In barracks, bedding consisted of a palliasse or a mattress, a pillow and a woollen blanket; all of which required frequent aeration and cleaning.

[See also: 27. Sergeant major; 30. Corporal; 48. Orderly; 182. Lodgings and the arrangements of the bedchamber; 183. The daily routine; 132. General disciplinary measures; 133. Regimental prisons; 205. Cleaning & maintenance (introduction); 242. Air quality; 254. Military hospitals.]

## 244. Sexual health

Dr Martin's manual recommended very firmly that loose women should never be allowed into the soldiers' camps or barracks, because soldiers neglected their duties in their company, and venereal diseases were propagated. This was standard policy in the army, but with France awash with prostitutes, this was easier said than done. The provisional field service regulation of 5 April 1792 (as modified 11 October 1809) stated *filles de joie* (pleasure girls) were to have their faces blackened with pitch, to be paraded around the camp and then sent home if they attempted to follow the army. The fact this clause was still relevant in 1809 perhaps indicates the problem had not gone away.

That said, Dr Martin recognised celibacy among soldiers was damaging not just to the men, but to society in general. If the state prevented men from marrying, this would inevitably cause the 'corruption of customs'. The authorities ought to make it easier for soldiers to marry he argued; after all, by putting obstacles in the way of marriage, the state was depriving itself of the subjects 'most appropriate to contribute to a numerous and healthy population'. True enough, the armed forces absorbed the strongest and healthiest young men, and only released them to civilian life when the 'fire of their youth' was extinguished. Reproduction was, Dr Martin argued, being left to the weaker members of society; to those unfit for military service. Far better, the doctor argued, for soldiers to marry young and have children, and for these children to be educated and fed, one day to succeed their fathers as soldiers.

[**See also:** 124. Marriages; 183. The daily routine; 187. The sergeant of police; 189. Duties of sentries at the gates; 254. Military hospitals.]

## 245. Physical exercise

Soldiers only ever took exercise at the end of spring, through the summer and at the beginning of the autumn. Having been idle through the winter, when the troops were suddenly exposed to continual activity in the hot season, they were not accustomed to it. This was believed to be the cause of numerous diseases, particularly the inflammation of the chest and haemoptysis (the coughing up of blood).

[**See also:** 39. Regimental children; 105. Velites; 212. Training (introduction); 218. Gymnastic and fitness exercises.]

## 246. Guard duty

Guard duty was damaging to the health due to the discomforts inseparable from standing outside in the extremities of the climate without shelter, and without sufficient men to ensure everyone could take a proper rest from service. The problems were worse when the post was near a fetid swamp, or when the air was filled with damp or contaminated vapours. In peacetime it was possible to prevent some of these inconveniences as there was more freedom in the choice of the posts. If a guard post was required on wet ground, it was necessary to raise the post clear of the water and dig drainage channels around it. If the air was damp, the air could be improved by fire and fumigations. In swampy ground, the sentinels ought to be warned to have eaten prior to service and to keep walking constantly while on duty. These men needed to be well dressed and relieved frequently. The same precautions were required in hospitals where malignant diseases reigned. In the intense cold, sentinels were advised to keep walking and not to be allowed to fall asleep lest the cold killed them.

[**See also:** 139. Honouring dignitaries; 183. The daily routine; 185. The police guard; 227. Duties in camp; 229. Outpost duty.]

## 247. Marching

During marches the health of the soldier was exposed to a number of dangers which resulted from the heat, cold, humidity, and dust. In peacetime, it was possible to avoid making the troops march in the full heat of the sun, putting regiments on the march before dawn and having them rest during the hottest part of the day.

On the march soldiers were cautioned against drinking brandy or iced water. They should only drink water acidulated by vinegar. To protect the men from dust, or the brilliance of snow, one should cover the face with a piece of crêpe attached to the front of their caps. When soldiers were extremely tired, they ought not to be forced to continue, but allowed to drop out and rest then be picked up by the rearguard. After forced marches, soldiers ought to wash their feet with a little brandy. Bruises and chilblains on the feet could be prevented by means of slippers (*chaussons*) coated with oil or grease.

One of the most dangerous discomforts was caused by the carrying of weapons and baggage. Soldiers should not be made to carry their muskets in too uniform a manner on long marches (i.e. not at 'shoulder arms'). The heavy burdens suspended from belts crossed over the breast sometimes caused a compression which resulted in a number of serious illnesses. From the examination of dead soldiers, there was often a black furrow across the chest caused by the belts digging into the skin.

[See also: 56. Weight of arms and equipment; 79. Haversack; 155. Marching & manoeuvres (introduction); 221. On the march; 223. Night marches.]

## 248. Forced marches

Although forced marches were not considered harmful in themselves to the health of the soldier, there was no doubt that during wartime service they could give rise to various serious illnesses. During forced marches the soldiers were usually obliged to leave behind their baggage and ammunition wagons; as a result they were obliged to overload themselves with provisions, or risk lacking these on the way. However, by overloading themselves with weapons and supplies, it was unlikely the soldiers would march very quickly. Without the supply train there was likely to be a great deal of marauding during the march. In order to best prepare men for the rigours of a forced march, it was recommended to practice them occasionally, even in peacetime.

[See also: 159. Route pace; 195. Brandy; 221. On the march ; 228. Provisions.]

Conscript wears his pokalem cap under the shako. The soldier to the rear has wrapped the lock and trigger in a protective cover. He is also wearing his shako sideways. (Beyer)

## 249. Bivouacs

Rather than obliging troops to spend a night in the bivouac, it was better for their health to make them continue to march. If they did rest on the ground it was feared the 'vapours of the earth' and those of the atmosphere would be damaging to health, causing rheumatism, catarrhal affections, and side stitches.

[**See also:** 84. Tents; 226. Arrival at camp; 229. Outpost duty; 234. After the battle.]

## 250. Battles

It was found soldiers who were exhausted before going into a battle were less likely to survive wounds. Battles and skirmishes fought nearer the end of the campaign tended therefore to be more deadly than those fought at the beginning, when the men were healthier. The wisest generals avoided delivering battles after a long march and never allowed their troops to fight on an empty stomach, adopting the Roman custom of eating a light meal before fighting.

Wounded soldier being evacuated from the
battlefield. (Beyer)

The care given to wounded men during the battle also had a great impact on
their chances of survival. The longer before the wounded were bandaged, the
more difficult it was to cure them. It was also necessary to have sufficient medical
officers, stretchers and carts for transporting the wounded. It was often the case
that defeated armies were obliged to withdraw hastily and to leave the majority
of their wounded behind, even without having had time to bandage them. In Dr
Martin's opinion, humanity dictated the need to remove the wounded as soon as
troops began to give way lest they were trampled by the fugitives. Humanity also
demanded care was taken to care for enemy wounded and all hostilities ceased at
the entrance of the hospital.

At the end of a battle soldiers ought not to be allowed to become drunk because
the joy of the victory, the despair of the vanquished and the fatigue of combat
would exacerbate the effect of the alcohol and lead to great disorder.

[See also: 231. Battle tactics; 234. After the battle; 251. Interment of the dead; 254. Military
hospitals.]

## 251. Interment of the dead

There was a great hurry to bury men and horses killed in battle, although one had
to take precautions to ensure men really were dead. It was necessary to bury them
in the deepest possible pits because the exhalations of corpses without a grave, or

Aftermath of fighting in a cemetery.

those buried without enough earth were deadly, not only for the army but for the countryside surrounding the battlefield.

[**See also:** 126. Registering deaths; 128. Assistance for wives and orphans; 234. After the battle.]

## 252. Sieges

Besieged soldiers were exposed to a great number of potential health hazards. If the besieging force lacked sufficient weapons to batter the place into submission, the most effective weapon was to blockade the fortress and reduce it to submission by starvation. As fresh food began to run low, the soldiers were forced to live on a diet of salted meat, mouldy bread and dried vegetables, thus increasing the risk of scurvy. As the men were denied exercise, their health would begin to fail. Then, as the air began to turn bad as the defenders were forced to bury corpses inside the city the risk of 'disastrous ravages' increased.

In order for a besieged city to resist for a long time without the garrison losing its health, the number of troops ought to be limited; just enough to guard the various posts, with enough men to ensure the guards were able to rest and be supplied with healthy food. The soldiers needed to be exercised as frequently as possible, to maintain their health by the movement of the body. Reserves of food ought to be built up before the start of the siege and as many 'useless mouths' ejected from the city as possible. Distributions were to be carefully regulated, consuming the most perishable foods first. Vinegar should be mixed with the food and drink, particularly sauerkraut and other vegetables prepared in a similar way. Precautions should be taken to prevent wells from drying out, and above all to maintain the quality of the air by ensuring the dead were buried in deep pits as far away from the city centre as possible and to light fires of wood and coniferous materials.

[**See also:** 97. Flags as signals; 134. Military justice; 192. Bread and biscuit; 202. Preparing broth from bones; 217. Practising field works; 228. Provisions; 233. Duties of sub-officers in battle.]

A cantineer offers a wounded soldier a tot of brandy. Although sutlers could make their fortune on campaign, there are many examples of them waiving payment for alcohol on the day of battle.

## Chapter 32

# Medical Treatment

### 253. Medical treatment in garrison

When a man fell sick the surgeon and sergeant major would sign a hospital ticket which was given to the captain. The sergeant major would gather the sick man's possessions in his haversack which was sealed with a band of paper. If the man died, the haversack was opened by the sergeant major in the presence of the captain.

[**See also:** 14. Surgeon major; 15. Surgeon aide; 183. The daily routine; 254. Military hospitals.]

### 254. Military hospitals

The treatment of the wounded was confided to doctors, surgeons and pharmacists. Each hospital would have a chief medical officer for each of these three branches of medicine.

There were three types of hospital: permanent, temporary and mobile. In addition to these were establishments for soldiers at spa towns, including those at Barèges, Bourbonne-les-Bains, Acqui and Aix la-Chapelle. When a military hospital was not available, soldiers would be referred to civilian hospitals. Wherever possible soldiers were to be housed with other soldiers in order to better follow the regime of a military hospital, and officers were treated separately from the men.

Permanent hospitals were located in the interior for the service of the military administrative divisions. In wartime they received the wounded sent home from the front. They were staffed by senior nurses, cooks, pharmacists, with one nurse (*infirmière*) per twelve men. These hospitals were furnished with wooden beds, with mattresses, sheets and blankets. The patients were not allowed to retain their weapons, money, uniform and linens. These possessions were put into safe keeping and would go to family if they died. On arrival the patient would be escorted to a bed. If it turned out he was not ill or injured the surgeon of the guard would notify the chief medical officer.

Instead of uniforms the patients wore long linen shirts. One in twenty-five of these shirts had openings on the back and sleeves. The openings were secured by ties and allowed surgeons easy access for examining wounds. The wounded were also issued with linen bonnets, and had access to greatcoats. Linen used in the treatment of venereal disease and scabies was made of unbleached linen. Those suffering from sexually transmitted diseases were issued with special pantaloons made of waxed canvas. These were changed every ten days.

Each patient had his own plate, a bowl, a jug for medicinal drinks, a bigger one for drinking water, and a chamber pot. Meals were at ten o'clock and four o'clock. The daily ration was half a kilo of meat, two thirds of it beef and the rest veal or mutton. When the season permitted, the meat was cooked in a soup with edible plants and was served without bones. Patients were also issued with half a loaf of bread, half a litre of wine, along with salt and vinegar as required. Some might be fed boiled eggs, prunes, and milk. The wine could be red or white, but not the most recently produced.

Temporary hospitals were established in wartime only. They were located to the rear and flanks of an army for the use of soldiers attached to the various corps. Facilities were naturally more rudimentary than in permanent hospitals, but there were instructions for soldiers not to be left on the floor, but to be put in beds, or at least on planks on trestles, with a mattress, canvas sack and blanket. The most gravely ill patients would receive a mattress. Every soldier was provided with four shirts, four night caps, two woollen bonnets, and a greatcoat or bedchamber robe. Each temporary hospital was required to have at least one bathtub.

The mobile hospitals were attached to the army and offered first aid to casualties. Known as *ambulances* these field hospitals were formed of a central depot and various sub-components which were attached to individual divisions. Within each division there might also be ambulance sections which accompanied the forward posts and detachments. They were typically composed of one or two caissons with sufficient medical equipment and supplies to administer sufficient first aid for a light action. Known as the flying ambulance (*ambulance volante*), the section would be positioned close to the action during combat to provide urgent assistance where required. The surgeons employed were typically lightly mounted with their equipment carried in a portmaneau.

At regimental level, according to the decree of *14 Fructidor XIII* (1 September 1805) every regiment had an ambulance caisson with first aid supplies. Each contained two mattresses, six stretchers made from belts, a case of surgeon's instruments, 50 kg of lint, 100 kg of linen bandage, a pharmacy chest. The contents of a caisson were considered as a reserve for the wounded only, and were not to be used on light injuries. This vehicle was pulled by four horses, and had to be able to carry at least six wounded men.

On the day of battle the ambulance depot would position itself behind the centre of the army, as close as possible without being exposed to enemy attack. The divisional and section ambulances were carried to the centre and on the wings. Regimental surgeons would position themselves as close to the action as possible and act as a first assembly point for the wounded. When possible, the wounded would be taken to the nearest field hospital. The usual formality of the wounded requiring a formal doctor's note was relaxed. Soldiers would be admitted on presentation of a wound (the formalities of hospital administration resumed the day after a battle). In order to account for the wounded, in the four days after an action it was necessary for an officer of each regiment to visit the hospital to identify the wounded and to record their entry into hospital.

As the wounded began arriving, the medical officers at the ambulances would perform first aid and, out of necessity, emergency operations such as amputations and trepanning. The wounded were to be kept off the ground and left on planks, or straw to protect them from the humidity of the ground. Every day a portion of the wounded would be evacuated to the nearest temporary hospital. The lightly wounded cases were released back to their regiments as soon as possible. The chief surgeon would ultimately decide which cases were too seriously wounded to move. The convoys of wounded were accompanied by surgeons and each hospital was provided with a number of assistants called *commis aux evacuations*, charged with accompanying the wounded from one hospital to the next.

[**See also:** 14. Surgeon major; 15. Surgeon aide; 126. Registering deaths; 183. The daily routine; 253. Medical treatment in garrison.]

# Alphabetical Table of Articles

# Select Bibliography

Anon, (Attributed to Heffmeyer), *Livret de commandements, ou Tableaux synoptiques des manoeuvres d'infanterie, par un Major d'infanterie.* (Strasbourg: Levrault, ND) (given as 1815)

Berriat, H. *Recueil méthodique et raisonné des lois, décrets, arrêtés, règlements et instructions actuellement en vigueur sur toutes les branches de l'état militaire.* 4 vols. (Alessandria: Louis Capriolo, 1812)

Bardin, Étienne-Alexandre. *Mémorial de l'officier d'infanterie.* 2 vols. (Paris: Magimel, 1813)

Bardin, Étienne-Alexandre. *Manuel d'infanterie, ou Résumé de tous les règlements, décrets, usages, renseignements propres aux sous-officiers de cette arme.* (Paris: Magimel, 1813)

Bardin, Étienne-Alexandre. *Dictionnaire de l'armée de terre, ou Recherches historiques sur l'art et les usages militaires des anciens et des modernes.* 17 vols. (Paris: J. Corréard, 1841–1851)

Damesme, A; Varinot. *Cours d'administration militaire, à l'usage de MM. Les élèves de l'école spéciale impériale militaire de Saint-Cyr.* (Paris: Magimel, 1810)

France. *Ordonnance du Roi, pour régler le service dans les Places & dans les Quartiers, du premier Mars 1768.* (Paris: Imprimerie Royale, 1768)

France. *Règlement concernant l'exercice et les manœuvres de l'infanterie: du 1er août 1791.* (Paris: Imprimerie Royale, 1791)

France. *Règlement provisoire sur le service de l'infanterie en campagne 1792, du 5 avril 1792.* (Paris: Imprimerie Royale, 1792)

France. *Règlement concernant le, service intérieur, la police et la discipline de l'infanterie du 24 Juin, 1792.* (Paris: Imprimerie Royale, 1792)

Keralio, L-F.G.; Lacuée, J-G; Servan, J. *Encyclopédie méthodique. Art militaire.* 4 vols. (Paris, 1784–1797)

Martin, Jean Jacques. *Manuel de l'officier de santé.* 3 vols. (Paris: Amand Koenig, 1801)

Quillet, P.N. *État actuel de la législation sur l'administration des troupes.* (3e édition) 3 vols. (Paris: Magimel, 1808)

# Illustration Credits